Jack O'Connell
Seattle
28 mai 1985

The Bronze Age in
Barbarian Europe

1 Ritual scenes and chariot, Scandinavian engraving, Kivik stone, Skåne (Sweden)

The Bronze Age in Barbarian Europe

From the Megaliths to the Celts

Jacques Briard

Translated by
Mary Turton

Routledge & Kegan Paul
London, Boston and Henley

First published in France as
L'Age du Bronze en Europe barbare
© *Éditions des Hespérides, 1976*
This translation
first published in 1979
by Routledge & Kegan Paul Ltd
39 Store Street, London WC1E 7DD,
Broadway House, Newtown Road,
Henley-on-Thames, Oxon RG9 1EN and
9 Park Street, Boston, Mass. 02108, USA
Set in Monophoto Apollo
and printed in Great Britain by
BAS Printers Limited, Over Wallop, Hampshire

British Library Cataloguing in Publication Data

Briard, Jacques

The Bronze Age in Barbarian Europe.
1. Bronze age – Europe
I. Title
936   GN778.2   78-41159

ISBN 0 7100 0086 3

Contents

Contents

Contents

Illustrations

Figures

Table and maps

Acknowledgments

Illustrations have been reproduced from the work of the following scholars: no. 29 after J. D. Evans, 33 after Cazalis de Fondouce, 37 after Abbé Breuil, 41 after H. Schubart, 46 after Medunova-Benešova, 48 after Klopfleisch, 54, 55 after Saint-Just Pequart and Le Rouzic, 56 after E. V. Wright and C. W. Wright, 69 after Annable and Simpson, 77 after Kossac, 127 after C. Schaeffer, 145 after S. Marinatos, 147 after P. Gelling, 149 after P. V. Glob, 151, 152, 153 after H. de Lumley, 154 and 157 after J. Abelanet, 171 after W. Kimmig, 173 after R. Wyss, 3, 202 after P. Gelling and H. E. Davidson.

The author and publishers wish to express their gratitude to the following persons and institutions, who have kindly allowed them to reproduce the photographs of which the numbers appear in brackets: Hermitage Museum, Leningrad (22), J. Clottes (30), Dr J. Arnal (34, 137, 138, 161, 195), Professor P.-R. Giot (57), Musée Calvet at Avignon (61), British Museum (72, 169, 200), P. Marcel (73), G. Rosselo-Bordoy, Director of the Majorca Museum (128, 181), F. de Lanfranchi (136, 143), Professor E. Atzeni and the Istituto di Antichità de Cagliari (139, 142, 144), H. de Lumley (155, 163), the Musée des Antiquitiés Nationales at St-Germain-en-Laye (170), M. Geantet and the Musée de Nîmes (31), G. Verron (182), C. Hughes (162), National Archaeological Museum of Cividale-del-Friuli (103), Dr V. Kondic, Director of the National Museum of Belgrade (92).

The photographs nos 15, 20, 58, 59, 60, 63, 64, 65, 93, 94, 95, 131, 141, 171, 172, 173, 188, 190 are the author's; all the rest are the property of Éditions des Hespérides.

We thank the prehistorians and museums who have generously allowed us to photograph their collections, notably: Dr I. H. Longworth, Conservator, and Dr R. J. Harrison, Assistant, Department of Prehistoric and Romano-British Antiquities at the British Museum (nos 18, 47, 70, 71, 78, 79, 96, 97, 98, 99, 122, 123, 183, 184, 186), Dr G. Körner, Director of the Museumsverein für das Fürstentum at Lüneburg (12, 13, 82, 83, 84, 90), Professor Ahrens, Director, and Dr G. Tromnau, Conservator, of the Helms Museum at Harburg (80, 174, 193, 194), Römisch-germanische Zentralmuseum at Mainz (14, 45, 164, 176, reproductions 5, 6, 7, 10, 16, 44, 49, 76, 91, 108, 175, 180), M. Vié, Conservator of the Musée de Narbonne (17), the National Museum, Athens (23, 24, 25, 26), Professor P. Graziosi, Director of the Istituto Italiano di Preistoria at Florence (reproductions 27, 35,

125, 150, 159), Sig. A. Aspes, Conservator of the Natural History Museum, Verona (reproductions 28, 52, 160 and originals 51, 100, 101, 158), M. de Loye, Conservator of the Musée Calvet at Avignon (32, 178), Professor E. Ripoll Perello, Director of the Archaeological Museum, Barcelona (models 36, 39, 129, 130, originals 42, 102, 132, 133, 134, 189, 196), the Musée d'Archéologie et d'Histoire de Lausanne (50, 115, 165, 167, 177), the Musée d'Art et d'Histoire de Genève (53, 81, 126, 166, 179, 201), M. l'abbé Burg, Conservator of the Musée de Haguenau (85, 86, 88), M. and Mme G. Laplace, Conservators of the Musée d'Arundy (87, 178, 197), M. R. Joffroy, Director, and J. P. Mohen, Conservator, of the Musée des Antiquitiés Nationales at St Germain-en-Laye (11, 89, 179), Fru E. Munksgaard, Conservator of the Danish Prehistoric Collections, National Museum, Copenhagen (104, 105, 106, 107, 109, 110, 111, 112, 113, 114, 116, 117, 118, 119, 120, 121, 156), the Musée Borely at Marseille (124), the Musée Archéologique de Perpignan (196), A. Coffyn (19).

Drawings were made by N. Ung-Tien (1, 4, 62, 68, 77, 140, 145, 199), Y. Onnée (8, 9, 21, 33, 37, 38, 40, 41, 43, 46, 48, 66, 69, 168, 185, 187, 191, 192, 198), and C. de Cruzel (2, 3, 56, 146, 148, 202; maps 1, 2 and 3).

The translator wishes to thank Brendan O'Connor for invaluable advice on metallurgical techniques and Bronze Age weaponry.

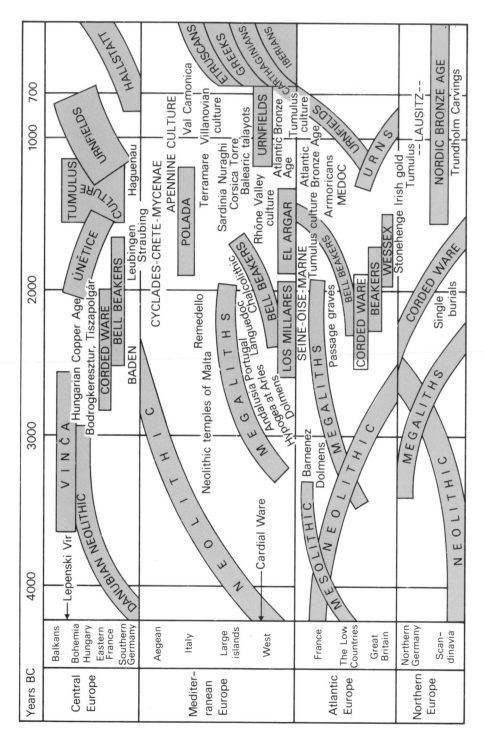

Chronological table: European cultures from the Neolithic to the early Iron Age

Introduction

'Barbarians' and the Bronze Age

Greeks and Romans called all who were not of their world 'barbarians', so in geographical terms 'barbarian' Europe confronts the classical Mediterranean world. To be chronologically exact the peoples known as 'barbarians' appeared in the Bronze Age at the time when the first archaic Aegean cultures were evolving. They continued down to about the sixth century AD and the term 'barbarian' for the general public conjures up first and foremost the hordes which engulfed the decadent Roman Empire and put an end to its hegemony.

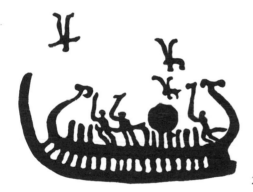

2 Scandinavian rock carving, Bohüslan (Sweden)

For a long time any art or any cultural feature alien to the Hellenic or Roman world was held in contempt and the epithet 'barbarian' acquired a pejorative meaning. All the great literate civilisations of antiquity – Egyptian, Mesopotamian and others – formed an integral part of the cycle of classical civilisations. By contrast everything that happened among the non-literate peoples to the north and west of the Aegean was of no consequence and can be apprehended only vaguely in the lines of ancient and often tendentious texts.

The first reactions against this view began to appear in the early nineteenth century. Already the romantic moralists' enthusiasm for the innocence ascribed to the 'noble savages' had stimulated a desire to know more about exotic peoples. Travellers and early ethnographers were revealing these little-known worlds. Progress in archaeology and the discovery of prehistory were to facilitate the pursuit of research into the past. Soon a whole mass of evidence concerning these vanished peoples came to light as a result of the excavations which were becoming ever more numerous all over Europe. People were forced to acknowledge the existence of ancient cultures – with no writing – differing from the classical cultures in many respects, yet as deserving as they of the name of 'cultures' and no longer justifying the unflattering overtones of the term 'barbarian'.

So the genesis of the most distant periods of human history was unfolded. The complex emergence of the genus Homo and the splendour of Palaeolithic rock paintings soon held great crowds enthralled. The more recent ages of prehistory were not so readily acknowledged outside the circles of specialists and initiates. Little was known of the Neolithic which witnessed the appearance of polished flints, the invention of pottery and, above all, the discovery of agriculture and animal husbandry. The Metal Ages – Copper or Chalcolithic appearing in Europe in the third millennium; Bronze beginning about 2000 BC, and Iron in the millennium before the birth of Christ – were often mis-timed; many people are still unaware that the period of Gaulish independence was the end of the Iron Age.

And yet from the period of the most ancient potters and builders of dolmens to that of the first sallies of Celtic horsemen, a whole amazing mosaic of original civilisations succeeded each other in Europe, from the Russian steppes to the Atlantic seaboard, and from the Aegean Sea to the meadows and icefields of Scandinavia.

The aim of our work is basically to conjure up the way of life of these Europeans living in the Metal Ages, to describe their social and religious customs, and to catch a glimpse, through the material objects they have left us, of the way their minds worked and their beliefs evolved. We are not aiming at a complete inventory of all the proto-historic civilisations of Europe, nor at a scientific treatise that enumerates and discusses the material proof of the existence of Bronze Age cultures. We will be content, rather, to describe the most typical groups, trying in particular to delineate scenes of everyday life in the light of the most striking excavations and the most famous monuments. The element of reconstruction may well be greater at times than is usual in scientific accounts: but reconstruction is, nevertheless, possible for there is an abundance of basic evidence, so that we need not fall back on the gratuitous assertions or the cheap sensationalism of fashionable 'archaeological' novels.

First of all we must define this Bronze Age more precisely. The concept dates from the middle of the nineteenth century. As a result of the work of the Dane, C. J. Thomsen, prehistory was divided into three great sequences: the Stone Age – which was later sub-divided into Palaeolithic, or more ancient, and Neolithic – the Bronze Age and the Iron Age, which takes us to the end of European prehistory. So the Bronze Age is the one in which for the first time man made use of metals – that is to say intensive use of them, for we shall see that a few timid attempts to do so were made in Neolithic times. After the discovery of gold and copper, a blend of copper and tin known as bronze was invented, which made the casting of tools much easier. This Bronze Age is usually dated between

2000 and 800 BC for 'barbarian' Europe. But it soon became clear that development did not occur uniformly. The Mediterranean or Danubian regions were the first to learn to use metal: copper appeared there at least from the beginning of the third millennium. In northern Europe the blacksmiths and foundrymen awoke later and the Nordic Bronze Age did not reach its full flowering until the middle of the second millennium – but then what richness emerged! On the other hand, this Nordic Bronze Age seemed to last for ever – until well into the first millennium when central Europe had long been forging iron swords.

From the end of the last century 'Bronze Age' studies proliferated: by the Englishman, John Evans, for the British Isles; by the Swede, Oscar Montelius, for the Nordic countries and Italy; by the Frenchman, Ernest Chantre, for France. A. and G. de Mortillet's *Prehistoric Museum* provided scholars and collectors with a catalogue of objects in which bronze axes were well represented. Their illustrations were based partly on the treasures already gathered together in the brand new Musée des Antiquités Nationales founded by order of Napoleon III. Shortly before he disappeared in the maelstrom of 1914, a great French scholar, Joseph Déchelette, published a *Manual of Prehistory*, one of the best-known volumes of which was devoted to the Bronze Age. J. Déchelette rounded off in masterly manner a whole first cycle of studies and research based on meticulous analysis of finds and attempts to link them with classical or proto-classical ethnic groups such as Iberians or Ligurians. For a long time Déchelette's work was a veritable Bible for French writers, and, curiously enough, they thought the last word had been spoken. So research in France went through a period of stagnation lasting throughout the second quarter of this century.

However, other authoritative voices were raised giving new life to archaeological thought. The Australian, V. Gordon Childe, provided the impulse for a study of the 'Neolithic Revolution', which saw man acquiring new and rational ways of feeding himself through the conquest of agriculture and animal husbandry. Excavations and inventories constantly revealed the riches of Europe's past. Great, unsuspected cultures were brought to light, like the Urnfield culture which had covered all Europe in the Bronze Age with cremation cemeteries, where the ashes of the dead were collected in pottery vessels and buried in the ground. The origin of these many brilliant cultures was commonly explained at that time in terms of 'migrations' or 'folk movements'. The source of all culture was sought in the east, although sturdy defenders of native Nordic or central European origins raised their voices in protest throughout.

In recent times, archaeological researchers have seen a proliferation of modern analysis techniques being applied to archaeology. In particular, F. Libby's discovery of the radio-carbon method of dating has completely revolutionised prehistoric chronologies and, by the same token, the grand framework of archaeological thought: at last, using a physical procedure, we can date civilisations whose exact position had been difficult to determine previously.

A lot has been said about the 'radio-carbon revolution'. There has indeed been a profound revolution in the basic ideas of archaeological science, even more so than in the

3

methods of study. For example, ^{14}C has made it possible to prove that many Western civilisations had appeared very early and that, for example, the great dolmens of the so-called megalithic period had been built in the Atlantic regions well before the Egyptian pyramids or the tombs and palaces of Mycenae. But application of the ^{14}C method and the use of radio-carbon dating raise certain difficulties – we examine these closely in the Appendix.

3 Lur players, rock carving, Bohüslan (Sweden)

A 'second ^{14}C revolution' as Colin Renfrew calls it, has taken place in the last few years: the chronological scales imposed by dendro-chronology force us to push back all our ^{14}C dates. These latest dates, combined with the results of archaeological work, show clearly that the origin of so-called 'barbarian' cultures goes back even beyond the third millennium. It seems impossible now to deny that these, too, in very ancient times and well before the Aegean lands, played a great part in the origins of European civilisation.

Chapter 1

The Discovery of Metal

How did the barbarians come by metal? Simply by looking for new jewellery in which prehistoric people took such delight. They were unable to resist the soft green charm of malachite or the deep blue of that other copper carbonate so aptly named azurite. The accidental fusion of these two lovely minerals probably led to the discovery of the first copper metallurgy. The barbarians were victims of the eternal fascination of gold, grains of which were carried along in profusion in virgin streams. It was the Age of Gold, dreamed of by the ancient poets and philosophers. Morcover, copper appeared spontaneously at that time in variegated seams of copper-bearing strata where a natural alchemy kindly brought to the surface copper salts which had been cunningly fashioned in the depths. A whim of nature or a wink from the gods? Whatever it may have been, this red stuff, copper, could be crushed between two stones or transformed by the blows of men; the plaques, wires, even twisted fringes were so many technical inventions which captivated the earliest metallurgists. Beads of gold and copper became more and more widespread and soon the function of mere adornment was exceeded and the first metal punches were hammered into shape.

The first Anatolian coppers

These appeared around 6000 or 7000 BC somewhere in the region of Çayönü in eastern Anatolia, and in a world which was not yet acquainted with pottery! The appearance of metal *earlier* than the classic pottery-making Neolithic was disturbing, unforeseen in the chronologies which had been patiently constructed for a century. It must be admitted that the first small articles made were not of a kind to revolutionise traditional economic life. Before the real flowering of the Metal Ages much patience would be needed, and much anonymous and unrecognised fumbling in order to move beyond the simplest hammering of unrefined metal. Only in the Americas would the early metal workers be able to draw on abundant natural copper. The ancient east and youthful Europe had to learn to win and transform the metal, to reduce the ores which at first were oxides, then carbonates, and finally, by means of more and more complicated firing techniques, to bring about the complex transformation of the sulphides. Then came the invention of smelting and casting which meant that new forms could be created and the material could be modelled as fancy dictated. Towards the fourth millennium BC, this threshold had largely been crossed by the peoples of the Iranian lands where a whole range of tools had already been created: simple, flat-bladed axes, axes pierced vertically as they are today, hoes and adzes for the peasant and the carpenter, chisels for the joiner, punches for the shoemaker. The dissemination of these objects could not be contained and, from the Near East, they spread to Europe, no doubt by the age-old route of the Aegean and up through the Balkans.

The discovery of copper metallurgy was gradual and took some millennia to complete. The copper carbonates, malachite and azurite, were the first to be used because they are easily smelted. Later the copper sulphides, requiring higher temperatures for reduction, were roasted. It was later still, in the second millennium, that it became possible to reach the temperatures needed to extract the commonest metal, iron. So everywhere Iron Ages are preceded by a Bronze Age.

The first coppers were not always pure. They were often mixed with considerable quantities of impurities – more than 1 per cent and sometimes as much as 4 or 5 per cent of the whole. The impurity most frequently detected by modern analysis is arsenic, but antimony and silver, common in the South of France, and nickel, frequently found in Alpine coppers, are also found in the fabric of the earliest metal objects. On the surface of the seams these mixtures occur naturally, but the metalworkers very soon learnt to manufacture them. To the pure copper they added 'regules', compounds very rich in arsenic or antimony. Thus they obtained a metal that was harder than natural copper.

One difficulty in working copper was its high melting point – over $1080°C$. That is why the discovery of tin is of prime importance. By adding this metal which melts at $232°C$, an alloy was obtained that was much easier to cast. So a bronze containing 40 per cent tin is liquid at $720°C$; normal bronzes have a tin content between 7 and 25 per cent according to their use. At the end of the Bronze Age, lead was being added to copper; but brass, composed of copper and zinc, was not in current use until the Roman period. The presence of zinc in a prehistoric object is exceptional, and is indeed one of the criteria by which fakes are recognised.

The idols of Lepenski Vir and Vinča

It was a revelation for the academic world when, in 1960, radio-carbon dating disclosed the great antiquity of Neolithic European cultures prior to the fourth millennium – that is 1000 to 2000 years before Crete, Egypt or Babylon. The corrections made by dendro-chronology to the radio-carbon dates only accentuated this time lag. Controversy was lively between those who held to the classical views and the 'revolutionaries', firmly convinced of the great antiquity of the Danubian cultures, for example, in comparison with the Aegean world. There was no gainsaying the evidence, and recent discoveries have shown the existence of very early centres of original cultures all along the Danube.

The most spectacular disclosure was the outcome of excavations at Lepenski Vir from 1965 to 1968. This site, downstream from the 'Iron Gates', consisted of small trapezoidal houses, from which a population of hunter-fishermen kept watch over the awesome whirlpools of the great river, in the sixth millennium BC. These homesteads were to suffer a curious fate: the recent construction of a large dam gave rise to an exemplary dig, followed by the complete reconstruction of the identical village some 10m higher up. The twentieth-century architects were given the task of reconstructing a village of the sixth millennium BC. It dominated the modern township, which is now submerged, with roofs stripped of their tiles and leafless trees appearing above the water like a vision from the Apocalypse.

4 Fish-man idol, Lepenski Vir (Yugoslavia)

Lepenski Vir's originality lies in its statuary which has no equivalent in the sixth millennium, either in the Aegean or elsewhere. The little stone huts were guarded by strange idols with heads of fish-men. So, original artistic creations could germinate in 'barbarian' brains. The tradition was maintained for several thousand years.

Everyone had his gods or his goddesses, and there is no lack of them in the brilliant Vinča culture which flourished, essentially Neolithic, from around 5000 to 3000 BC in what is now Yugoslavia. Very soon it evolved highly developed agricultural techniques, learned no doubt from the Near East with which it had continuous contact. Wheat and barley were grown there and they even discovered millet as a crop plant, for the first time in the Balkans. Large settlements, like the one at Vinča near Belgrade, grouped together farmhouses with several rooms, built of wooden beams and daub. At the centre of the dwelling the hearth or baker's oven symbolically occupied the place of honour. Burials were scattered within the village itself or clustered outside in large, simple necropolises which reflect no great social divergences. The bodies were crouched, recalling the position of the embryo in the womb; mankind returned to sleep in the bosom of the Great Earth Goddess. The pottery shows a high degree of skill with fine pedestal vases and differences in style, which can be used to establish chronological sequences. Ornamentation was simple. First bone was used – readily to hand – but also, more surprisingly, seashells: the spondylus imported from far-off Aegean shores. Here is an example of the amazing trading links which flourished as far back as the Neolithic, and continued throughout the Bronze Age all over Europe.

5 Statuettes from Cernavoda (Romania)

At Vinča the cult of the Mother Goddess is found again, having spread from Anatolia to the Danube. A plentiful series of clay statuettes groups together shapes with marked sexual characteristics, bearing witness to a cult of fertility and abundance. Much more aesthetically pleasing are the works of art, often symbolic, which evolve towards masks or heads of birds. There are statuettes of women, sometimes in pairs, mothers with children – the unending theme – and, in addition, busts or reproductions of faces. And what faces! A long, pointed nose and two big, slanting, almond eyes stand out from an elegant, triangular face with a narrow chin. The hair is often just suggested with very many variations of hair-style. It is tempting to equate them with that famous 'Parisienne' of the Cretan palace at Knossos: amazing artistic parallels, which are found again in a Neolithic statuette from a neighbouring Romanian group: the famous thinker of Cernavoda, pre-figuring Rodin's famous work, but 6000 years earlier.

This Vinča group in its earliest phases is typically Neolithic. As it evolves its products and its life-style remain basically Neolithic in spirit; but metal is making its appearance very discreetly. These civilisations which are in the Neolithic tradition but in which metal – more often copper than bronze, incidentally – is being introduced, without noticeably disrupting society and the way of life, are often called Chalcolithic. The word has grown old, worn out by passionate quarrels about the real status of these hybrid civilisations, and

6 Head of an idol, Vinča (Yugoslavia)

7 Ceramic idol, Priština (Vinča
culture, Yugoslavia)

is no longer fashionable: in fact its very right to exist is disputed on the grounds that it
stands for an erroneous concept.

The word Chalcolithic – from the Greek *chalkos* (copper or bronze) and *lithos* (stone) –
has a synonym of Latin origin, Eneolithic – *aeneus* (of copper or bronze) – for the Latin
speakers did not distinguish the metal from its alloy any more than the Greeks did; this
latter word is frequently used by central European authors.

At Vinča metal is found – Chalcolithic then – in the form of small beads or awls, which
until recently were thought by many to be imports from the Near East. Recent finds show
that from this period, about 3500 BC onwards, the exploitation of the first seams of copper
was in full swing in Europe – no doubt at the instigation of Anatolian prospectors who had
just discovered the rich copper deposits of the Balkans. In particular, Transylvania,
Bosnia, Serbia and Macedonia possessed valuable copper deposits which, moreover, were
easy to work.

The work of the Yugoslavian archaeologist, Borislav Jovanović, has made known the
mine at Rudna Glava, in eastern Serbia, which was exploited at a very early date. Near the
river Saska Reka a vast hollow, 30 to 40m deep, is the result of ancient magnetite and
copper workings, no doubt medieval. But this open-cast mine cuts across traces of even
older workings in the form of some ten vertical or slanting shafts, sometimes lined, which
follow the seams of copper. Shaft number 7, the best preserved, shows some safety

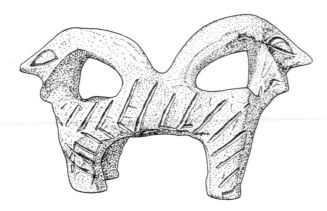

8 Ritual vase, Rudna Glava copper
mine (Vinča culture)

measures with a starting platform at the top and small dry-stone walls to guard against rock
falls. The shafts are 1m 60 to 1m 80 wide and 3m 20 deep. The surprising thing was to find
fragments of pottery in these workings: amphorae and handled vases, typical of the Vinča
culture. Better still, 12m down in the rubble of a trench that had been destroyed, a ritual
vase was found, complete with two 'protomes' or busts, with human faces modelled on the
Vinča idols, and with pointed noses and almond eyes. So the good Lady of Vinča protected
the miners at Rudna Glava in their perilous work. This is important because it shows
copper being worked by a Neolithic group, and the working is indigenous as the presence
of regional idols shows. This ore extraction was remarkable for the period since there were
some twelve shafts in a group.

Moreover, deposits of copper objects were soon to appear, evidence of the first
manufactured surpluses intended for commerce. The first stocks were of beads – in lots of
thirty – then tools. The deposits at Pločnik, which is also in Serbia, include flat or shaft-
hole axes in tens, massive copper bracelets and even large 'fork-shaped pins', modelled on
the Anatolian spirals. Before long copper manufacture was to become more widespread,
particularly to the north of the Danube in present-day Hungary.

The Hungarian Copper Age: Tiszapolgár and Bodrogkeresztur

No, it is not a tongue-twister, but the names of two great Hungarian necropolises
representing successive phases of the brilliant Hungarian Chalcolithic or Copper Age,
around 3500 to 2300 BC. Funeral customs, and hence social life, do not seem to have
evolved significantly. Great cemeteries are still found in which the burials do not indicate
any notable social stratification. On the other hand, animal husbandry seems to have
become very important and the tombs provide evidence of this. At Oszenvitan, one burial
contained the skeleton of an adult, aged about forty, with a few funeral pots and, in
particular, quarters of veal and several sucking pigs, indicating a healthy appetite for a

corpse! The settlements show a similar increase in livestock – sheep, cattle, horses, goats, and even domesticated dogs.

Was the metal, as an element of barter or trade, the source of all this wealth of animals, or did groups of men turn to animal husbandry and metallurgy at the same time, leaving a more sedentary and agricultural way of life to others? However that may be, metal was to become more and more abundant. The first imitations of Anatolian products – small ornaments or tools in the early Tiszapolgár phase – were to be succeeded in the Bodrogkeresztur phase by original products: axe-adzes, copper implements with central shaft holes and a double edge, axe on one side and adze on the other. This was a new invention, a hybrid deriving from the stone axe-hammers of Danubian type, and the more distant Eastern adzes of Sumer; it was the first original European metal product and the first example of a trade which flooded over into neighbouring regions, reaching Bulgaria, the Caucasus, Dalmatia, and perhaps even France and Germany in the west, if we are to trust some finds of the last century. A new feature in the composition of these coppers is the high degree of purity. As a result of research by some German writers, such as E. Sangmeister, it has been possible by means of spectrography to distinguish metallurgical groups in the whole of palaeometallurgic Europe. The Hungarian group is E 00, which may be translated 'almost free of impurities'. They used an exceptional ore but these sorcerer's apprentices had a remarkable technique as well.

Hungarian developments in metallurgy were paralleled to the north and west of that country. All along the main communication routes a Chalcolithic phase appears in countless peoples, transforming the old Neolithic civilisations. It would be tedious to catalogue them all, but a few groups display remarkable innovations. One such is at Aichbühl in south Germany, where large, wooden houses bear witness to a sensible use of the resources of the temperate forest. The woodman was to play an important part in Western barbarian civilisations for a long time. Another group, at Baden, a site to the south of Vienna, spread out widely through Austria, Hungary and Czechoslovakia. This one displays a balance between the search for metal, animal husbandry and improving agricultural traditions. The ard, a primitive type of plough, was known to them and

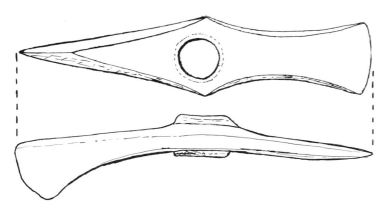

9 Copper axe-adze,
Hungarian type

increasing use was being made of the wheel. A whole series of little clay votive chariots testifies to the use of four-wheeled vehicles, like small carts, in contexts dated to 2500 BC in Hungary. They are reminiscent of the solid wooden wheels found in the peat-bogs of northern Europe, notably in the Netherlands. These chariots must have been pulled by teams of oxen, which were more suited to the traction of these first fragile vehicles than were the fiery little horses of the steppes, which were still wild and being hunted, although, from the time of the Neolithic in Switzerland, bits made of horn and antler are evidence of a probable beginning of domestication.

10 Clay votive chariot, Budakalasz (Hungary)

Still in the Baden cultures, a few objects give us a clue as to religious rites: votive horns and, in particular, strange clay drums, huge earthenware jars across which animal skins were stretched by means of a host of little teat-screws or rings. Some folk eddies are discernible in the evolution of the settlements, which now include high places that could more easily be defended. The appearance of a few cremations in the cemeteries may indicate new populations with different rites. This was the period, towards 2500 BC, when Europe was in fact about to be overrun by new, very mobile groups. Some of these were the Corded Ware peoples.

The migrations of the Corded Ware peoples

Around the middle of the third millennium BC a whole series of more or less related peoples were to be found in a vast region stretching from the great Russian steppes to northern and western Europe. These populations, too, were 'Chalcolithic' in the sense used by older writers, enjoying a pastoral and agricultural life-style in the Neolithic tradition, but with the introduction of something new, heralding the New Age: if they did not know metal, at least they made stone imitations of it, and the funerary rites underwent a profound change. Archaeological jargon has heaped various names on these peoples, deriving from their tools (almost entirely of stone, as in the Neolithic period which immediately preceded them), or their most typical pottery or their funeral customs. In Saxo-Thuringia there is talk of 'corded people' – a strange, grammatically indefensible term. It is a daring ellipsis recalling their ceramics with 'corded decoration', based on impressions of cord and incisions. In Denmark we find the Single Burial people, for these new arrivals brought the rite of individual inhumation in contrast to the great collective dolmens, known as 'Giants' Tombs', which gathered all the members of the community together in death. In Sweden we have the Boat Axe culture (boat-shaped stone axes), which shows another facet of these cultures; these magnificent stone battle axes were deposited in tombs so frequently that these groups were sometimes called the Battle Axe cultures. Finally, in Russia, an eponymous site some 300km from Moscow was chosen for their name: the Fatyanovo culture.

This brief list, for there are numerous sub-groups or derivatives, shows in the first place how widely dispersed these probably pastoral populations were, and we are lost in conjecture as to their origins. Years ago, convinced Germanists – a great many of them! – saw the cradle of these peoples in Saxo-Thuringia and described an Indo-European expansion, to which we shall return. Others supported the theory of a religious revolution in the area of the Netherlands, but they do not carry much conviction. Nowadays it is generally agreed that their origins are scattered in the distant steppes of Russia or south-east Europe. It is true that one of the main features of these groups is the combat or battle axe – a stone, shaft-hole axe, reminiscent of the first copper objects originating in Anatolia and Iran, which reached Europe via the Caucasus or the Balkans.

Detailed analysis of the Corded Ware peoples reveals regional peculiarities in each group. It might give the impression of a static mosaic of peoples, and this may, in fact, have been true of the final phase of their evolution. But, at the outset, the groups from Russia probably had difficulty in forcing their way through the territories they were spreading into. Violent clashes no doubt occurred in that melting-pot of populations. In any case, these migrations of the Corded Ware peoples, peaceful or not, played a major part in spreading ideas at the dawn of the Bronze Age.

But what were these tides of Corded Ware people bringing with them? In the first place, as we have seen, single burial. Individualism was asserted even in death. Man was no longer an anonymous member of a community: he became an individual. The contrast with Neolithic customs and their collective tombs is plain – with the dolmens and gallery graves in Brittany, the underground cists and hypogea in the Marne and South of France, the 'giants' tombs' of northern Europe and even the great democratic cemeteries of the vast Danube plains, where no notable differences in the richness of the burials are found. The tombs of the Corded Ware people vary from group to group, from the most ancient which were still simple funeral trenches to the tumuli of which the Low Countries provide some famous examples, thanks to the remarkable excavations of Professor A. van Giffen, who was one of the pioneers of excavation techniques. Careful trowelling, the use of quadrants, and the dismantling of the mounds with surgical precision led to the uncovering of strange rituals. The corpse was placed in a grave in either a crouched or an upright position. Then a hut of osiers, shaped like a beehive, was constructed over him. Finally the whole thing was covered with a circular tumulus surrounded with wooden stakes. These peculiarities were to be imported into England to contribute to the religious monuments of stone or wooden posts foreshadowing the great Stonehenge.

The battle axe and Schnurkeramik

Battle axe – what a marvellous name for an instrument designed to smash skulls! But were they always functional? Their very beauty, due to a choice of the most suitable rocks for polishing, and their symbolism, make it doubtful. They are symbols of power, for the glory of their owners, who are never parted from them, even in death. Several remarkable features are to be found in certain of these axes, in particular the often very close imitation of metal tools, to the extent of suggesting, by means of a rib running lengthwise, the seam at the join of the two halves of a mould, which is characteristic of copper artefacts. The Corded Ware people at least knew of the existence of metal and of certain types of tool, which were beginning to be common in certain areas. Then, too, in Russia, Sweden and Finland, there were those polished stone, boat-shaped axes, in which the cutting edge formed the prow; they brought together two symbols, the boat and the axe. And so we see appearing in the religious myths of the very early Bronze Age, objects that glorify travel – boats, canoes, and, a little later, wheels, carts and horses.

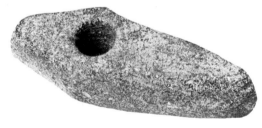

11 (above left) Stone axe. Battle Axe culture
12 (above right) Battle axe, North Germany
13 (left) Boat-shaped axe, northern Europe

The battle axes were placed in tombs but they also gave rise all over western Europe to imitations and to series of objects in the form of 'hammer axes', also in stone. Some battle axes are made of copper, including the handle – an unheard-of luxury; these fine axes, like the ones at Trévé and Kersoufflet, were exceedingly rare gifts, offered by people living along the middle Rhine and in Brittany.

As for the Corded Ware itself, archaeological detective work is carried out by following the chronological evolution and interrelationships of small variations in the pottery; this gives a good indication of technical 'marriages' with products from other groups. Among the Corded Ware peoples of western Europe and Germany we find

14 Corded ware beaker, Wiesbaden (Hesse)

amphorae and, more especially, little beakers with a silhouette like the letter 'S': this is the *Schnurkeramik* of the German authors, the Corded Ware of the Anglo-Saxons, a terminology which recalls the frequent use of cord in the decoration. These pots were to undergo many variations and a blending with another, later group, the Bell Beakers.

The problem of the Indo-Europeans

The Corded Ware peoples brought new ideas and changes in funeral rites. What was the economic effect of their migrations? They helped the spread of metal, which they imitated so well in stone. It is generally thought that they were groups of itinerant herdsmen, for they spread a new kind of husbandry which implied a constant quest for new pastures. Earlier Neolithic groups were more tied to the soil, more sedentary and preferred to pen their cattle. The Corded Ware people moved about with theirs, occasionally settling and forming stable communities in favourable places. In areas like the Low Countries, they even seem to have halted on sandy territory, which had never previously been settled: this suggests peaceful relations with the Neolithic peoples and ethnic juxtaposition rather than mixtures.

Since the word is so frequently heard, can we include the Corded Ware or the Battle Axe peoples in the Indo-European group? Some have believed firmly that they belong

15

there. The theory even had its fanatics such as that founding father, Kossinna, who long ago insisted on the pan-Germanic origins of Europe, or Professor P. Bosch-Gimpera, who, in a very long dissertation, made almost half the populations of prehistoric Europe Indo-European. It was even assumed that it was groups related to the Battle Axe peoples who brought destruction to the Mediterranean regions around 2500–2000 BC, penetrating as far as Greece and Troy. This destruction demonstrates the appearance of a new phenomenon at this particular moment: the development of pillage and insecurity, and this was partially linked with the discovery of metal. Indeed, if the sacking of Neolithic villages only brought in a few measures of wheat or foodstuff, a few cattle or some polished axes, that of the earliest communities of metal-working pastoralists was much more fruitful. Raids on ever larger animal populations and on the collections of metal treasures, copper and gold, which, though small in quantity, had a high commercial value, were extremely worthwhile. Every new technical achievement has its drawback. Metal production, which implied storing surplus stocks not for immediate use, brought in its train a rise in banditry.

To which of the Indo-European groups might our Corded Ware peoples have been related? Perhaps those raiders of the Aegean in the third millennium had some link with the Achaeans. Perhaps we should look for a more distant kinship, with the Hittites or their ancestors. But archaeological-philological speculation is a very difficult art. Some authors would rather see the first Indo-Europeans in the region of the Neolithic Danubian tribes, earlier than the Corded Ware peoples. The skein is far from being unravelled.

The 'Bell-Beaker explosion': flux and reflux

If there is one type of pottery which, by its beauty and its unusual geographic distribution, quickly drew the attention of archaeologists, it is the Bell Beaker ware. This name is given to a whole range of varied forms: rimless bowls, shallow cups, beakers, well-fired, coloured red or black and decorated with bands of geometrical motifs, combed, corded or stamped. But the commonest, most classical basic shape is a bell-like beaker, whence the expression 'Bell Beaker', with an S-shaped outline, and a flat or slightly curved base. This type of vessel is ornamented with horizontal bands alternately smooth and decorated with slanting incisions, sometimes encrusted with white and stretching from the rim to the base. The execution of this pottery, which is often faultless, makes it one of the peaks of ceramic art.

This remarkable production which is dated to around 2000 by radio-carbon (b.c.), or even earlier ('uncalibrated' dates) – in other words to the period of the so-called 'Chalcolithic' cultures – is found in abundance in the Iberian peninsula, where it was studied very early on, but it is also found in France, the British Isles – where the vessels are called 'beakers' – in Belgium, the Netherlands, Germany and Poland, where hybridisations with the Corded group already described occur. By the Mediterranean route it reached southern France, Sardinia, Italy, Czechoslovakia and Hungary. The first works, such as A.

16 Polypod bowl of Bell Beaker ware, Baden (south Germany)

15 Bell beaker, megalithic burial at Kerbors (Brittany)

17 Bell Beaker ware from Languedoc, Boun Marcou (Aude)

18 British beaker

del Castillo's, described a folk migration, originating in Spain and bringing a knowledge of metal to Europe through a whole network of small traders. The Bell Beaker is often accompanied by little copper, tanged daggers, sometimes called 'western daggers' – to distinguish them from the more complicated daggers of Únětice and of the northern Bronze Age or the Aegean cultures – and by small gold objects, little beads or pendants.

At first a Mediterranean origin for the Bell Beaker culture was sought. The shape of the vessels was similar to the calabash and to African esparto vessels, made of alfa grass or other vegetable fibres. Archaeologists like V. Gordon Childe even hinted at the possibility of remote Egyptian influences. As for the ornamentation, first traces of it were found in the *pointillé* decoration of ancient Iberian Neolithic ceramics. All these ideas are outmoded now and it is thought that the origin was probably located in Portugal, although for a long time there was support for an origin somewhere in central Spain.

Very soon it was noticed that the bell shape had given rise to the development of a host of secondary groups. The most typical was the group of 'beakers' in Britain where, in another context, a particular physical type was found. The Beaker people had round heads, brachycephalic, and were buried in round tumuli (the 'round barrows'), while the descendants of indigenous Neolithic peoples were dolichocephalic – that is they had long heads, and were laid to rest in long tumuli or 'long-barrows'. This curious correlation between the shapes of the tumuli and the craniums that they covered provided a talking point in archaeological gatherings all over Europe at the turn of the century.

A. del Castillo's classic theory was taken up by the great Australian archaeologist V. Gordon Childe, who described the Bell Beaker people as small, armed bands of merchants roaming Europe in search of precious materials like amber and callaïs; they traded small copper and gold objects which were much admired by the Neolithic peoples. It was tempting to imagine their way of life: small, armed groups, always on the move, perhaps making use of horses or mules, although there is no evidence for that.

Their armament, on the other hand, is well known: they had at their disposal little copper 'western daggers' but, more significantly, they were good archers. In their tombs are found highly sophisticated barbed and tanged flint arrowheads. Their archers' wristguards, which protect the skin from injury when the bowstring is released, consist of a rectangular plaque of bone or slate which is attached to the wrist with linen or leather thongs. Copper javelin heads, originating from Palmela in Portugal, are occasionally found in western Europe, Brittany or Vendée.

The jewellery includes small gold objects, little clothes fasteners or spirals. But the Bell Beaker groups in Portugal exported more important jewellery like the great necklaces with massive gold cords. Little is known about their dress, apart from the buttons or toggles made of bone, stone or amber, which fastened the items of clothing; they had a V-shaped perforation through which the thread passed and are regularly found in tombs.

The metal goods are limited, at least, in the tombs – a few awls or punches – but it seems likely that many of the flat copper axes found singly or in hoards should be ascribed to these early metallurgists. Perhaps they even taught the first rudiments of metallurgy to the Neolithic peoples.

They also exported their pots. These have sometimes been seen as tankards for beer or a fermented drink, on the strength of a few grains of millet found at the bottom of a Portuguese beaker. It is a very bold suggestion but it poses the eternal question of the trades which have left no trace: salt, drinks, perhaps the first alcohols, trade in which may have been very important then as now. We have well known examples of this from more recent periods: did not the 'Celtic thirst' give rise to trade in luxury goods like situli and bronze vessels, and was there not an amazing trade in wine amphorae in antiquity? Be that as it may, the Bell Beaker people mingled easily in the communities they visited. Perhaps, in addition to their trading stock of copper and gold, they had the smooth tongues of commercial travellers which gained them admission even into the burial chambers: traces of them have indeed been found under individual tumuli in the Netherlands or Bohemia as well as in the chambered tombs of southern France and the passage and gallery graves of Brittany. Often, like the cuckoo, they slept in other men's beds.

The increasing numbers of discoveries and studies recently have only reaffirmed the

19 'Western dagger', Bell Beaker culture, Le Moustier (Lot-et-Garonne)

complexity of the Bell Beaker problem. It is true that the homogeneity of the basic shapes suggests a phenomenally rapid spread which could justify the expression 'Bell Beaker explosion' which is sometimes used. A. del Castillo's original theory envisaged an expansion radiating outwards from the Guadalquivir towards the Atlantic zone through Portugal, Brittany, the British Isles and the Netherlands. North Africa was reached via the Mediterranean. Finally, patience won a route through Sicily, Sardinia and Italy to central Europe. The detailed study of the ceramics has opened the way to subtle distinctions. A very pure style with fine, even, alternating bands, known as pan-European or maritime, did in fact spread from Portugal to Brittany and northern Europe. But how complex the more evolved forms became, with contrasting decoration including incisions, grooves, 'zip fasteners', and even corded decoration borrowed from the Battle Axe people! What a mixture!

At one time a dual origin was suggested: on the one hand in Spain, on the other in Bohemia and Moravia. This 'parallel' theory, formerly supported by the Italian, Palliardi, has recently been taken up again by a young British researcher, R. J. Harrison: a sound argument, based on relatively early radio-carbon dates for some Dutch vessels, gives food for thought; however, the theory has few supporters.

The controversy over the Rückstrom

The great debate on the subject of the Bell Beaker culture keeps coming back to the *Rückstrom* theory launched by E. Sangmeister about 1960. *Rückstrom* means reflux: the movements of the Bell Beaker people are thought not to have been one way only, but to have consisted of a dual movement of flux and reflux, which is hardly surprising for a movement of Atlantic origins. From Portugal they would have reached Brittany, Holland, the Rhine and arrived in Bohemia to inspire the development of a group there. Much cross-fertilisation with the Corded Ware peoples would then have occurred and a vast return

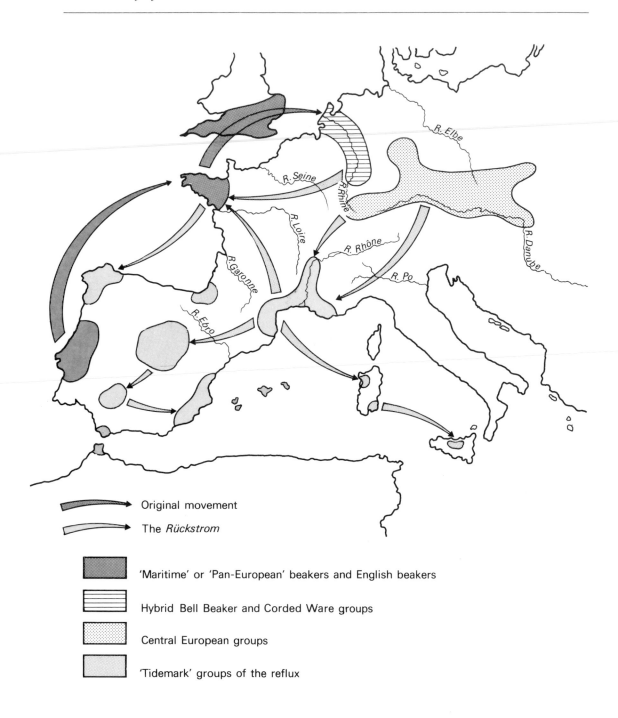

Original movement

The *Rückstrom*

'Maritime' or 'Pan-European' beakers and English beakers

Hybrid Bell Beaker and Corded Ware groups

Central European groups

'Tidemark' groups of the reflux

1 Migrations of the Bell Beaker peoples: the *Rückstrom* (after E. Sangmeister)

movement, marked by more complicated pottery with more varied decoration, would have pushed down the Rhine valley and the Atlantic coast, scattering many tide marks on the way; these may be found in plenty in Brittany, in the Pyrenees and even in Spain. The theory, which is seductive despite its vagueness, received the approval of many archaeologists – in itself something exceptional.

However, the last had not been heard of these restless Bell Beaker folk who were to stir many minds yet. E. Sangmeister's theory was scrapped; impossible chronologies in the Corded Ware–Bell Beaker relationships were pointed out: a beaker which should have been a derivative was shown by radio-carbon to be earlier than its supposed model, which was embarassing, to say the least. Sangmeister himself then revised his opinions. The famous return current was said to have split in two: a true *Rückstrom* which brought the Bell Beaker, crossed with Corded Ware peoples from the north-west back to the south and west of Europe, and a '*Zustrom*', running parallel, showing a flowering of central European Bell Beaker groups, which, in turn, sent derivatives back towards Spain. Moreover, some Czechoslovakian archaeologists had already begun to think that the origins of the earliest Bohemian or Moravian Bell Beaker peoples should be sought in the late Neolithic civilisations of north-west Yugoslavia (Vučedol group).

But the Atlantic ebb and flow, too, was challenged, and H. N. Savory even wanted to know if the first Bell Beaker people were not simply Corded Ware people. Corded decorations have, in fact, been found in the Bell Beaker burial at Gâvres in Brittany, studied by J. L'Helgouach and dating from the mid-third millennium: however, the Bell Beaker ware, an intrusion according to the excavator (it is known as a secondary re-use), could be later and belong to around 2000 BC. On the other hand, a typical decoration has been accepted as very early among the great Bell Beaker series of southern France and the Pyrenees, which J. Guilaine's work has made available for study. So it is not so simple: we are a long way from the charming notion of little Bell Beaker groups roaming Europe on their donkeys. Some major phenomenon has occurred which is difficult to distinguish. The heated debates of the specialists, which are difficult to follow at times, show what a complicated problem it is to reconstruct the great trends of ancient civilisations.

Belated Bell Beaker groups lingered on, mingling intimately with the early Bronze civilisations. In Holland there is the Veluwe group with their, at times, rather angular Batavian pots. They even adopted the funeral customs of the Corded Ware peoples, with stockaded tumuli. In their homes they used huge bell-shaped 'pot-beakers' for storing food. In England the Beaker groups were to display great powers of survival, well into the Bronze Age and, more particularly, they were to play a major part in the birth of the early Bronze Age Wessex culture. They were to be responsible for the first monuments composed of wooden or stone circles – the henges – and the earliest phases of the astronomical temple at Stonehenge.

The Bell Beaker phenomenon overflowed into North Africa, further proof of its vitality. A few pieces of pottery and a series of very characteristic daggers have come to light there, as for instance the one at Cap Chenoua near Algiers, described by G. Camps.

This is important because a metal industry was to continue for a very long time in Africa, using styles apparently derived from metal forms invented about 2000 BC by the Bell Beaker folk. Still further afield, Mauretania has provided a whole series of arrow and javelin tips which are curiously reminiscent of the weapons at Palmela. It is odd that subsequently other technical innovations which mark the progress of Bronze Age metallurgy in Europe rarely crossed the straits of Gibraltar. Some weapons – very few, it is true – and some cave drawings provide evidence of a tentative development of proto-historic industries in these regions, where much remains to be discussed.

To sum up, the Corded Ware peoples, and, later, groups of Bell Beaker folk, closely intermingled at times, caused an extraordinary ferment in the beginnings of Bronze Age Europe. They brought with them social and cultural innovations, the development of trade and contacts between groups of human beings as well as considerable novelties in the economic sphere, the development of animal husbandry in the case of the Corded Ware people, the knowledge of metallurgy in that of the Bell Beaker folk. Nowadays the 'new archaeology' tends to play down these 'migrations', preferring to look for the evolution of group cultures within a more local framework. But it is nevertheless indisputable that something of importance happened near the beginning of the second millennium and its repercussions were felt right down to the Mediterranean world. Ah those Indo-Europeans!

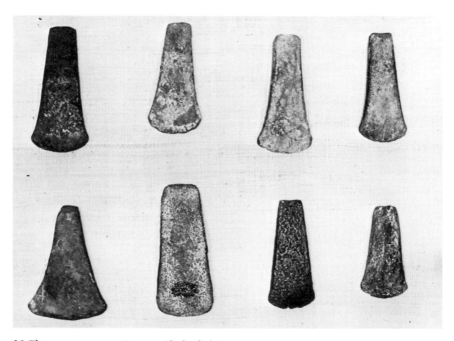

20 Flat copper axes, Breton Chalcolithic

The kings of the kurgans

Before turning to the new civilisations which will mark the early phase of the Bronze Age, let us take a quick look at the south-eastern fringe of Europe. Some tribes from the steppes created ephemeral and very strange kingdoms there, as a result of contacts with the great empires of the East. They are roughly contemporary with our Bell Beaker and Corded Ware groups and, like them, belong to Neolithic traditions by their way of life and to the new age by the appearance of metal and unusual funeral rites – hence the appellation Chalcolithic in the older writers.

In the steppes to the north of the Caucasus, between the Caspian Sea and the Black Sea, in Kuban, the great plain swelled up into huge mysterious lumps known, by popular tradition, as kurgans. For the first archaeologists, who had something of the treasure hunter about them – but of course things have changed! – these enormous mounds, more than 10m high, must inevitably conceal magnificent objects. And for once it was true! The Maikop excavation in 1843 revealed to the astonished world the existence of marvellous barbarian royal houses, unprecedented in Europe and dating from the middle of the third millennium BC.

Beneath the great mound at Maikop a sacred stone circle surrounded the royal tomb of timber. There were three compartments: to the south lay the remains of the prince, sumptuously adorned; to the north, each in its own recess, a man and a woman, more modestly dressed, no doubt the most devoted retainers accompanying the king on his last journey.

The prince was covered in ochre. There was nothing surprising in this, since this tradition, dating back to distant Palaeolithic times, had been preserved in many Russian Neolithic groups. Red ochre was associated with purification, the colour of fire and also of blood. After the corpses had been sprinkled with ochre, the flesh decomposed but the ochre remained to adorn the skeleton with its symbolic red glow.

The crouched position of the body was perfectly normal, but less normal was the amazing luxury surrounding the deceased: copper arms, hundreds of gold or silver appliqués, vases and precious stones. On his head the prince had a diadem ornamented with small gold rosettes. The most extraordinary item of furniture was a large dais: the uprights were gold and silver tubes with massive gold bulls as handles and the cloth which formed the canopy was embellished with countless gold and silver appliqué animals and discs – a processional dais of which a king of France could have been proud! The silver vases with repoussé ornamentation proved unrivalled in their decoration. The composition combines landscapes with mountains, palm trees and a spring cascading from a lake above processions of animals. The style is naive with the heads amusingly deformed. The selection of animals is surprising and has something of a Noah's Ark atmosphere about it. The little hairy horse of the steppes is there – the Przewalski as scientists call it – wild boar, bear, wild sheep and goat, but there is also a lion being ridden by a bird, a panther and a kind of great bustard.

The unexpected appearance of these animals calls the East irresistibly to mind. Were these silver vases imported or is the primitive technique more indicative of local imitation? The question remains unanswered and may be repeated in connection with the copper objects deposited in the tomb: an adze of pure Sumerian style and an axe-adze which foreshadows analogous types found in Hungary at Bodrogkeresztur.

The tomb at Maikop is not an isolated example and other burials in the same region confirmed the magnificence and royal character of the tombs. They provided hitherto unpublished documentation on clothing. The burial at Novosvobodnaya, formerly Tsarskaya, included a complete wardrobe: first a cloak of black goatskin, the hairy side out, then a camel-hair coat trimmed with black, and lastly a linen tunic edged with purple. That was the royal robe, the coronation coat. The tombs at Novosvobodnaya are interesting too, because of the way they are built: they are small cave-like constructions of stone slabs, compartmentalised and in one case topped with a ridged roof, apparently copying the house types then in use.

21 Silver vase from the Maikop kurgan (Kuban)

The kings of the Kuban were undoubtedly very rich: they traded in cattle – animal husbandry was very important in those societies – and particularly sheep; but it may be that they were mining for the very first time the mineral deposits of the Caucasus. Indeed we should not insult these princes by believing their wealth to be simply the fruits of plundering raids outside the Caucasus on the great highly developed cities such as Alaca Hüyück, or the even more distant Tepe Issar in Iran, or perhaps even Troy, eternal and magnificent! Affinities with the Kuban group have indeed often been sought in these sites, but the Maikop vases remain undeniably native in style.

Russian archaeologists have discovered dwellings near these kurgans. The common people remained poor, living in big huts of willow daubed on both sides with clay. Evidence for agriculture takes the form of traces of soil cultivation, the use of sickles with flint blades, and of querns. Moreover, quantities of animal bones testify to stock raising. Luxury was reserved for a small élite.

The steppe civilisations

The Scythian civilisation has often been mentioned in connection with the early kurgans; it was to dawn more than a millennium later, in the same regions and with the same barbarian wealth, appropriate to these 'royal hordes', to quote the felicitous phrase of E. D. Phillips. In spite of the great difference in time scale, there are some disturbing similarities in the animal art.

If Maikop appears to be a privileged moment, a glow of oriental magnificence in the midst of the other, more drab steppe cultures, it was not without its successors. Leaving aside the parallel with the Scythians, in Transcaucasia there is a group of kurgans with equally rich grave goods, dated by A. Montgaït to the eighteenth century BC. There, too, gold and silver vases were deposited. At Trialéti, for example, the richest chiefs of the pastoral tribes were buried on their massive four-wheeled carts. Quarters of animals were deposited in their tombs for the great journey but, in addition, there were fine examples of the goldsmith's art: thus a shallow gold cup with filigree decoration and encrusted with turquoise was a piece which a Renaissance artist would not have scorned. The processional theme returns in these vessels: stags this time, but in addition, some quaint characters with animal heads and tails marching past with cups in their hands. At Kirovanan lions were engraved on gold cups, still with large, clumsily executed heads.

22 Gold bull from the Maikop kurgan (Kuban)

25

If we accept the Russian archaeologists' arguments, social differences can be sensed between Maikop, which practised human sacrifice, and Trialéti; the former knew slavery which required human chattels to follow their master even into death. It was a class-ridden society. At Trialéti sacrifice was not known; there were no longer distinct castes although considerable differences in fortune persisted, to judge by the inequalities in the grave goods. Evolution towards a more socialist world was slowly taking place.

In their gold and silver vessels, Maikop and Trialéti carried on a tradition of animal art which had its roots in the distant world of Sumer. This art was to be renewed and reach new heights with the Scythian civilisations. The other regions of western Europe were able to produce equally fine gold vessels, but the decoration remained purely geometrical. The Bell Beaker cups from Rillaton in England and Eschenz in Switzerland would have simple ornamentation consisting of regular curved lines of gold leaf, whereas later, in France, circles and discs – probable solar symbols – were to decorate the vases at Rongères or the cone at Avanton.

So we find the two basic trends of barbarian art once more: the old geometric style with symbolic motifs in the west and a more vivid, concrete art persisting in the Danube regions and at times up into northern Europe.

Chapter 2

Mediterranean Awakenings: from the Aegean to Andalusia

It is commonplace to assert that the eastern Mediterranean at the beginning of the second millennium was an amazing crucible whence flowed the most brilliant civilisations. Overflowing with their vast wealth, as V. Gordon Childe put it, the great empires of Egypt or Mesopotamia turned their eyes towards the Aegean and Europe, often drawing renewed vigour from the dynamic populations of the coasts and islands. Ships were setting out from the trading posts of Lebanese, Syrian or Anatolian merchants, loaded with weapons and jewels made of that copper which was already contributing to the wealth of the island of Cyprus. The famous Cypriot curved-tanged daggers and the massive torcs of Byblos were exported as far as central or Atlantic Europe.

23 The 'Warrior Vase' from Mycenae

They were the exchange currency for tin; the recent invention of bronze was to lead to a new quest for deposits of tin, and the richest lay in the unknown lands of barbarian Europe. A by-product of this contact with the northern peoples was the discovery of that strange, fascinating substance, the fossil resin called amber – the 'electrum' of the ancients. The need for these and many other products fostered trade, barter and even envy, rapine and a move towards monopolies. The tribute exacted by intermediaries on the way was, after all, a new means of subsistence. We may imagine how bitter was the struggle for supremacy in the Mediterranean and how control of the seaways became a major preoccupation for the great men of the day.

In the Aegean power passed in succession from the Cyclades to Crete and then to Mycenae.

The Aegean: the Cyclades, Crete, Mycenae

The first in date were the civilisations of the Cyclades, around 2200 BC. They are the least well known, but two series of artefacts were enough to immortalise them: the little rowing boats with the emblem of a fish displayed on their high prow, carved on vessels shaped like frying pans, and the delicate white marble idols with fine stylised faces. Who is not familiar with the superb marble heads in the Louvre or the museum in Athens and the musicians playing a double flute or a lyre as they charm their flocks or their shepherdesses in bucolic settings? These island people were only spare-time artists; they were small-time pirates first and foremost.

Crete took over from them, with its world of wonderfully frescoed palaces, its leaping bulls and bare-breasted goddesses brandishing serpents. Twice the kingdom of Minos attained an apogee followed by brutal destruction. From the second, around 1400 BC, it was unable to recover.

24 'Frying pan' with an illustration of a ship, Siros (Cyclades)

25 (*above*) The harpist, a marble idol from Keros (Cyclades)
26 (*above right*) Marble idol from the Cyclades

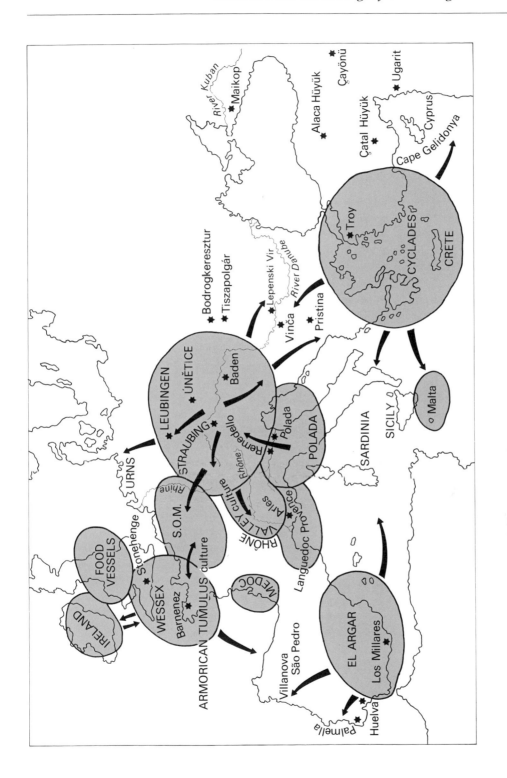

2 Europe in the early Bronze Age, with Neolithic and Chalcolithic sites

Mycenae then became the mistress of the Aegean, with its harsher world of citadels, war chariots and tombs of masculine, bearded warriors, in which the romantic H. Schliemann thought he had discovered the famous heroes of the *Iliad*. Mycenae, with its daggers encrusted with gold and niello, portraying hunting scenes and wars, with its expressive cameos celebrating the hand-to-hand combat of kings, also fell victim to man or the gods, despite its power and wealth, in a 'second end of the world', conjured up in masterly fashion by H. van Effenterre.

These Aegean tales have been so often told that it would be pointless to go into them again at length, but we must bear in mind the contributions these civilisations made to the birth of the western world. They are indisputable, but it may be that some of them have been overestimated by scholars, dazzled by the prestige of Crete and Mycenae. Modern methods of analysis, for example radio-carbon dating, have demonstrated recently the very great antiquity of the Atlantic architectural civilisations, like that of the megaliths. In the Mediterranean, too, there were centres of culture which pre-date those of the Aegean and we shall consider, among others, one of the most famous: the enigmatic civilisation of the Maltese temples.

Megalithic cultures

The term 'megaliths' has been given to a number of monumental constructions, consisting of undressed, widely spaced stones. The simplest are the menhirs, which are simply standing stones (often arranged in alignments, cromlechs, etc.). Dolmens have characteristic horizontal stone slabs supported by low walls or other upright stones. The gallery graves are a kind of elongated dolmen. The hypogea, walled with stone slabs, or carved out of rock, the navetas of Minorca, the great cupola burials of Andalusia and Portugal, etc., are also 'megalithic'. The funerary purpose of these monuments is generally evident: they are mainly collective tombs, common in the Neolithic.

The term 'megalithic constructions' has been extended to include other monuments exhibiting the same kind of widely spaced stone construction – these are the so-called Cyclopean walls, an allusion to the strength of the legendary Greek monsters – but are not necessarily funerary in purpose: there are religious edifices such as the great temples of Malta or Stonehenge, or even civil or military buildings: the talayots of the Balearic Islands, the nuraghi and torres of Sardinia and Corsica, etc.

The fourth millennium witnessed the development of a great religious phenomenon: the inauguration of new funeral rites, linked with the appearance of megaliths. The first signs appeared along the Atlantic seaboard where the first great dolmens were constructed. Very soon the megalithic civilisations stretched from Scandinavia to Iberia. Their beginnings and their spectacular spread across the whole of western Europe are one of the most contentious problems of prehistory. The dissemination was so rapid and the relationships were such that a 'megalithic religion' has been postulated, spread by

27 The 'Recumbent Goddess' from the hypogeum at Hal Saflieni (Malta)

'missionaries' up and down the Channel and the Atlantic: they are supposed to have celebrated a new cult based on grandiose monuments to the dead and representations of sacred horns and goddesses associated with the fertility cult. Unfortunately, religious concepts and funeral rites are still largely beyond our grasp.

This wave of megaliths, which was to cover the west through more than two millennia, developed above all in privileged areas – Brittany and the Iberian peninsula in particular: we shall study these later. Southern France was also affected by the new faith, but a little later. Much more ancient and honoured and perhaps even the source, or, at least an important staging post in the spread of the new faith, were the megalithic temples of Malta.

Malta: 1000 years before the Pyramids

The little Maltese archipelago occupies a key position between Sicily and Tunisia, between the two Mediterraneans – eastern and western. Malta's role in history – at the time when it was the main base of the Knights of St John of Jerusalem, who had sworn to defend Christendom against the infidels of Turkey and the Barbary coast and never to lower their banner – is well known. The fortifications of Valetta still bear witness to that glorious past. But some 5000 years earlier, Malta was an extraordinary centre of architecture, which was misunderstood for a long time, perhaps because of the mystery surrounding its monuments.

This very ancient Maltese civilisation has some basic features common to many western Mediterranean civilisations: the use of artifical caves dug in the ground to bury the dead (a formula which led to the hypogea and the constructions with 'Cyclopean' walls). Here we are witnessing the beginnings of Mediterranean architecture. The use of small circular walls gives rise to the round huts of the villages, but it also allows defensive walls provided with bastions and even the building of actual towers. All this architecture, Mediterranean in origin, was soon to be found on the coastal fringes of Iberia and southern France, and especially in the islands. Because of their natural isolation these islands were to

31

develop very individual features: the Corsican torre and statue-menhir cultures, the Balearics with their taulas and navetas, Sardinia with its gigantic nuraghi and little votive bronzes. But none of these civilisations was to flourish until late in the Bronze Age, towards the end of the second millennium. Here, in Malta, remarkable architecture arose much earlier: the great temples appeared around 2800 BC and ceased quite abruptly about 2000 or 1800 BC (using 'conventional' [14]C dating).

And yet this civilisation had no knowledge of metal (it arrived after the temples were abandoned and is found in them, as an obvious intrusion, brought by new arrivals). Thus they represent an essentially Neolithic – or, in the hybrid sense of the term, already discussed – Chalcolithic civilisation.

The dating of monuments in the Maltese archipelago has proved to be a fascinating problem which at times has generated some heat. The chronological criterion by which the final phase of the construction of these temples was assessed, remained, until quite recently, simply the style of certain stone altars: these blocks were decorated either with animal friezes or with elegant spiral motifs, the prototypes of which were sought in the neighbourhood of Crete or Mycenae. This led to the belief that the final fitting out of these great temples had taken place around 1600 BC. But recent works by J. D. Evans and D. H. Trump included radio-carbon dates which were a revelation if not a source of consternation for many people. The most ancient showed a Neolithic occupation of the island in the region of 4200 b.c. uncorrected, or around 5000 BC in corrected dates. The temples are more recent (they do not begin until the so-called 'Ggantija' phase), and their dates, according to D. H. Trump, range from 2000 to 2800 b.c. or 2500 to 3500 BC (corrected radio-carbon dates).

As the same author observes, the great pyramids of Egypt go back only to 2575 BC and the first Cretan palaces were not built until after 2000. Which means that the early phases of the Maltese temples pre-date the great classical civilisations by a millennium or more. For the British archaeologist, Colin Renfrew, this is a weighty argument which underlines the importance of the revolution, brought about by radio-carbon dating, in our overall view of prehistoric civilisations. He even heads a chapter on the Maltese temples, 'The world's first stone temples'. In this striking fashion he emphasises the importance and antiquity of the monumental architecture of the island; its builders – Neolithic men! – seem to be the forerunners of the whole cycle of Mediterranean civilisations. Perhaps they were even the instructors of the Minoan and Mycenaean architects.

Despite this respectable antiquity we may be permitted to ask whether the architecture of Malta is the first or only one of the first in the prehistoric world. The clay or plaster structures which appear in the pre-Sumerian or Anatolian world from 7000 or 6000 BC, with their celebrated bull's head temples at Çatal Hüyück, are earlier than the Maltese. As far as stone building is concerned, however, Malta remains the earliest, but only in the Mediterranean world: for from 3500 b.c., or 4000 BC, the first dolmens and tumuli were being raised in Brittany and also the great tholoi such as Barnenez, which we will discuss later.

The Mother Goddess and the great trefoil-plan temples

The monuments of Malta, in an early phase, consisted of classical hypogea, simple tombs carved out of the rock. They were to evolve into extraordinary monuments, under the influence of other buildings also open to the sky: the megalithic temples which were to become more and more complex: the climax (the so-called Tarxien phase) has multi-chambered hypogea like the one at Hal Saflieni, as vast and complex as the great open-air temples at Ggantija or Hal Tarxien.

Archaeologists have always been surprised by the astonishing convergence of the Maltese monuments with western European types of architecture, as for instance, the megalithic tombs. Between an enclosed world, like that of a Mediterranean island, and a series of continental civilisations, evolving in a complex manner, many similarities have been found: the construction of semicircular façades in front of the entrances, the use of corbelled coverings, the use of 'porthole slabs' as doors. These slabs have a rectangular perforation which has been interpreted in various ways: prosaically, as a hole for communication purposes, to pass stones through from the temples for modification, to pass offerings or perhaps, even, in the last resort, corpses; more spiritually as a symbolic opening, the 'soul hole' or *Seelenloch* of the German archaeologists. This perforated slab was to be found again in western Europe – around 3500 in the dolmen tumulus at Barnenez, a millennium later in the passage graves in Brittany or in the gallery graves of the Seine-Oise-Marne culture in the Paris Basin.

28 The 'Headless Lady', temple of Hagar Qim (Malta)

The cult associated with these funerary or religious monuments is the same, too, that of the Mother Goddess. In Malta, according to J. D. Evans, stylised heads of the old common Anatolian stock turn up again, together with some profiles – like the ones at Hal Tarxien – that are worthy of Matisse. A little later the opulence of the 'obese goddesses' would appear, the 'headless lady' of the Hagar Qim temple or the 'recumbent goddess' of the Hal Saflieni hypogeum, this last lady wearing a skirt somewhat reminiscent of the Sumerian style. And so we see these agricultural and pastoral peoples in Malta preoccupied with the same religious problems as the Atlantic civilisations and proposing the same

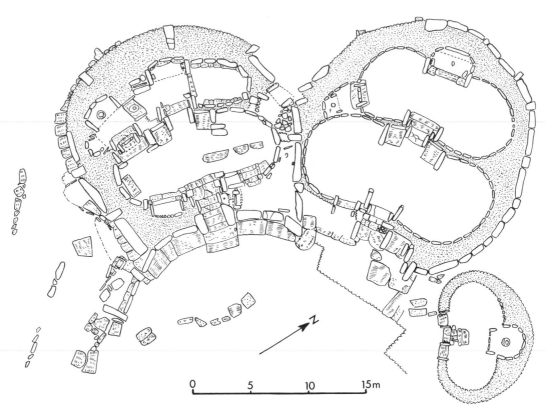

29 Plan of the Temple of Mnajdra (Malta)

solutions both from an architectural and a religious point of view. The pastoral nature of the Maltese civilisation is borne out by frescoes portraying goats, pigs and oxen as well as by the bones of religious and funerary offerings.

The Maltese temples are some thirty in number of which a dozen are still well preserved or partially restored, like the one at Hagar Qim, giving us some idea of the ancient splendour of these master works. The area covered by these monuments varies from a few square metres up to the exceptionally large Hal Tarxien which exceeds 5000m². It is true that the type of structure lent itself to a process of successive extensions. The basic plan is of a façaded building with a central entrance leading to a series of chambers. The earliest examples have a simple trifoliate structure: two round chambers on either side of an absidal passageway. At Ggantija on the island of Gozo, the plan is more complicated with two lateral antechambers in front of the trifoliate sanctuary area.

The classical interpretation of the Maltese megaliths is that they were temples, on account of their size, their many rooms, which could serve different stages of some ritual, and also because of the sacred courtyard in front of the temples, where, in exceptional circumstances, larger numbers of the faithful could foregather. Finally, the bones collected in them are overwhelmingly those of animals and are, it seems, the remains of offerings. The occasional human burials are due largely to later re-use of the sites, but when the temples were being used for religious purposes the dead were buried in hypogea, and the main cult was that of the Mother Goddess, protectress of crops and herds. In order to win her favours these pastoral people, with the firm faith of country folk, did not hesitate to devote a considerable amount of time to building and embellishing the houses dedicated to her.

However a question mark has been 'raised over this traditional interpretation by recent studies of the social organisation of the Maltese temple builders, which suggest territorial or even aristocratic differentiations. In the first place, Colin Renfrew shows that the distribution of the Maltese temples is not haphazard but is arranged in groups of two, three or four in well-defined territories, like so many small diocesan centres. A group of two temples at Ggantija seems to dominate the island of Gozo, whereas in Malta itself five groups can be considered to be religious centres of as many well-defined territories. This implies a distribution of spiritual, and, no doubt, also of temporal power between large units of authority associated with the temples. Thus a religious aristocracy could have dominated a common people of peasants and megalith builders.

This idea fits in perfectly with the views of J. D. Evans, who takes as his starting point the internal organisation of the temples themselves. Its extreme complexity, with altars, annexes, corridors, huge open spaces, etc., is evidence of a complicated ritual. It required a specialist caste of priests, solely occupied with the demands of the faith; but from being officiators, these priests may well have become administrators as well, and even the representatives of the gods on earth. The great excavator of the Tarxien monuments, Sir Themistocles Zammit, noted as early as 1916 that some of the clay statuettes could represent the priests themselves rather than the gods. The furthermost rooms of the religious monuments would have been the shrines where the priests played the part of oracles, as at Delphi. And, of course, they would receive certain small material rewards in the normal course of things.

The great megalithic civilisation of Malta seems to have come to a very abrupt end. Themistocles Zammit saw it as the result of some natural catastrophe, possibly an epidemic. It has also been suggested that men arrived from the mainland, armed with metal implements, daggers and copper axes and murderous arrows carved from razor-sharp obsidian – for in Malta a metal culture followed that of the Megaliths – but the reasons for the abandonment of the trefoil temples remain swathed in mystery.

There is no doubt that Malta was the great ancestor of all the western Mediterranean architectural civilisations, but it is difficult to define the role, if any, that she played in the spread both of religious ideas and of construction techniques. In any case, it is disturbing to find in Sardinia 'giants' tombs' with monumental entrances and crescent-shaped open spaces, which recall some of the structural features of Malta. We must not forget, either, the remote links with the west which we mentioned previously.

Dolmens and statue-menhirs in southern France

The South of France enjoyed very early and brilliant Neolithic civilisations. There, too, radio-carbon dating has pushed back the emergence of these new cultures, which were notable for the development of animal husbandry, agriculture and pottery. Following the work of V. Gordon Childe, the great archaeologist, these profound economic changes were known as the 'Neolithic Revolution'. This term emphasised the importance of this upheaval, but implied an element of violence, whereas, on the contrary, the replacement of a hunter-gatherer economy by agriculture and animal husbandry was a gradual process.

30 Dolmen from the south of France (Gabaudet, at Issendolus, Lot)

In the Near East, the first Neolithic societies appeared very early, around 8000 BC. In the South of France, the work and excavations of M. Escalon de Fonton have led to the recognition that, in sites like Chateauneuf-lez-Martigues, Bouches du Rhône, sheep were being raised as early as the sixth millennium, starting, probably, from captured local varieties. The invention of pottery followed shortly and very soon there were differentiations into individual styles which made the recognition of regional schools a possibility. In Southern France, for example, Cardial ware predominates in the early Neolithic, so called because the pots were decorated with the edge of a Cardium shell. At l'Abri de Chateauneuf-lez-Martigues, M. Escalon de Fonton was able to date Cardial ware to 5570 BC, making it the earliest pottery in the western Mediterranean, according to G. Bailloud. Soon, during the middle Neolithic, around the fourth millennium, other pottery styles appeared; Danubian from central Europe, the pots decorated with punched or applied motifs, and Chassey ware, with fine, round-based pots, taking its name from the Camp de Chassey in Saône-et-Loire.

Towards the end of the Neolithic, the Megalithic wave broke and was of great importance in Languedoc and Provence, which it did not reach until the beginning of the third millennium, a little later than elsewhere.

But what an abundance of monuments! J. Clottes has reminded us that half the dolmens on French soil were to be found between Provence and the Quercy region. They are very varied: from small stone boxes or 'cists' to galleried graves, sometimes surrounded by a mound or tumulus, to the passage graves with an entrance passage, etc.

Despite difficulties of interpretation (for these monuments were often re-used for burials at later periods – and, again, most have been plundered by treasure hunters) a classification can be made, based on the grave goods, which are very varied; on the basis of the pottery, in particular, numerous local styles can be defined. Some derive from Chassey ware, for example the Ferrières group in Languedoc decorated with incised chevrons. The Fontbouïsse culture, named by Dr J. Arnal from a site in Hérault, has yielded some fine pots with channelled decoration in a metopic arrangement. This group is particularly famous because the settlements are known and were recently catalogued by X. Gutherz: they are the first real 'villages' of Mediterranean France with groups of large huts inside low dry-stone walls: Conquette, at St Martin de Londres in Hérault, is a good example.

All these groups who buried their dead in megaliths are often placed at the end of the Neolithic, but more often in the Chalcolithic, a term we defined in the previous chapter, and which is still regarded with respect in southern France because it describes these

31 Divinity with 'the object', statue-menhir, Rosseironne (Gard)

Copper Age cultures rather well: they were societies in which metal was unknown, or hardly known (there are a few rare metal objects in the Fontbouïsse group), but they were contemporary with metal-using cultures and in any case were more sophisticated – in their pottery, their stone tools, their settlement types and, particularly, their funeral rites – than traditional Neolithic groups.

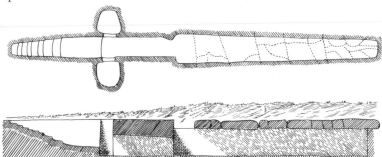

32 (*left*) Stela at Lauris (Vaucluse)
33 (*above*) Plan and section of the 'Epée de Roland', a hypogeum near Arles

Another feature of the Chalcolithic in southern France is the presence of carved stelae and statue-menhirs. These are found isolated, with no associations, notably in the departments of Gard, Tarn and Aveyron. They are distributed in groups in several localities and a study of them would be beyond the scope of this work. Let us recall their broad characteristics: the head of the divinity is schematic, sometimes sunk into the shoulders, at others quite separate. Some of them carry crossed axes, crossed swords or some unidentifiable cult symbol. The hands are crudely executed and lie across the belly. Often breasts are featured, or a many-rowed necklace, and the waist is enclosed in a big pleated belt. East of the Rhône, one distinctive group has stelae associated with cremation burials. Some, in particular the necropolis at Trets, Bouches du Rhône, have yielded a whole series of broken, carved slabs. They are unique in having the representation of the goddess surrounded by a geometric decoration composed of chevrons or lozenges and covering the whole surface of the stone.

The hypogea of Arles

The Chalcolithic of southern France does not only have passage graves. Where the rock was soft enough to be hollowed out the dead were laid in artificial grottoes or hypogea.

The tradition of hypogean burial spread throughout the Mediterranean. In Sicily there are the Conca d'Oro tombs; in Sardinia, at Anghelu Ruju, bulls' heads are often carved over the entrances: this is a relic of a Mediterranean cult which found its climax in Crete.

Some hypogea were to appear in Provence in the Chalcolithic. Imposing monuments as they were, they attracted the curiosity of treasure hunters who frequently plundered them, rendering their study more difficult. Popular tradition either saw them as fairy graves or linked them with the legend of some, often ill-fated, hero. At Arles, we have the 'Epée de Roland', while the hypogeum at Crottes à Roaix in the Vaucluse was said to be a cemetery of the Knights Templar, recalling some grim settlement of scores in history.

A hypogeum is a large cavity, hollowed out of the ground and covered with capping stones. It is essentially a funerary monument: witness the skeletons that have reached our times despite the countless more or less well-intentioned visitors who have come to disturb them down the millennia.

The most famous and impressive group is at Montagne de Cordes, a few kilometres to the north-east of Arles, towards Fontvieille. It has been repeatedly described by archaeologists of the south, and the latest works of G. Bailloud or J. Courtin have given a new insight into these huge tombs. For they are really very large: the overall length of the Hypogée des Fées, otherwise known as the 'Epée de Roland', is 42m and the burial chamber alone measures 25m in length. It must have been built with a view to epidemics and wars. The plan of the 'Grotte des Fées' ('Fairies' Grotto') is the most complicated of the series, for between the approach passage and the main chamber it has an entrance hall with two small circular apses, giving the monument a general cruciform appearance, whence the name 'Epée de Roland'. The chamber is hollowed out of soft rock – in geological terms 'myocene molasse of the Burdigalian'. The maximum width of the large hollow is 3m. The walls slope inward at the top to support a series of large capping stones. The other hypogea in the Arles region, Bounias, Le Castellet, Coutignardes and La Source, show similar large chambers, trapezoidal in cross-section, hewn carefully and evenly from the rock: a real work of art. Apart from Arles, the only tombs worth mentioning, according to Courtin – and they are often very modest – are at Sausset-les-Pins in Bouches du Rhône, Cairanne in the Vaucluse and Mollans and Roaix in Drôme.

The furnishings of these monuments are identical with those of other Provençal dolmens: fine flint daggers, polished on one face, and flaked arrowheads. In the higher levels, like those at Mollans, it is worth noting the sophisticated barbed and tanged arrowheads, associated with ceramics of the Bell Beaker people; they had been there too!

But it is the hypogeum at Roaix, excavated by J. Courtin, which yielded the richest and most complete furnishing, with two, clearly separated, levels of occupation. In the lower level were flint blades and daggers, sharp flint arrows and items of adornment amongst which stone and shell predominated: 2312 calibrated beads of limestone or mollusc shell, 185 of soapstone, 2 of callaïs – a rare and noble rock – about 30 other beads, 2 of dentalium, not to mention the numerous objects found out of context in the spoil of previous digs. For the earliest treasure hunters the use of a sieve was entirely superfluous.

In short, we have some thousands of stone beads for just one modest copper bead made by rolling up a small metal tube. The date (^{14}C) of this collection is 2150 b.c. or 2600 BC. The lower level, showing an extremely tentative appearance of metal, is covered by a metre of sterile sand. The upper level, on the other hand, sheltered a layer of superimposed skeletons, legs folded under, arms across their chests (about a hundred of them) clearly deposited at the same time. 'A war layer,' says J. Courtin, 'traces of the bloody affray of 2090 BC, if we are to believe the (conventional) radio-carbon date.' With the skeletons were found Fontbouïsse pottery and flint tools, placing this level firmly in the Chalcolithic of southern France.

'Aegean trading posts' in the west

The classical explanation of the appearance of new Chalcolithic or Bronze Age civilisations in the west involves the arrival there of Aegean or Anatolian prospectors. It has even been suggested that actual colonies were founded in the Mediterranean zone. The stay of the colonists may have been only temporary and marked by the discarding of a few material traces as, for instance, jugs with everted lips, typically Cycladean, and found in the neighbourhood of Marseilles and in the Balearics. Numerous Cypriot daggers have been recorded at various spots. But during the last century so many antique objects were imported into France that the authenticity of this trade is very doubtful, particularly as the theory has not stood up well to the shock of radio-carbon dating, which at many western sites has yielded dates earlier than those of the classical eastern civilisations.

However, small walls reinforced by circular towers have been seen as the remains of permanent settlements of Aegean origin: Stuart Piggott draws a parallel between the fortified walls of Los Millares in south-eastern Spain and those of Chalandriani in the island of Syros, dated to the third millennium. He also compares them with the Portuguese earthworks at Villa Nova de São Pedro to the north of Lisbon and even with Le Lébous in the South of France. A radio-carbon date for carbon from Los Millares places this feature around 2340 BC. This early interpretation saw the ramparts as built by Aegeans in search of copper ore.

But let us examine these fortified walls in detail, in the light of the recent publication of the Le Lébous site by its discoverer, Dr J. Arnal, who had the pleasure of adding to the number of remarkable discoveries made in his commune of St Mathieu-de-Tréviers in Hérault, some 20km from Montpellier.

From the top of its ridge, invaded by scented herb scrub, the site controls two great traditional axes, one leading from the coast to the Cévennes and the other from the Rhône to the Atlantic or into Catalonia. Le Lébous had an eventful history which Dr Arnal has reconstructed. The settlement, first used in the Chalcolithic, was destroyed by the people of the Bronze Age and then transformed into a tumulus burial ground by the men of the Hallstatt period; it was re-used by Roman agriculturalists in the fourth century,

34 Tower at Le Lébous, a Chalcolithic fort destroyed by early Bronze Age invaders

plundered, inevitably, by the invading Visigoths, and all this without taking into consideration repeated depredations caused, amongst other things, by tilling and the constant tramplings of flocks and herds. Paradoxically the fallen stones of the Roman ruins served to protect the earlier traces.

But we will go up to the 'castle' and visit it with J. Arnal as our friendly guide, ignoring the song of the cicadas and the scent of the herbs in the garrigue. It is a huge trapezium; the measurements of two of its sides are well known – 70m and 48m – but the others are less certain. The walls are not thick, 1m on average, rarely more and, near the bastions, they are reinforced. Seven towers have been distinguished and four others are surmised. They are perfectly round, as though they were drawn with a compass; and carefully constructed with large foundation blocks, although in the walls themselves the size of the stones was less rigorously exact. The average internal diameter of the towers is 2.5m. Within the protecting wall, there are the remains of huts of a plan similar to that of known Chalcolithic houses in the area: large rectangular dwellings with rounded corners, 12m long and 4m wide. They were probably roofed with large flat stones.

The shepherds of Fontbouïsse

As for the inhabitants, they were, quite simply, our good herdsmen of Fontbouïsse, the local Chalcolithic people we have already mentioned, with their characteristic pottery: carenated vases with pastilles, incisions, channelling, pinched cordons and handles with an applied design, often four in number and opposite each other. There were few imports in this series. The only indisputably 'foreign' element is the vase of Bell Beaker ware, still being used, only two sherds of which have been found. The tools were still lithic, flints, polished axes, but a few copper rods and a ring prove that we are well into the Chalcolithic and this is confirmed by the eponymous site at Fontbouïsse which is richer in local copper.

There are plenty of details to throw light on the domestic life of the Lébous folk. There was the water chore – water had to be fetched from a spring some 400m away. Their diet – mainly animal – is known: at present, specialists, like T. Poulain, are able (when the diggers have extracted all the tiny pieces of bone, which used to be casually thrown away) to enumerate the animals eaten and to determine their age and whether they were the fruits of hunting or of animal husbandry, etc. It is affirmed that the animals consumed at this site included principally sheep (36 per cent) but also wild rabbit (23 per cent), ox (21 per cent) and pig (10 per cent). Ox, sheep, goat and dog were domesticated and pig partly so, whereas wild horse, wild boar, stag, magpie, red partridge and even mole were hunted.

Pig and sheep were eaten young, unlike ox which was the small 'peat-bog' breed. Veal must have been prohibitively dear, even then. Patient study of the bones has made it possible to recognise signs of removal of the flesh, of jointing and cooking and even of uses after cooking: the teeth, particularly the incisors, were made ready for use as pendants and long bones were sharpened to make punches. A few of the bone remains are hardly mentionable: there were human bones mixed in with the animals in the kitchen refuse, in the shape of a few tibias and femurs hidden at the back of a hut. It seems that cannibalism was practised, at least occasionally and perhaps in secret. Agricultural pursuits are less well known, but a few traces, preserved in some pots, indicate the use of a compact, round-grained wheat similar to present-day soft wheats, according to J. Erroux.

The discoverer of Le Lébous has compared it with the sites at Los Millares in Spain or Villa Nova de São Pedro in Portugal, although their defences were more impressive. It is perhaps closer, according to J. Arnal, to the small fortified villages of Sardinia and the

35 Rock carving, Val Camonica

Balearics. Le Lébous, then, seems to show a local adaptation of a type of fortifications which was widespread in the Mediterranean. But, if the age of the settlement is unanimously recognised as Chalcolithic, that of the ramparts has recently given rise to controversy: X. Gutherz does not hesitate to compare Le Lébous with medieval fortifications, which have not been widely studied as yet. However, the overlapping of huts and ramparts seems indisputable according to J. Arnal's publications and reconstruction. It is still difficult to settle the question but further study will elucidate it.

The local herdsmen of the Fontbouïsse culture, who occupied Le Lébous, abandoned it in 1920 b.c. (that is about 2400 BC). But other dates from other Fontbouïsse-type sites suggest an earlier occupation. In any case Le Lébous was destroyed by people of a bronze culture, who wore bulb-headed pins and carried little triangular daggers made of bronze. Some of them, no doubt, came from the north, as we shall see, by way of the Rhône valley. But that is another story. . . . We must carry on westwards and tackle the celebrated 'trading post' at Los Millares, which may well have had more direct links with the world of the Aegean traders.

The fortified site of Los Millares

In the Iberian peninsula and all along the Atlantic face of Europe, megalithic religion raised numerous grandiose collective burial places from the fourth millennium onwards, notably passage graves with chambers often capped with large flat stone slabs, but also tholoi and these were capped with smaller corbelled slabs.

36 Model of passage grave and tholos, Cueva del Romeral (Antequera)

These tholoi contain Neolithic goods: pots, polished axes and flints, but from 3000 onwards a few small copper objects begin to appear: awls or punches, notably in south-east Spain. They are interpreted as the earliest material objects resulting from the discovery of local mines by prospectors from the eastern Mediterranean.

The importance of these metal-bearing layers – and no doubt their exploitation by the natives, who turned their hand to trade as well – led to the flowering of a brilliant copper civilisation in the Almeria region with the renowned site of Los Millares at its centre. In time and in spirit (and in spite of the relative abundance of the metal) the civilisation is still 'Chalcolithic'.

Los Millares is a settlement fortified on one side by a wall with bastions towering 70m above the Rio Andarax. Carbonated wood taken from under a collapsed section of town wall yielded the date already mentioned of 2340 b.c. which is still much debated: dendrochronological correction pushes back the date of the earthwork by several centuries to somewhere around 3000. If Le Lébous, by its dimensions and type of occupation, can only be thought of as a large Chalcolithic village in Languedoc, Los Millares is on a very different scale, that of a town, fortified with thick walls, capable of withstanding a long siege, thanks to an aqueduct bringing water from more than a kilometre away. Moreover, it is not an isolated site and other neighbouring hills also have walls which bear witness to a complete defensive system. A whole necropolis with tombs mainly of the tholos type lay close to the entrenched camp. Some of these burials, which have been very well published by Professor M. Almagro and Professor A. Arribas, have been dated to 2340 b.c., which agrees with the dates obtained for the rampart.

The Almerian culture

Los Millares is no isolated phenomenon: there is the whole Almerian culture which blossomed not only on the east coast but towards the west as well, in Andalusia and what is now Portugal. Fortified sites are plentiful, dominating the rivers which lent themselves to

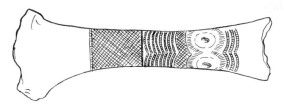

37 Phalange with eye decoration, Almizaraque (Almeria)

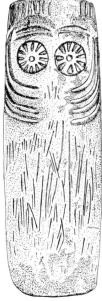

38 The 'Goddess of Los Millares', stone idol (Estremadura)

trade and communications. Many are established near mining districts, a fundamental source of the economic prosperity of these 'new rich' copper people.

This copper industry gradually replaced the old Neolithic tools which were still in use: polished axes, daggers, arrowheads and flint sickles. But flat copper axes were already plentiful, as were awls and chisels. The daggers were short with ribbed blades, tanged and notched, and that curious Bronze Age weapon the long-handled dagger, or halberd, was making its appearance.

Los Millares is interesting because its tholoi show a religious phenomenon lingering on: despite their step up the social scale, its inhabitants had preserved the faith of the megalith builders, or, at least, most of them had, for there were a few tribes in the Almerian complex who did not continue the tradition of great collective burials in tholoi.

A new element is the great increase in idols representing goddesses, based on a combination of geometric motifs with certain essential features suggesting the Mother-Goddess: a head emphasised by schematic shoulders, and above all, eyes. The 'atropophaïc' eye motif reappears in many civilisations as a protection against bad luck, and these eyes are stylised in the form of a sun or a rose window or as simple enigmatic perforations against all kinds of backings. There are small plaques of schist decorated with chevrons and triangles, limestone bactyls or cylinders, funeral pots and even bits of human bone, phalanges re-used as amulets. This style can be found, too, in the statue-menhirs of Gard and Aveyron.

The Chalcolithic civilisation of Los Millares seems to have come to a sudden end around 2200, during what was certainly a period of generalised destruction, since it was then that Troy II was sacked, at the other end of the Mediterranean. Los Millares, the first great metal culture of the Iberian peninsula, was to hand over to those restless Bell Beaker peoples who have left traces in Los Millares itself and also at Villa Nova de São Pedro where they apparently settled in the smoking ruins of the Almerian fortifications. The vigorous Bell Beaker culture went on developing the copper industry and founded a long-range export trade.

It marks the closing of a cycle of Iberian copper age civilisations. Afterwards the Chalcolithic was to disappear but the deposits were far from exhausted and the discovery of bronze brought to this still privileged land of Almeria the blossoms of the first real bronze cultures at El Argar.

Early bronze in Andalusia: El Argar

The development of a bronze industry in Spain is linked with the presence of both tin and copper deposits. Tin is particularly plentiful in Galicia and the Asturias, in the north-west of the peninsula, while there are numerous copper deposits both in the north-west (Asturias) and in the south with the rich mines at Rio Tinto near Huelva or in the province of Almeria. Some signs of prehistoric exploitation have been found at Cerro Muriano in the

Sierra de Cordoba, where the copper ore was attacked on the surface, using huge grooved stone pounders. At El Argar itself there is ample evidence of the existence of local foundries; stone moulds, waste from castings and crucibles have been found in plenty, showing clearly that the metal was cast on the spot.

The importance of El Argar was revealed by two Belgian engineers, the brothers Henri and Louis Siret, who worked on the site around 1885. The vast quantity of their finds supplied countless museums in Europe with Argaric bronzes and pottery, and Belgium, their homeland, was not forgotten as the collections at Brussels and Ghent testify. It must be admitted that the 650 pots and 2000 metal objects they found were enough to prompt a generous share-out.

The site at El Argar is a small plateau, dominating the Rio Antas, 12 km from the sea. There was a big fortified village, which unfortunately was largely destroyed before the archaeologists realised it was there. But a large necropolis remained, containing some thousand individuals, and this yielded enough material for us to reconstruct the customs and economy of the El Argar culture. From the thousand burials discovered, Professor L. Pericot Garcia estimates that the site was occupied for about three centuries by a population of several hundred.

It was not an isolated settlement, for some forty similar, though less important, establishments are scattered along a coastal fringe of about 75km. Moreover, throughout the peninsula weapons and pottery types have been found which are often Argaric in style but in non-Argaric contexts, reflecting other less well known cultural groups of the early Bronze Age; the excavation work of H. Schubart gradually revealed one in south-west Spain. This latter group, for example, produced chests, megalithic tombs with circular structures and a strong Chalcolithic tradition, marked by copper tools, but new forms of pottery which already belong to the early Bronze Age. El Argar is certainly the best known group, because of its exceptional position and also because it was discovered very early and became the object of careful study; but, as always, there is no end to the complexity of human groups when one gets down to details. Sometimes prehistorians are accused of being too meticulous in their analyses and of cheerfully sub-dividing small cultural groups on the strength of the most trivial pieces of material. But the fact is that large-scale phenomena like the spread of the Bell Beaker culture are rare. More often, in a period when communications were fraught with difficulties, many groups remained exceedingly diverse and defeat our attempts at synthesis.

The necropolis at El Argar shows a radical change in the funeral customs of Iberia somewhere between 2000 and 1800 BC. It reflects profound upheavals in the social structure. The development of metallurgy created a different division of labour and new hierarchical criteria. As all over Europe, the tradition originating with the Corded Ware peoples prevailed and individual burial became the rule. The great collective tholoi, built for a whole tribe, vanished; and so did the Mother Goddesses. Customs change!

Burials now often took the form of individual inhumations under tumuli – in some cases double inhumations: mother and child or husband and wife, united in eternity as in life – where the bodies were sprinkled with ochre, a very time-honoured rite. In the centre of the tumulus the skeletons were buried in trenches or little chests, 85cm long at the most, which implies some strange gymnastics to get the wretched corpses inside. The term a 'forced position' was never more appropriate.

But in another funeral rite – the most widespread – it is even worse: inhumation in jars. The deceased was thrust unceremoniously head first into a large oval-shaped urn 40 to 70cm high, together with the funeral offerings. L. Siret surmised that the pots must have been assembled on the spot, from a few large parts. In some cases the practice of removing the flesh from the cadavers before final burial may have prevailed. The jars often have a row of small teat screws under the rim which may have served a dual purpose, both decorative and functional in that they held fast the cloth cover of the vessel. A flat piece of pottery, a limestone plaque or some old worn quern was placed on top of the cloth.

39 Reconstruction of an Argaric jar burial

This method of burial in jars is rare in Europe. It is found occasionally in Bohemia but chiefly in the early Bronze Age of the Near East. The jars at El Argar could be a further indication of ethnic diffusion from the eastern Mediterranean. At a later stage the rite of urn burial was often practised in Europe, but it seemed more practical then to cremate the bodies first.

Amongst the grave goods, metal appears much more frequently, although flint and polished stone are still in evidence. It is still mainly copper which was only gradually ousted by bronze. The period of metallurgical experimentation is not yet over. Gold is used for the adornment of women and of weapons, but it is on silver that the reputation of El Argar rests. L. Siret collected no less than 320 silver objects in the necropolis alone. But we need not be too impressed: it only amounts to a few kilograms of the precious metal. Nevertheless, it is the most significant production in Europe – in barbarian Europe, that is – leaving aside the treasures of Mycenae and the occasional distant copies of oriental vases

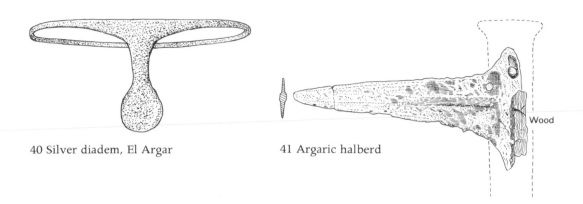

40 Silver diadem, El Argar
41 Argaric halberd

Wood

dotted about the Russian steppes. We should not forget either, that, unlike gold, silver deteriorates very easily: it becomes tarnished, black and often crumbles to a powder. So the quantity recovered by the archaeologists is certainly considerably less than the original deposits.

In El Argar silver was used to make small items of jewellery: little spirals, necklaces of rolled silver wire, beads, some of which were fish-shaped. But the most original product was the paletted diadem, made to adorn the forehead of the wives of minor chiefs or rich merchants, and consisting of a bandeau round the head from which hung the central palette. In some cases, it seems, the palette pointed upwards, towards the crown of the head. Was this a random feature of the grave goods or may we hazard ethnographic comparisons? Was it some kind of symbol: palette turned down for nubile women and up for married women or widows? There is a corresponding fashion for the poorer women consisting of cloth bandeaux with small ornaments attached. This fashion was to continue a very long time, if we think of the jewellery of present-day Berber women or of our own fair hippies. Modest copper tools were deposited with the diadems, little punches or awls used in sewing or tattooing.

In the men's tombs there is a variety of weapons: the daggers are riveted and of a style that was to increase in length to give large, flat-bladed or leaf-shaped swords, also found in Brittany and not very practical as weapons. They could be simply symbolic and are sometimes richly ornamented: an Argaric weapon from the Asturias has the hilt entirely covered in gold leaf with repoussé decoration. It is tempting to think of Mycenae. Another novel weapon, which was to remain in vogue for a long time in the early Bronze Age, is the halberd. At El Argar the blades are triangular, broader at the base and with a strong central rib and numerous rivets, which were a necessary precaution if these 'pick weapons' were to deal violent blows. The halberd is still a surprising weapon. Involuntarily, perhaps, we are reminded of the inoffensive symbolic weapons carried today by the Swiss guards in churches. But with a good handle, this axe-dagger became as cutting a weapon as the 'faucart' of the Chouans. And in the Bronze Age, halberds were popular. They are often found made of copper containing arsenic in many early Bronze Age centres, in Spain,

France, Ireland and, with bronze handles, in Saxo-Thuringia. In Romania magnificent gold replicas are to be found; and, finally, many cave drawings show little Bronze Age men handling the weapon with great dexterity and obvious satisfaction. Halberds also figure on rocks in the Atlas region of North Africa as well as on countless Iberian sites, and the rocky slopes of Mont Bego or Val Camonica in the Alps. They are a classic feature, too, of cave engravings in Bronze Age Scandinavia; in fact it can be said that the presence of a halberd in a series of engravings is grounds enough for dating them to the Bronze Age. Halberds were used most of all in the early bronze period. Later, when the casting of open sockets had been mastered, spear heads were often preferred, but ceremonial halberds persisted in northern Europe. Fighting techniques are constantly evolving and being perfected from age to age! Certainly the spear required much less intensive training than was needed to handle a halberd.

The range of tools at El Argar show little sign of evolution. The axe-blades remained simple, though occasionally rims began to appear, and chisels were still the commonest tools. There was no revolution here.

The pottery is worthy of attention: it is well-fired as might be expected from a metalworking people, skilled in the use of hearths, and it displayed new forms. Besides the carenated bowls and vats, elegant chalices and pedestalled goblets, with a black, often burnished surface, are worthy of note. One might be tempted to see them as imitations of metal goblets, perhaps silver which at times oxidises, taking on a black patina. So these pedestalled vases of El Argar could have been copies of exceedingly rare and precious vessels imported from the east.

42 Argaric vases

El Argar was less renowned than Los Millares, but its influence in the Iberian world was still considerable. There is no doubt that this culture had somewhat sporadic contacts with the eastern Mediterranean; this is suggested in particular by the custom of burial in jars, but also by the presence of blue glass beads which originated in Aegean or Egyptian workshops. In return El Argar gave rise to a number of trading posts in the Mediterranean islands, notably the Balearics. But its influence was felt towards the Atlantic as well and

49

seemed to be characterised by trade in silver. Silver jewellery from Brittany, the rings from the forest of Carnoët, the pins of Ploumilliau, the vases of Melrand and Saint-Adrien could have come from south-eastern Iberia. The silver rivets in the sword at Cissac in Gironde would mark a good relay point. Other silver pins or beads in the French Midi as well as pins in northern Italy could be indications of other Argaric trade routes.

The El Argar culture was a worthy daughter of the brilliant Iberian Chalcolithic cultures; but seems to have quietly died out leaving no heirs. The Iberian decline was marked by a period of stagnation in the middle Bronze Age around 1400–1200 BC. It was not until the flowering of the Atlantic bronze in the late Bronze Age that the Iberian peninsula found a new economic and cultural prosperity. What happened, then, in 1200? One of the reasons for the wealth of El Argar had been in part her enduring trade relations with the east. The fall of Mycenae, the great human or natural upheavals which affected the eastern Mediterranean at that period, no doubt had a damaging effect even as far off as Iberia. After these Mediterranean catastrophes, the Iberian people needed time to adjust to the idea of an Atlantic European community.

Chapter 3

Continental Awakenings: the Leaven of Únĕtice

Únĕtice, the Aunjetitz of early writers in the Germanic tongue, is primarily a necropolis to the north-west of Prague and in the heart of Bohemia. But, beyond that, it is a beacon light in the beginning of European prehistory. There is hardly a phase of early bronze metal civilisation which is not known by that name. So, why Únĕtice?

In the heart of Bohemia

First of all, it was there, at the very beginning of the Bronze Age, around 2000 BC, that the earliest original creations of the barbarian world were produced, in the aftermath of the final Anatolian ferments. This production subsequently gave rise to a long string of descendants. The earliest sophisticated flanged axes came from Únĕtice, the earliest triangular daggers came from Únĕtice, the first of the richly varied series of continental Bronze Age pins which were to delight generations of distinguished typologists, also came from Únĕtice. From then on, the epithet 'Únĕtician' replaced 'Aegean' or 'Anatolian' in archaeological descriptions and enjoyed the same lustre. It had long been predictable that Únĕtice would play a major role in the rise of metallurgy since it exploited, or, at least controlled both the Balkan and Alpine copper deposits and Bohemian tin resources. Moreover, it controlled the trade routes which led northwards for the traffic in amber.

But this industrial wealth only partially accounts for it. Únĕtice also embodied the coming together of new ideas and social structures, which were to shake the European Neolithic to its foundations. In that crucible the last Aegean influences clashed with cultural contributions from new groups like the Battle Axe people from the north and with the heritage left by the powerful Bell Beaker groups in Bohemia and Moravia. Únĕtice was to participate in the transformation of the emerging new world and to leave its mark on it more clearly than either the Atlantic or the Mediterranean groups, not by the violence of the changes it brought, but by their duration and their dispersal westwards and northwards. Many cultures were to spring from Únĕtice, and it is astonishing that more attempts have not been made to see a 'protoceltic' phenomenon in the 'Koine' of Únĕtice.

Like all the other Bronze Age centres, Únětice was to witness the end of the old Neolithic rites and the fertility cult, symbolised by the Mother Goddesses, but was to preserve here and there the symbol of the horn, associated with the development of cattle-raising. The social structures, which can be traced by studying the burial grounds, are neither markedly hierarchical nor matriarchal nor collectivist. We are witnessing the birth of a world that was more individualist, but also more violent; the proliferation of weapons and the appearance of fortified, hill-top villages bears witness to this. This world was at times more difficult to grasp through its art which was inclined to be abstract, preserving the 'old European geometric style' of decoration for its weapons and pots. We will start by studying its earliest origins.

The eastern torc-wearers

C. F. A. Schaeffer, professor at the Collège de France, is not only the brilliant leader of French archaeological expeditions to, among other places, Ras-Shamra, the ancient Ugarit in northern Syria, but also the man who published the grave goods of the *Tumuli of Haguenau Forest (Tumulus de la Forêt de Haguenau)* in Alsace. This rather unusual twofold archaeological activity in Syria and Alsace led him to wonder about the connections between the civilisations of the two areas, which had been thought previously to be totally separate. He noticed the presence in both places of massive thick necklaces or torcs with small rolled ends. These ornaments were found at a very early stage in Lebanon and Syria but they reappear in an Early Bronze Age tumulus at Donauberg in Haut Rhin. A whole range of intermediate types was recognised successively in Austria, Italy, Bohemia, Hungary, south Germany, Würthemberg and Alsace. It seems very much as though a considerable trade took place, starting from the Syrian coast and moving up the Adriatic towards central Europe. For C. F. A. Schaeffer this was the result of the activities of a group of wandering metalworkers, the torc-wearers.

Towards the end of the third millennium, in fact, groups of metalworkers specialising in the manufacture of new types of objects, spiral bracelets and club-headed pins, were living in centres like Byblos in the Lebanon and Ugarit in Syria. But their most remarkable product was a massive torc made of a round rod, the ends of which were hammered flat and then curled round. These torcs, sometimes representing some hundreds of grams of metal, could be either items of adornment or an elegant way of commercialising copper or bronze. In a word, they were ingots, and even ingot-torcs. They were offered to the gods in the temples and, on occasion, they adorned the divinities. Thus, the second level at Ras-Shamra yielded a delightful pair of silver statuettes representing gods, adorned with gold torcs round their necks, dated by C. F. A. Schaeffer to 2100–1900 BC. Later other stelae also show engravings of gods wearing torcs. But in spite of these sumptuous offerings, the gods would not be placated; natural catastrophes, earthquakes and wars ruined, in the full sense of the word, the settlements of the Syrian and Lebanese coasts. Perhaps this

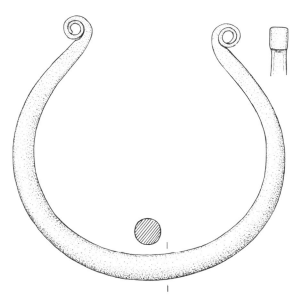

43 Copper ingot torc

prompted the torc-wearers to set out for more clement and peaceful lands, unless it was the new need for ore, particularly tin, that lured these metalworkers to their European voyage around 1800 BC.

C. F. A. Schaeffer's attractive theory, which was finally worked out in 1949, is, of course, only a theory. It assumed the movement of a small band of metalworkers through the unknown land of Europe. If vast migrations of countless, well-armed peoples, like the Corded Ware groups, are conceivable, the movement of small bands is much more open to question. They could have been decimated by the first flight of arrowheads even before they had taken the first metal torcs out of their canvas bags. No doubt many objects exported over considerable distances, like, for example, the famous 'Egyptian' beads which were quickly imitated in Europe, reached their ultimate goals after successive 'swaps' between neighbouring tribes. It is undeniable that native centres, copying the products originally imported from the east, developed very rapidly. At Únětice they probably learnt very quickly to cast the famous rolled torcs, found in tens and hundreds within the confines of that civilisation. They are so numerous that they cannot be considered simply as imports. Moreover, these famous ingot-torcs soon met competition from other, specifically European, types of ingots: the *Spangenbarren* or *Rippenbarren*, small elongated bars, sometimes curved at the ends, which are found in isolation or in hoards as far away as France (ingots from Widensolen in Alsace or the Fonts-Gaidons hoard near Bourges).

Finally, the possible contribution of Anatolia to the civilisation of Únětice was, no doubt, restricted to a few metal objects which served as prototypes. In the Chalcolithic groups we have been studying it would have stopped there. The unique quality of Únětice was that from these few models it created an original metallurgy and civilisation.

Metallurgy: inception and explosion

Those best placed to judge the birth of the Únětician culture are the Czechoslovakian archaeologists; and perhaps it is no bad thing to see how it is described by the renowned Neustupny dynasty, Jiři and his son Evzen, who have made the study of the prehistory of their country a family tradition.

The Neustupnys tend to dismiss influences from distant civilisations and, in fact, Únětice was subject to very few. Its evolution, which was slow at the start, quickened later and can be divided into several phases. The only perceptible influences stem from the Corded Ware people – fairly slight – and above all from the Bell Beaker peoples. In the first place, the Únětician necropolises were set up in places that had been occupied by the Bell Beaker folk – either living or dead. Then the grave goods of Únětice show a certain connection with those of the Bell Beaker groups; without going into detail it is possible to quote certain pottery types, common to both groups: small, handled pitchers, water or milk jugs, and especially the curious polypod vessels fitted with a series of little feet.

The early Únětician phase seems to be mainly Chalcolithic but the second phase sees the appearance of eastern metal types: Cypriot pins and even some blue glass 'Egyptian' beads. So there are certainly contacts with the Mediterranean world.

45 'Únětice axe' and halberd from Bavaria

44 Únětice-type cup (lower Austria)

The final phase at Únětice, the most classic, coincides with its most flourishing period: there is an explosion of metallurgy with a host of copper, bronze or gold ornaments and the appearance of amber. The pottery, which is very characterisic, includes small cups with the handle attached, oddly, at the base. The mastery of metallurgical techniques has opened the way to the casting of fine flanged axes. Outstanding among the weapons are fine, metal-handled daggers, decorated with geometric motifs – a product that was to be copied all over Europe, as far away as the Rhône valley, northern Italy or north Germany. Evidence of technical progress is plentiful: hollow bronze handles could be cast and fixed with great rivets to separately cast blades. The scabbard itself was made partly of decorated bronze and partly of leather or cloth. Weapons were manufactured in series and hoards of about ten daggers have been found, as at Horomenice. This is industrial production! As for pins, the knot-headed Cypriot type was joined by pins with ring- or clover-shaped heads as well as the celebrated Únětician pin with a small perforated head. Spirals and massive torcs were the mainstay of adornment with countless varieties of beads.

But we must not be under any illusion about the total metal production. The sum total of known or supposed deposits is quite small even so. E. and J. Neustupny reckon that metal extraction and casting could not have occupied large groups of metallurgists, and that the economy in general was mixed, still based on agriculture and animal husbandry. So how did these Úněticians live?

Social and religious structures – funeral rites

We are beginning now to know something of the domestic life of the Únětice groups, their neighbours and later derived groups. Numerous recent excavations have made it possible to approach some idea of their social and religious structures.

Villages were often established on slopes or small hills and the uncertainty of the times made it necessary to protect them with palisades of wooden stakes and large ditches. The houses, 5 to 10m long, were built of wood and daub. The floor was wooden except for the hearth which was of beaten earth. A comparative refinement consisted of decorating the rough wall plaster with geometric motifs, which is evidence of some slight interest in improving the domestic environment. Some vases or bronze objects seem to have been placed on shelves or in specially prepared niches.

The villages were built according to fairly strict rules of layout, which implies a coherent social organisation. A concrete example is provided by the detailed excavation of the settlement at Barca in eastern Slovakia. The houses were clustered inside a double bank with roadways, 2.5m wide, which might have been laid out by survey. But it is the interior arrangement of the twenty or so houses that is the most revealing. We find some large huts with a single hearth, suitable for a large family with a lot of children. Other houses have two separate rooms, but only one hearth; the children grew up and slept separately but food was prepared communally. Finally, other dwellings have two rooms, each with a hearth; newly-weds lived with their parents-in-law, while waiting to move into something better – human problems do not change.

Occasionally some of the structures seem to have had a religious purpose. In the Romanian Otomani group, a wooden construction fitted over a thermal spring suggests the possible existence of a temple associated with a water cult. The Chalcolithic and the Bronze Age in Europe have other examples of wooden-raftered sanctuaries. The peat bogs of the Netherlands have revealed similar structures linked with animal cults. The menhirs and durable stone structures are well known as monuments of Neolithic and Bronze Age religion, but the important part that wood may have played in building sanctuaries at that period is often forgotten, because it disappears so quickly in the soil.

55

At Únětice, or in the Otomani culture, religious and domestic art became more abstract. Only very rarely are clay figurines found; these are little clay pigs or cattle which might just as well be children's toys as votive amulets. Human figurines became rare; a few are known, vaguely outlined and adorned with crescent-shaped necklaces in *pointillé*, but we are a long way from the beautiful idols of Vinča.

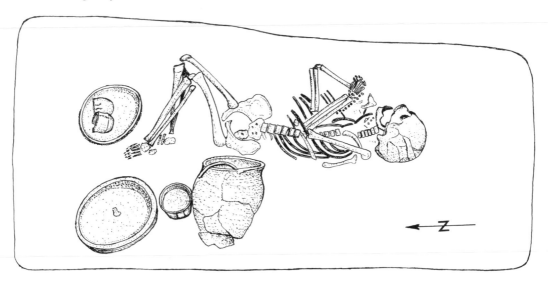

46 The 'contracted position', Bell Beaker tomb, pre-Únětice (Moravia)

A study of the necropolises is, as always, very instructive. The usual contracted position is found again, the dead looking eastwards at their last sunrise. On the whole grave goods do not suggest big social differences: the stage of princely tombs, monopolising for eternity the wealth accumulated by the tribe, has not yet been reached. On the other hand, a certain number of curious facts are worthy of note: for example, the presence of cremated babies or children lying beside the adult skeletons. Perhaps the children were sacrificed after the death of their mother. There are double and triple tombs as well. J. and E. Neustupny do not think it can be a case of simultaneous death of several members of a family every time; rather they suggest that one or two servants may have been sacrificed for the occasion when the patriarch or petty chief departed to join the Sun God. In a desire to probe further, an analysis of the distribution of groups within the necropolis was attempted. The most penetrating studies seem to distinguish small series of about twenty burials, two-thirds of them adults. This suggests small patriarchal groups of about twenty people over three or four generations. Several patriarchal units might be associated. The roots of these new structures are to be found in the earlier Chalcolithic populations.

Other funeral rites are revealing: fragments of querns and daub from the huts were deposited with some of the dead, whose houses were burnt after their death. Animal offerings were deposited: at Hole'sov in Moravia a man's skeleton was accompanied by the heads of five oxen. This must have been an attempt to win the favour of the dead man, an important stockbreeder, by sacrificing five of the finest beasts in his herd.

Some peculiarities also appear in the funerary structures: inhumations in jars or pithos, originating in Anatolia, are known, but do not reach the proportions they attained in that other early Bronze centre, El Argar. Here, too, we may ask whether the continuation of this originally Mediterranean rite does not reflect the arrival of some ethnic group. For everyone wants to be buried in accordance with the principles instilled in his country of origin. Men may adapt to many changes in their lifetime, but death is too serious a matter to allow them to deny their native traditions. We must draw particular attention, too, to the appearance of the first tumuli and the first tombs with tree-trunk coffins, a fashion which was to become established in northern and sometimes western Europe.

A disturbing detail among the funerary offerings is the wearing of small rounds of cranium as amulets. So the rite of trepanning was known in Únětice; throughout prehistoric and primitive societies we find it persisting and it was still in force in the Middle Ages, as witness the Breton tombs at Saint Urnel in Finistère, dating to around 1000 – AD this time! The trepanning at Únětice shows that these primitive people were already looking inside the head for the secrets of human motivation. Was it a treatment for mental illness or a wish to acquire some of the abilities of a dead man by taking a sample? For once we will eschew the usual ethnographic parallels.

To come back to earth, what were the gastronomic preoccupations of the people of Únětice? The raising of stock, sheep, pigs and cattle was held in high esteem. There is nothing exceptional apart from the much more frequent appearance of the horse. From being the huntsman's quarry, as he was in early Palaeolithic times, he has at last been tamed. This definitive victory in the early Bronze Age is a major step forward in the economic and military development of ancient and proto-historic societies. Bridle bits proliferate, implying riding and perhaps the replacement of the ox by the horse for drawing carts. Hunting brought in, as it does everywhere, an assortment of large and small game, stag, boar or rabbit. Agriculture did not develop much technically. The bronze plough could not yet be numbered amongst men's inventions and the primitive wooden ard was still being used, sometimes fitted with a polished stone ploughshare. Fishing techniques improved with the appearance of metal hooks, curved spikes of copper or bronze. Fish was supplemented by turtles and large mussels, the shells of which are found in heaps round the settlements.

So life at Únětice remained relatively hard, essentially pastoral and agricultural despite the additional wealth brought in by metallurgy. Indeed, in spite of their organisation, the villages were still far removed from the urban structures of Greece or Crete. The skill of her smiths allowed Únětice to acquire a little gold, a few simple spirals at first, then more elaborate jewellery, Transylvanian crescent pendants or basket-shaped earrings. Nordic amber was beginning to circulate, accompanied no doubt by some imported Mycenaean objects which we shall come to; but it stayed on a modest scale. At Únětice itself there were no famous accumulations of wealth for the benefit of a favoured few, tribal chiefs, big businessmen, princes or petty monarchs. This would not always be the case in the groups which derived from it.

Relations with Mycenae?

Then there are those mysterious little clay discs deposited in the tombs; the disc was an all-important symbol in Bronze Age mythology and a multi-purpose symbol, since it may be sun, wheel or magic circle. It suggests the sun, fire and chariots for transporting both the living and the dead. This perennial Indo-European myth was to culminate in the Chariot of Apollo suffused in the glory of the Great Sun. It is a long tradition. Here we need only call to mind the fine chariot from Trundholm in Denmark with the horse pulling a magnificent golden disc.

Finally, there are small objects of bone or antler, decorated with spirals, typically Mycenaean and datable to 1600 or 1500 BC; more ink has flowed on their account than on that of any other artefacts. For the word Mycenaean has been uttered and controversy begins, or rather, continues: the Quarrel of the Ancients and Moderns. The Ancients place the development of Únětice somewhere between 1800 and 1500, with lively contacts with the Achaean world at the end of the period, and it must be admitted that the rings, discs and occasional decorated bit mountings are not isolated; their distribution can be traced in Czechoslovakia, where K. Tihelka has drawn attention to those at Cesavy and Veterov, as well as in Hungary at Tiszafured, at Vattina in Romania or Vinča in Yugoslavia, taking barbarian Europe as a whole. On the other side there is Alakakhen in Turkey, but, above all, Kakovatos or Asine in Greece. A distribution like that could not possibly be fortuitous. And yet the resolutely Modern, challenging shadow of Colin Renfrew, the 'apostle' of the radio-carbon revolution, rises up to 'calibrate' – in other words, joyfully and dendro-chronologically to correct the date of 1895 b.c., obtained by ^{14}C for the Únětician site of Prasklice in Czechoslovakia. This leads to the fixing of the first stages of Únětice well before 2000 and makes the copying of Mycenaean objects problematical. If there was copying, it happened the other way round!

But consideration should not be limited solely to dating criteria. Other arguments make it difficult to increase the age of Únětice too much. If it is true that the Aegean component in the rise of barbarian civilisations has been given too much weight in the past, at the other extreme an ultra-regional position would be equally unacceptable. Probably the life of Únětice was very long. Born out of the first great Chalcolithic civilisations around 2000, it could still shelter groups that survived into the age of Mycenaean expansion. But the last word has not been spoken in the changing world of archaeology. It would be sad if everything were finally settled.

Únětician expansion – Leubingen and the Straubing group

The prestige of Únětice's metal products was enormous. The first stage of Únětician expansion consisted simply of exporting new types of weapons and tools to Chalcolithic groups. Triangular, riveted daggers were exported over considerable distances, replacing the Bell Beaker tanged or notched blades. They can be traced as far as Holland with the little dagger of Bargeroosterveld, a bronze blade with a wooden handle decorated with little bronze nails. This type of decoration, which was known in Mycenae, was to enjoy a great vogue in the Atlantic civilisations of Brittany. Únětice was also the starting point for the trade in ingot-torcs which reached eastern France. In fact it is probable that Únětice took over from Anatolia in that field.

47 Únětice-type dagger, found in Italy

Other western groups in the early Bronze Age derived directly from the Bell Beaker or Corded Ware cultures, as for instance, the Adlerberg culture, south of Worms, where copper continued to be used for adornment but triangular daggers, copied from Únětice, were already appearing. There jewellery, which was unassuming, included shells of *Colombella rustica* imported from the distant Mediterranean shores, via the Rhône valley.

In the end the expansion of Únětice produced profiteers; a few potentates in Saxony were to lay hold of the new wealth for their own ends, act the part of petty kings and be buried under huge, princely tumuli. And so the rite of burial under tumuli, destined to great things, appears at the very beginning of the early Bronze Age; in the middle Bronze Age we were to see the 'Tumulus culture' give rise to swarms of the huge funerary mounds across the whole of central Europe – and even into western Europe. These little kingships, these 'diminutive kings' in the words of V. Gordon Childe, held brief sway and their tombs can be counted on the fingers of one hand. The most famous are at Leubingen and Helmsdorf. The Leubingen tumulus was excavated last century. It was an imposing mound, more than 8m high. The mortuary house, more than 4m long, was made of wooden beams forming a pitched roof covered with boards and then with thatch; this house had been built in a small trench dug in the ground. It must correspond to some of the wooden dwellings of the period, a kind of primitive log cabin with a lower, but thatched, roof. Since the Helmsdorf tumulus also covered an identical type of mortuary house, we may conclude that it was a widespread style of building.

The relatively rich and plentiful grave goods of these Saxon tumuli are so unusual in the Únětician territory that they have often been called 'princely burials'.

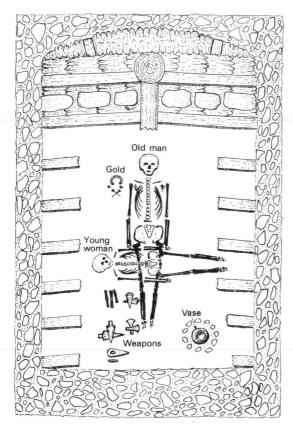

48 Reconstruction of the tomb at Leubingen (Saxony)

Two people were buried at Leubingen: at the bottom, lying along the axis of the tomb, was an old man; above him, level with his knees, the skeleton of a young girl lay at right angles to the axis of the tomb. So the two bodies lay in a cross formation. According to the earliest hypothesis they were two members of the same family who happened to die on the same day; but in view of what has been found in cemeteries at Únětice, sacrifice seems a more likely hypothesis. The old patriarch of Leubingen would have insisted on taking this young fifteen-year-old girl with him to provide pleasurably for his leisure in the after-life: ritual sacrifice of the last woman the great chief had chosen or voluntary suicide of a loving wife – it is easy to embroider. But the difference in age makes it seem likely that if one of the deaths was natural, the other probably was not.

It is the grave goods that have attracted most attention from the archaeologists: an unusual quantity of weapons for the grave of one man; axes, halberds, daggers and a small hammer-axe, fashioned in serpentine or polished stone; this first collection of weapons fits in well with the 'princely' view, as does the richness of the jewels, a massive gold torc, decorated with engraved cross-hatching and two fine pins, in the classical style of Únětice but also of gold. Some small spiral earrings, and tubes of helicoid wire completed the gold jewellery. For the period it was indeed an exceptional collection in barbarian Europe!

What was the source of this wealth? First there were in existence potentates capable of inspiring obedience and fear to such an extent that they were able to syphon off a certain amount of wealth. These chieftains, ruling over clans or bands, these kinglets, did not found dynasties: the phenomenon is isolated. The accumulation of goods was accidental but, nevertheless, something had happened: a source of gain had suddenly appeared, probably connected with the arrival of the Únĕtician bronzes. Are we seeing dealings in Únĕtician arms here, a type of trade that has always been lucrative? Did some astute middleman re-sell the first daggers and halberds for gold? Or did these traders take advantage of their position on one of the routes to northern Europe, to become magnates of the amber trade, which was already appearing in the final phase of Únĕtice? It must have been something of the sort. But it is strange to observe two convergent influences in the tomb: that of the Corded Ware groups with the Battle Axe and that of Únĕtice, which is very pronounced, with the pins and bronze weapons. Perhaps some petty chieftains, descended from the Corded Ware people, were quick to appreciate the value of the new metal products and suddenly grew very rich on the proceeds.

The rise of the Straubing groups in lower Bavaria shows another kind of Únĕtician derivative, still in the early Bronze Age. This is the appearance of another, very important school of metallurgy, which was to radiate outwards into Switzerland and France and to which we are indebted for some notable artistic creations: a host of bracelets shaped as spirals or helicoidal springs reminiscent of the celebrated neck rings of the giraffe-women in Africa. As for clothing, they invented innumerable little bronze trifles which jingled in dances and ceremonials. Jackets were decorated with curious little bronze cones or *tutuli* and skirts with a host of little cylindrical and spiral tubes. With this metal decoration the ladies' skirts tinkled delightfully. But Straubing did not devote itself entirely to high fashion. The people were serious metalworkers, well organised and producing an abundance of the famous ingots in the form of bars, bent at the ends. They have been found at times in staggering quantities – nearly 500 at Munich – which suggests organisation on an almost industrial scale, and well organised channels for removing the surplus production.

The Straubing people seem to have maintained social customs very close to those at Únĕtice. The cemetery is composed of flat tombs with the dead forced into a flexed position and with apparently no great distinctions of wealth or class. The 'princely element' is missing. So, even in a field that is restricted both geographically and chronologically, we can see the variety of social structures to be found in the small Bronze Age tribes.

The Rhône Valley people and the Polada culture

Únĕtice, which at the beginning had received some impulse from the eastern Mediterranean, radiated in its turn from Bohemia towards the Mediterranean world, but to

49 Rhône daggers (Valais and Lyon)

the west this time. Traces have been found in the form of imports, like the famous pins, flanged axes or rolled torcs. But soon regional schools of metallurgy were to spring up, which at first copied the early Únětician products, in particular the famous triangular, metal-handled daggers.

The Rhône culture is found in the early Bronze Age, in Switzerland and the Rhône corridor. It owed its fortune to the trade which grew up between the Mediterranean and south Germany. The new metal products were exchanged for something that seems laughable to our blasé modern eyes: the little Mediterranean shells – the famous *Colombella rustica* again – but with other bivalves as well. As Professor J. Hundt comments, maliciously, a lot has been said about the 'white shells' found in tombs, but this colour is in fact only a by-product of age, due to modification through the centuries. When they were new, the shells were multi-coloured, glittering and, in a word, utterly charming in the eyes of our barbarians. That is why in the renowned Römisch Germanisches Museum at Mainz, with its enthusiasm for living reconstructions of the past, a glass case contains a necklace of modern shells, brilliantly coloured and in marked contrast to the small whitened anvil shapes of the Bronze Age tombs. A lesson in interpretation on which many archaeologists might ponder!

The Rhône Bronze Age had its moment of glory with the manufacture of some admirable daggers, decorated with geometric motifs, crosses, triangles and chevrons, in a style that is both elegant and sober. They are found in the Rhône valley at Lyons, at Loriol in Drôme and on into the south at Nîmes in Gard and Sollies-Pont in Var. Some of them were exported to the departments of Isère and Basses Alpes. With this quality production, the Rhône valley people won their honours as metallurgists: they had assimilated

50 Disc-headed pin, Bex (Switzerland)

completely the lessons of their Únětician masters. Here, too, a new centre of original metallurgy was created. Both in Switzerland and in the Rhône valley axes would be made in a wide variety, verging at times on the fanciful; the first simple flanged models were followed by chisel axes or even strange elongated spatulas which some people have persuaded themselves were either simply for display, like the sabres of Napoleon's Old Guard, or for throwing like boomerangs, or, again – and this is perhaps the most plausible – for use as battle axes. In the end we have to admit that no one really knows how these 'spatula axes' could have been used.

Pins were used to fasten clothing and feminine – or masculine – vanity gave rise to a wish for originality. From the Jura to the South of France the favourites were trefoil-headed, sometimes decorated with cabochons. So each region, each important population group, can be followed throughout two millennia, thanks to the whims of fashion – and they say it is futile!

Únětician influence reached down into northern Italy as well, but there it was to meet well organised groups, descended from a brilliant Chalcolithic phase at Remedello, in which the Bell Beaker people, as in many other places, played a large part.

51 Pots with 'applied handles', north Italian Bronze Age

52 Polada-type dagger

One of the most attractive periods of this early Italian Bronze Age is characterised by the Polada culture. It carried on in large measure into the middle Bronze Age, when it spread out over a large area. It is known by a whole series of waterside settlements in Lombardy and Piedmont, often sited at the edge of rivers and lakes. Its position enabled it to control the trade moving from the Adriatic up into the Alpine valleys and passes. A unique feature of the Polada culture is the preservation of interesting relics of wooden objects in peat bogs, showing a wealth of wooden vessels for domestic use. Construction techniques of note include the use of beams skilfully assembled using mortice and tenon joints. Transport was by land and by river; canoes hollowed out of tree trunks have been found as well as sophisticated wooden cart wheels. The earliest wheels, in the Chalcolithic peat-bogs of the Netherlands, were solid with a central seating for the axle. At Mercurago in Piedmont, we can follow the evolution of technique in several models of wooden wheel. The solid wheel is opened up at first by removing two crescent-shaped pieces, and from there they moved on to a wheel assembled from several pieces, with a rim and spokes. So a whole successive gamut of technical inventions accompanied the progress in metallurgy which is often studied too exclusively, overlooking parallel developments in industries using perishable materials.

Still in wood, elegant curved bows have been found, sometimes nearly one-and-a-half metres long. Another curiosity is wooden arrows with club-shaped heads, intended either for training troops of warriors – the forerunner of blank cartridges – or to amuse children. Or perhaps – there are ethnographic parallels for this hypothesis – they were used for hunting small birds by stunning them rather than mutilating them as a flint tip would.

53 Trefoil pin (Switzerland)

The bronze workshops of Polada clearly drew their inspiration originally from central Europe, with their rolled torcs and Únětician pins. Flanged axes and metal-hilted daggers complete the equipment: but stone was still widely used as well.

In this north Italian group, Únětician influence declined and was limited to metalwork. Domestic life and particularly pottery remained firmly Mediterranean. A particular feature is vases from southern Italy with original handles equipped with 'spurs' and thumb-holes to give a good grip. These knobbed strap-handles – often *ad ascia* (axe-shaped) – were to enjoy a great vogue in the Mediterranean, particularly in the subsequent middle Bronze Age. They were to lead occasionally to a rather baroque style of pot, the most extreme examples of which were to display huge applied bosses, horns or even anthropomorphic shapes on top of the vase. A certain Mediterranean exuberance already!

Chapter 4

Early Atlantic Navigation and Megaliths

From the Neolithic age of 'shepherds with a megalithic religion' onwards, the Atlantic Ocean and its offshoots, the English Channel and the North Sea, were criss-crossed by fragile craft, daringly confronting the storms of the open sea. This is the only possible explanation of the various architectural similarities between megaliths in the south and in the north of Europe, the frequent exchanges of pottery and jewels or, again, the striking similarities between the dolmen art of the Iberian Peninsula, Armorica and Ireland.

These people could propel themselves over the sea. They were accustomed to observing the stars, as recent studies on the standing-stone alignments, stone circles or the great monument of Stonehenge have shown. But traces of their boats are virtually non-existent and we must turn to other documents to study prehistoric navigation.

The first boats on the Atlantic

Engravings on dolmens are not much help. But they do have some shapes which have been interpreted as boats. At Mané-Lud and at Locmariaquer there are horizontal lines turning upwards at either end – sketches, probably, of canoes or boats; attempts to interpret them as sailing-boats are more debatable. It needs a lot of imagination to describe the famous shield motifs with circles inside them, at the Dolmen of Pierres Plates in Brittany, as decorated sails: the classic interpretation, which is not necessarily correct, is that they represent the Mother Goddess. Other explanations have been given, either prosaic – a saucepan – or symbolic – the stag-beetle, guide of the dead, ferrying souls to Heaven. It needed all Dr Cariou's imagination to reconstruct on the basis of these same data a small megalithic vessel with a sail and oars. But why not give room for once to such an engaging hypothesis?

Peat-bogs and rivers have yielded traces of monoxylic canoes, in other words, dug out of a single tree-trunk. Oak was the most commonly used because of its durability, but in the Nordic regions canoes were fashioned in poplar which is easier to carve and can be modified, under heat, into a shape like a pea pod. These canoes were in use in the Neolithic period and the Bronze Age, but, like log rafts, could be used only on rivers or, in case of need, close to the coast.

Why were there no boats made of skins over a wooden frame? In Arctic countries, where there are very few large tree-trunks suitable for making canoes, the kayak or umiak keeps that tradition alive. The Celtic world used them for a long time, and if we think of the amazing conservatism of boat-building traditions, we may wonder if this one does not go right back to proto-historic times. A few coracles, big wicker baskets covered with leather or cloth, still sail some Scottish, Welsh and Irish rivers. The equivalent seagoing vessels – long slender curraghs – are bigger; the curraghs of Aran and the west coast of Ireland can carry four to six persons and freight. The tradition has been maintained even though tarred cloth is sometimes substituted for leather.

Between these present-day relics and the ancient world, Celtic navigation in historic times provides a staging post. Leather boats were used, it is said, when the Breton population migrated to what is now Britain around the sixth century, although folk tales prefer to picture saints crossing the Channel in stone troughs, a legend which may originate, perhaps, from the presence of ballast stones which were used to secure the foot

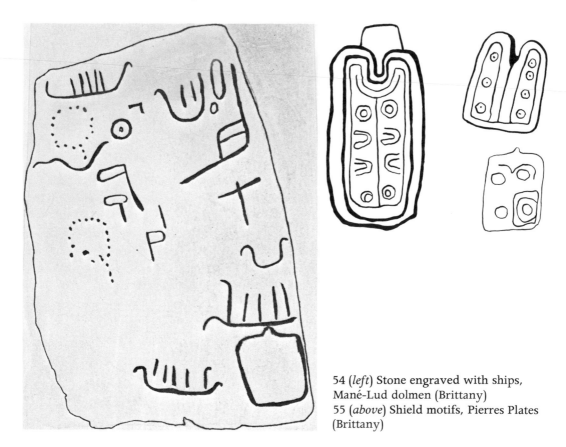

54 (*left*) Stone engraved with ships, Mané-Lud dolmen (Brittany)
55 (*above*) Shield motifs, Pierres Plates (Brittany)

of the mast in this light craft. That long voyages were indeed possible in these fragile craft is proved by the *Odyssey of St Brendan* told by the late lamented R. Creston, an expert in such matters since he was a marine ethnographer, and the recorder of Commandant Charcot's expeditions in the *Pourquoi Pas*. A series of ninth-century manuscripts, drawing on earlier texts, recounts the legend of Brendan, who is said to have reached Iceland and perhaps even Greenland, if not the West Indies, during his marvellous voyages around 550 AD.

The boat which accommodated Brendan, his fourteen disciples and victuals for forty days, was bigger than the modern curragh. We are given details of how it was built: oxhides were stretched over a frame of chestnut wood lashed together with pine roots; caulking was with a mixture of animal fat and pine resin. The oar was made of fir and the sail of hemp soaked in boiled oak bark to prevent rotting. In that way the boat was fitted out for its long voyage.

Wooden boats must have been used too. Late Bronze Age rock carvings in Scandinavia show high-stemmed boats with keels extended to form a beak. The prow and the poop were decorated with animal heads in the tradition that was to last till the days of the Vikings.

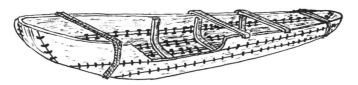

56 Boat from North Ferriby (Yorkshire)

Traces of wooden boats are exceedingly rare. However a discovery in 1946 caused a sensation in England: remains of two prehistoric boats had been reported at North Ferriby in Yorkshire. At the same spot, in the muddy bed of the river Humber, a third skiff was discovered at low tide in 1963. All three boats were of the same type, made of wooden laths stitched together: so it would seem that the method of assembly, used in curraghs for pieces of leather, was also applied to wood. The North Ferriby boats were successfully reconstructed. The wooden laths, shaped with adzes, measured a maximum of 35ft, which would give a boat 9 or 10m long; three seats could be fitted giving a carrying capacity of at least six or seven persons; but the boats were still primitive in conception, with no keel or helm. Their wood yielded a radio-carbon date of 750 BC, putting them in the late Bronze Age.

Finally, history too tells us something of these Atlantic navigators. It is towards the end of the Iron Age that classical texts describe large wooden vessels in the Atlantic zone. Caesar recorded the defeat of the Veneti at sea in 56 BC somewhere near Morbihan. He was impressed by the massive size of these Atlantic ships. The vessels, 20 or 30 ft long, were of oak with iron bolts; the sails were of raw hide and they had heavy iron anchor chains; the bows and sterns were exceptionally high to withstand the buffeting of the Ocean. Nevertheless Caesar conquered them with his Mediterranean galleys, thanks, he says boastfully, to his astuteness in cutting the halyards from the yards, using scythes, and immobilising the ships by stripping them of their sails. R. Creston, the ethnographer and a passionate admirer of the Celts, disagrees, claiming that the defeat of the Veneti was due to a mean trick of the gods who made the winds drop, becalming their vessels at a crucial point in the battle!

Successors of these great vessels sailed the gulf of Morbihan down to our own day, in the shape of large ships (now almost vanished) called 'sinagots'. If a model like that has endured for 2000 years, it is not improper to think that there may have been heavy wooden ships on the south coast of Brittany some centuries before the Veneti. The intense maritime traffic of Bronze Age Brittany must have needed such vessels.

Did the Mediterranean peoples, many of whom are islanders and therefore sailors, venture through the famous Pillars of Hercules around 1600 BC, to sally forth over the great Ocean? The swift galleys of the petty Cycladean pirates and even the Minoan or Mycenaean boats with sails and oars were hardly suitable. The high Atlantic tides were daunting to Mediterranean sailors. The great adventure on to the Ocean was more an exploit for heroes like those celebrated in the legend of Hercules or the Homeric poems. The myth of the Golden Apples of the Hesperides has sometimes been seen as a legendary reference to Ireland, with its wealth of gold, but we should not forget that, even in the middle of the fourth century the Massalian Pytheas was called a liar when he told of his Hyperborean voyage to the British Isles and Iceland. And yet the Atlantic world shows evidence of contacts with the Aegean world, even if all light did not always come from the east, as was formerly maintained. Exchanges were probably made through a combination of stages by land and sea, starting from the Mediterranean and involving a variety of peoples who discovered a new source of revenue in the transaction.

Trade must have been heavy in the Bronze Age along the coasts of the English Channel, for it formed a kind of land-locked sea, a Mediterranean of the north, across which Irish gold, Baltic amber, Galician, Breton and Cornish tin, Iberian copper – not to mention manufactured products and new metallurgical creations – were exchanged. A few gifts even arrived from remote eastern lands: daggers, precious vases, and particularly the blue 'Egyptian' glassware which competed with native products. Such a melting pot could not but give rise to original civilisations on either side of the Channel, and in fact these did emerge from the early Bronze Age onwards: this was the flowering of the Wessex and Armorican cultures. They developed where brilliant Neolithic civilisations had already flourished, characterised by the great stone monuments, or megaliths, that were attributed not so long ago to metal-using peoples. It is only gradually, in the wake of numerous modern excavations and, in particular, thanks to the support of radio-carbon dating, that the great antiquity of many of these monuments – generally earlier than the Bronze Age – has been driven home.

The great megalithic monuments

The brilliant megalithic past of Armorica is known chiefly from tourist postcards on which a menhir stands alongside the eternal dolmen. For a long time it was thought that these megaliths were relatively recent. We will not waste time on the flights of fancy of the Celtomanes who wrongly attributed them to the Gauls and took them to be phallic symbols and sacrificial stones. Not everyone has got over this yet and there are many who are still pleased to treat as 'Celtic' monuments that preceded the Celts by some millennia. They have also occasionally been attributed to the Phoenicians.

Yet, from the beginning of this century, the great prehistoric sequences were recognised and the succession from the Neolithic to the Bronze Age was finally established. From that time it was known that many dolmens must stem from the Neolithic, judging by their contents: stone axes and pottery but no metal objects. However it was conceded that the megaliths might have survived a very long time, and the 'stubborn pride' of the native, preserving and defending a deep-rooted faith, in spite of all innovations, was evoked. Some groups which were in fact Neolithic (like the large tumulus group in the Carnac region) were still difficult to date: their tumuli contained many dolmen-like chambers, but they were closed, like the well known Bronze Age vaults, and they even yielded polished stone axes with broad blades which were interpreted as imitations of flat copper axes. So all this seemed to suggest that they belonged to the Bronze Age. Finally to complete the confusion, metal objects were found in certain passage or gallery graves and it was not realised that their presence was due to later re-use.

The megalithic phenomenon had been wrongly considered as a homogeneous chronological whole: modern typological studies of the monuments and the grave goods have shown, on the contrary, a long and complex evolution down the ages. It is now known that the first megaliths, dolmens and large tumuli, date from the beginning of the Neolithic, whereas the gallery graves – or tombs with side entrances – are later, and date from the Chalcolithic. Some copper and bronze objects were in fact deposited in these and occasionally pictures of metal weapons were engraved on the walls.

Since 1960 a whole series of radio-carbon datings has clarified matters, proving the great antiquity, going back to before the Bronze Age, of the Breton monuments. The dating of chests from the tumulus of Saint Michel at Carnac by the physicist J. le Run, showed that this great monument had been built before 3000 BC. For his part, Professor P. R. Giot obtained a whole series of dates for the dolmens of Finistère: results from the tumuli of Ile Gaignoc, Ile Carn and Barnenez all agreed in going back to the fourth millennium, or even the fifth, if we take calibration into account.

This avalanche of unsuspected dates aroused astonishment at first in the archaeological world. For some it meant stupefaction and the reversal of opinions thought to be definitive. And so, some 2000 years before the great tholoi of Mycenae, little architects on the Atlantic seaboard had built great monuments in Brittany with corbelled roofs, a technique that had been thought to originate in the Near East. An invention, hitherto attributed to the great architecture of the classical world, had sprung from the brain of a 'barbarian'! Chronological scales had to be lengthened significantly.

The tumulus at Barnenez

Among the ancient monuments of Brittany, one in particular deserves a larger measure of attention: it is the great tumulus of Barnenez en Plouézoch. Situated at the mouth of the Morlaix river, it dominates the Kernelehen peninsula. Until 1955 it was just a heap of stones 100m long which the early archaeological inventories had overlooked. A heap of stones like that could not fail to attract entrepreneurs and one of them began to sell it as roadstone. The quarry was to suffer a strange fate, for soon a whole series of burial chambers was uncovered in the very heart of the tumulus: some classic, covered with a large capstone, some covered with a corbelled roof of small flat stones. Thanks to the energetic action of P. R. Giot, this 'megalithic Parthenon', as he was sometimes pleased to call it, was saved. Paradoxically, the partial destruction of the monument allowed a clearer view of this extraordinary series of tholoi, sectioned in such a way as to show clearly the use of corbelling in its construction. But the vandalism had been halted just in time.

57 The Barnenez tumulus, aerial view

In reality the monument was divided into two tumuli, with an overall length of 72m and a width of 18 to 21m. The earliest covered five passage graves and the second six burials! The quarrying had in fact only cut into four of the passage graves. The others were intact and I remember the emotion of discovering an unviolated tholos and entering it for the first time with my friend, J. L'Helgouach. We had opened up a long gallery filled almost to the top with stones, to arrive eventually at the heart of the monument. It was breathtaking. The tholos structure was intact. The circular vault was glistening with a

58 The Barnenez tumulus, cut open during quarrying, showing the tholoi in section

myriad faceted, shimmering beads: drops of water which had condensed on the schist and granite capstones: an unforgettable moment in an archaeologist's career!

The graves at Barnenez have long passages of 8 to 12m, some of dry-stone walling and others revetted with stone slabs. The chambers are circular and one of them is double: that is dolmen H, at the centre of the tumulus, and the one with the most engravings showing axes, with or without handles, a bow, and wave-like marks, perhaps representing the sea. The grave goods were not numerous and were essentially Neolithic: pottery, arrowheads, polished axes. Later the Bell Beaker people came through this way leaving a few sherds of the finest pan-European style, and a little tanged dagger of arsenical copper. In one of the galleries a few large sherds of cordoned ware provided evidence of a final use in the Bronze Age. One of the chambers seemed to have been re-opened in historic times and the discovery of an enormous hearth suggests some kind of occult practice.

The monument is no less remarkable from the outside: to the west the shape of the cairn, edged with large slabs, suggests the bow of a ship. The tumulus becomes a great vessel carrying the dead into the after-life. At the sides, terracing gives the monument the appearance of a Mesopotamian Ziggurat or a Mayan temple and this stimulated a great deal of imagination. Large monuments, whether of brick or stone, required this type of stepped construction if they were to be solid and stable, hence these surprising similarities.

Barnenez was built before 3500 BC, a revelation which, as we have said, amazed the supporters of a Mediterranean or, to be more precise, Aegean, origin for the megaliths. This type of dolmen with a chamber and a passage developed later in different ways. The dolmens became more complicated, either by adding side chambers or by lengthening the chamber; this led to the 'angled' or 'set square' dolmens. The development is complex, as we see from the works of J. L'Helgouach. Around the third millennium, at the approach of the Chalcolithic period, new types of megaliths, like the gallery graves appeared.

59 Gallery grave at Commana (Brittany)

The last megaliths

In the passage graves the chamber can be distinguished from the passage by its greater height and width. In contrast, in the later gallery graves, the height and width are constant. Another difference is the transverse stone slabs dividing the monument into chambers; often a small chamber or 'cella' is isolated in this way at the end of the monument. The deposits from the gallery graves are very varied; polished stone axes, flints, local or imported pottery and small copper and gold objects. The gallery graves at Prajou-Menhir in Côtes-du-Nord or at Commana in Finistère have engravings on some slabs: pairs of breasts with a necklace and pictures of weapons, axes and daggers. At Kerbors in Côtes-du-Nord one burial was stuffed full of Bell Beakers, a real potter's shop, according to some people. More probably it was the work of a group of Bell Beaker folk who, for once, adopted the rite of collective burial.

In this Chalcolithic period the passage graves continued in use and Bell Beaker ware was often deposited in them, sometimes accompanied by small copper daggers, as at Barnenez. Subsequently, in the early Bronze Age, the megaliths were used more sporadically. Sometimes individual coffers were made by removing the slabs. Much later still the passage graves were transformed into sanctuaries and passing Roman legionaries placed little white clay Venuses in them.

When the last megaliths were being built the knowledge of metal was advancing, even in Brittany. And yet Brittany was one of the high spots in the manufacture of polished stone axes: at Plussulien, in Côtes-du-Nord, for example, a hard volcanic rock called dolerite was shaped in large quantities over many acres. These rough cuts were later polished and transformed into axes which were exported all over Europe, as the studies of C. T. Leroux have shown. Even so, flat copper axes gradually replaced the axes of hard rock here too.

These copper axes were produced in great quantities in Vendée and Brittany, no doubt even before the beginning of the second millennium, but it is difficult to date these tools which are often found in isolation. The few objects with which they have been found associated are gold strap necklaces, a Portuguese type of jewellery, and some copper daggers, beloved of the Bell Beaker people.

Belated Neolithic cultures: Seine-Oise-Marne

The arrival of metal did not prevent the great Neolithic cultures from lingering on. Some had a long life, like the almost indestructible 'S.O.M.', the culture of Seine-Oise-Marne, which held sway over the greater part of north-west France around the second millennium. Its origin is the source of much debate: sometimes it is sought in the middle French Neolithic, sometimes in south German groups. Its culture is revealed chiefly by its burials which were collective and various in form: rectangular subterranean tombs, hollowed out of the limestone in Champagne; trenches with dry-stone walls; or again, in the central and north-west Paris Basin, buried gallery graves. These latter often have a long chamber, separated from an entrance hall by a porthole slab: it is through this that the

60 Gallery grave at Prajou-Menhir (Brittany)

souls of the dead depart, the *Seelenloch* already seen in Malta. Metal equipment is limited to a few beads or small pieces of imported copper jewellery. The pottery, which is poor, includes rather clumsily made 'flower pots'. But the flint tools compensate admirably for the absence of metal: fine daggers with flint blades, sometimes imported from workshops at Grand-Pressigny in Touraine, arrowheads in constantly changing shapes, sometimes tanged. Bone and antler are competently and artistically used, making fine polished or carved axe handles. Items of adornment include perforated axe-amulets, arc-shaped pendants, and small 'ninepins' of antler. Pictures engraved on the tombs exalt the cult of the axe and of the very ancient Mother Goddess, adorned with her heavy necklaces.

In short, a whole remarkable cultural style, which the work of G. Bailloud has made known to us. It illustrates the type of society which was basically Neolithic, or at most Chalcolithic, and hardly used metal, although metal was known to it: it carried on while all around the Bronze Age was well established.

61 Stela of the Rocher des Doms (Provence)

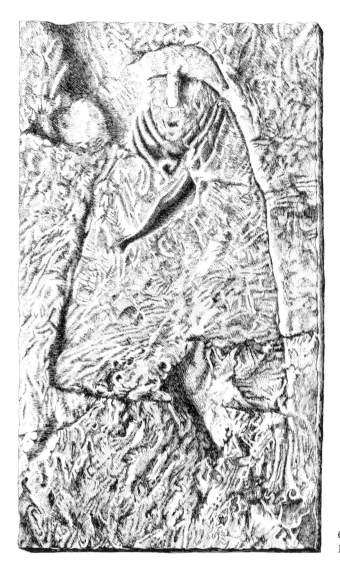

62 Funerary goddess, Seine-Oise-
Marne culture, Coizard (Marne)

Chapter 5

Western Burgeonings: the Princes of Armorica and Wessex

At the beginning of the early Bronze Age, that is in the first centuries of the second millennium BC, small groups, no doubt from northern Europe, arrived by the Channel seaways and settled on either shore, some in the south of the British Isles, others in the extreme west of Armorica.

Their journeyings have been followed with some uncertainty, thanks to sporadic discoveries of daggers in northern France and Calvados or a few tombs in Normandy. They are the originators, in Brittany, of the flourishing Armorican Barrow culture and, in England, of the Wessex culture. These cultures cover the whole of the early Bronze Age period and fade or degenerate from the beginning of the middle Bronze Age. They are characterised by the rite of individual inhumation, a recent rite, introduced by the Bell Beaker and Corded Ware peoples, which was to be generalised everywhere from the beginning of the Bronze Age. Only a few Neolithic groups, lingering well into the Bronze Age, went on practising collective burial, notably in megaliths.

But, in contrast with Chalcolithic inhumations in a simple trench, the tomb was now covered with a mound of earth or stones which was often imposing when compared with the size of the burial hollow. So the simple tomb became a great monument. But the practice of raising funerary tumuli was well known in certain Neolithic sites, even very early ones: around 3500 BC the coffers of the great tumuli in the Carnac region or the tholoi of the passage graves of the renowned monument at Barnenez, were covered with heaps of stones, or cairns. Later the multiple-chambered passage graves and the gallery graves were to be surrounded by a mound too. Similarly in Great Britain collective burials in the Neolithic long-barrows were replaced by the round-barrows of the Beaker tombs and the early Bronze Age burials of the Wessex culture, which we shall study later.

This funeral rite was destined to a great future: in the following middle Bronze Age period, that is from the middle of the second millennium, another centre of tumulus burials, originating in central Europe, was to spread westwards as far as eastern France, with distinctive groups in Alsace and the Jura. This central European Tumulus culture is often also called the Protoceltic Tumulus culture, a term which we shall discuss, or, more simply, the Tumulus culture. It must be clearly distinguished from the Armorican Barrow

63 Tumulus at St-Fiacre (Brittany)

culture, the Wessex barrows and also the Únětician barrows at Leubingen, all of which date from the early Bronze Age. These similar terms, which are classic in Bronze Age literature, refer not only to distinct periods but also to separate cultural entities. The earliest Armorican barrows are 'princely tombs' with imposing mounds. They degenerate at the end of the early and beginning of the middle Bronze Age into a poorer style. When this first western entity quietly faded away around 1400 BC, the great Protoceltic Tumulus culture from central Europe began to flourish, but reached only the eastern parts of France.

The petty princes of Brittany

The arrival of new populations in Brittany is disclosed by a scatter of barrows along the coastal fringe from Côtes-du-Nord to south Finistère. Some inland monuments like Saint-Fiacre en Melrand bear witness to penetration along the small coastal rivers. While some barrows are grouped in series of three or four, more often we find only one large monument, all that is left of the deceased's illusory domination over the surrounding territory. No doubt the land was shared out between the new arrivals. These imposing funerary mounds, 6 to 8m high and 30m in diameter, were intended to be seen from afar, but time and man have often robbed them of their early glory.

The rite of the wooden framed tomb was also imported from the north. After removing the top soil or digging a trench, a coffin hewn from the trunk of an oak, or a structure of planks and wooden sticks, was set up and the body, in its leather shroud, laid inside. The whole thing was covered with a heap of stones, and, under the earth from the mound, modern excavations often uncovered a 'bathtub' structure resulting from the collapse of the stones in the centre when the wooden burial chamber gave way. At Saint-Jude in Côtes-du-Nord, the central tomb had an additional covering of a roof of poles topped with straw and bracken. The deceased was sleeping in a mortuary house which was a replica of the unpretentious grass hut or thatched cottage then in use.

However, the influence of earlier, powerful, megalithic traditions soon made itself felt: the tombs were constructed with schist and granite slabs, making the 'dolmens under tumuli' of earlier authors. But the difference between these, and what we may perhaps term the 'true dolmens' with a permanent entrance, is considerable. The burials became inaccessible, enclosed and – most important – individual, in obvious contrast with the collective mortuary houses of the Neolithic. Even in death the individual took precedence over the group. Some chambers 4m long may have sheltered several skeletons, but these were for the most part the tombs of princes or potentates as the rich grave goods prove: great chiefs insisted on sumptuous burial with all their panoply and adornments.

64 Excavation of the tumulus at Kernonen en Plouvorn (Brittany): Armorican arrow heads, archer's wristguard, dagger (*centre*), bone pommel (*left*)

To illustrate these early Bronze Age princely tombs we will describe one of them, Kernonen en Plouvorn, in detail. In 1907 P. du Chatellier briefly reported a large tumulus, 6m high and 50m in diameter, at Plouvorn, Finistère. The excavation had yielded only 'a few fragments of bone and some shapeless bits of iron'. Subsequently the mound was three-quarters destroyed and almost vanished completely in 1961, when the owner of the land wanted to be rid of the bump which got in the way of his cultivations. As soon as the work of flattening it began, there was a subsidence which partially revealed what might have been a capstone. The central chamber was intact and the excavation was to prove one of the most rewarding of recent years in Brittany. A large trench was cut from the centre outwards laying bare the structure of the mound – a heap of yellow loam, becoming whitish towards the base and yielding, at the old soil level, quantities of natural iron precipitate, the 'shapeless bits of iron' reported by P. du Chatellier!

The central chamber 4.70m long and an average of 1.30m wide, was built on the old soil level. The dry-stone walls supported a huge block of granite which must have weighed 7 or 8 tons, with small supplementary lintels. Part of this covering had collapsed but the bulk of the grave goods was miraculously intact. The axis of the tomb runs south-east–north-west, and at the bottom, on carefully laid paving, was the mingled debris of a wooden floor and plant material. Some hazelnuts showed that the burial had taken place in autumn. The tomb furnishings were put in small oak coffers which had naturally collapsed under the weight of the soil that filled the tomb after a part of the capstone was broken.

Starting from the north-west there were three wooden coffers: the first contained the remains of three or four bronze axes, slightly flanged and so corroded that they looked like bone in places. By some phenomenon of natural electrolysis in the soil, the copper had partially disappeared leaving a white metal rich in tin salts. Some 50cm away a row of about twenty flint arrowheads indicated the great central coffer where the most valuable weapons were collected. Three great bronze blades arranged at right angles were lying in their scabbards of bark and hide. The wood of the small handles had partially decomposed, but around the hilt shone thousands of small yellow specks: they were tiny gold 'nails', in incredible numbers – about 15,000 altogether or 5000 for each weapon. In order to count them, soil from the excavation was brought to the laboratory and patiently sifted through very fine sieves for more than a month. Some were hardly visible to the naked eye; the average length of these 'nails' was of the order of 5mm and their diameter from 0.3 to 0.5mm. It was not a fortune for their total weight was no more than a few tens of grams. These tiny gold pellets were arranged in geometrical motifs forming circles round the rivets, and chevrons or vertical lines on the wooden handle, in the middle of which three large gold tacks had been driven and they, too, were surrounded by a circle of tiny nails.

Another peculiarity was the unusual presence of bronze pins between the scabbard and the blade of the daggers. The placing of these pins, usually reserved for garments, is inexplicable, unless they were there 'for emergencies'.

Amber was scattered liberally round the central chest: a dozen pendants in the shape of discs or trapezoidal cobbles. The skeleton (or skeletons) had left no trace of bone because the soil was too acid. They must undoubtedly have occupied the empty space at the west end of the tomb.

The final chest at Plouvorn held some forty flint arrowheads, a dagger with a bone pommel, and an archer's wristguard. This was a display article since it was made of amber.

Plouvorn is a recent example of the small princely tombs showing some opulence; some thirty such burials have been investigated in Brittany. Gold has been found in small quantities and so-called 'Armorican' arrowheads, elegantly barbed at the sides and very finely worked. So, at the dawn of the Bronze Age we find flint-working at its apogee.

Gold and silver

Gold was not only used to decorate weapons. Occasionally it was used to make small jewels, simple wires rolled into spirals or little twisted blades. An exceptional collection comes from the Forest of Carnöet, where in 1843, a tumulus was excavated under very odd conditions, which were quite customary in those heroic days of archaeology. One of the diggers, whose girth was rather excessive, had the capstone of the tomb broken so that he could get in. Another, who was dissatisfied with the share-out of finds, carried off the only bronze axe amongst the grave goods in his boot. But despite all this, the bulk of the goods was recovered and presented to the Duc de Nemours, who was visiting Brittany. The duke deposited the treasure in the Musée de Cluny where the Carnöet gold and silver rings can still be seen today. Indeed this unique tomb housed rings not only of gold but also of silver, a great novelty. The precious metal has also been found in the pins of the Côtes-du-Nord tumuli. Still more surprising are the silver goblet fragments which were found in two burials at Saint-Adrien and Saint-Fiacre. The silver was probably not local, since the silver-bearing lead of Brittany was not exploited, it seems, until the late Bronze Age. Silver in these early Bronze Age tumuli came, no doubt, from the Iberian peninsula where the El Argar culture was already producing it in great quantities. So Brittany was maintaining its relations with Spain, which began in the Neolithic and which we have already mentioned in the age of the megaliths.

Origin and kinship of the Armorican barrows

The origin of this Armorican Barrow culture in the early Bronze Age remains a mystery in many respects. The most frequent exchanges took place with their cousins in Wessex, where gold nails, bronze weapons and amber beads of a strikingly similar type are found. It has even been suggested that the famous small gold nails came from the same workshop. This is why British authors like Stuart Piggott looked to Armorica first for the origins of the Wessex culture. P. R. Giot held the opposite view, but nowadays he leans more towards a common Nordic origin whose starting point, nevertheless, remains far from clear.

The princes of Wessex and Armorica would have been the chieftains of small bands coming from the North Sea, a sort of pre-Vikings, landing all along the coasts; finding the country pleasant or profitable, they settled down. There are serious arguments in favour of this Nordic origin: first of all the tombs and daggers of Normandy form a stage in the journey and the first Breton tumuli are distributed along the coasts showing fairly clearly the route followed by the early Bronze Age arrivals. It is further along the line that things become confused.

P. R. Giot brings the anthropological argument to bear. Despite the small numbers of skeletons, which often dissolved in the acid soils of Armorica, some usable traces remain here and there. At Kergoniou there is half a cranium. Formerly it was thought that this was the memento of a heroic sword thrust, but for P. R. Giot, more prosaically, this reduction by half is due to the head being dissolved in the juices of the cadaver and does not preclude the recognition of the long-faced cranium characteristic of the proto-Nordic races.

Archaeology, too, produces some comparisons which seem to go along with this theory. Thus we find the 'princely phenomenon' again at Leubingen in Saxony as well as in Brittany. An even more interesting illustration of the connections between Brittany and North Germany is provided by the sword blades from the Forest of Carnöet; these long, flat swords have a white glaze which early excavators thought was silvering and which the first Bronze Age specialist at the Musée de St Germain, G. de Mortillet, saw as tinning. Modern analyses have decided otherwise: it is arsenic. A 30 per cent arsenic enrichment of the surface has given this strange appearance. This was a source of some astonishment to the modern technicians of the Centre Technique des Industries de la Fonderie who carried out the micro-analysis: right from the earliest steps in metallurgy in the early Bronze times, the art of enriching certain parts of the blades with arsenical powders or regules was known. It was not an isolated phenomenon: Professor J. Hundt recognised it on the blades in the Gau-Bickelheim hoard in Rhine-Hesse. The shape of these swords too is reminiscent of the Armorican type. So between two distant European communities relations probably existed which led to the spread of the same sophisticated techniques. The Common Market is not new!

Finally we must report finds of some sherds of Bell Beaker ware in the soil of these early Bronze Age tumuli and this cannot be fortuitous. So, here too, the Bell Beaker element, left over from the Chalcolithic, may have played a part alongside Nordic influences, in the beginning of the Armorican Barrow culture. The fine arrowheads and wristguards, which are similar to those of the Chalcolithic, support the idea. Radio-carbon dates, as well, place the Armorican tumuli mainly around 1900 to 1700 BC, or in a period which lies astride the end of the Bell Beaker culture. And there is the analogy with Wessex, where, as we shall see, the Bell Beaker influence is much in evidence.

The new social classes

These new arrivals in the early Bronze Age shared out the territory of Brittany to the west of Morbihan amongst themselves. They seem to have lived side by side with the native population who had been building gallery graves there since the Chalcolithic. On the other hand they did not penetrate far into the great megalithic centres like Carnac, which were already over-populated; but they exchanged a few gold ornaments on occasions, like the small circular gold boxes found in Morbihan, and these were very close to Wessex ornaments in style.

What exactly were the relations between the newcomers, with their tumuli, and the natives? Bronze Age men needed a large work force to build their great earthen tombs. Did they press the local population into 'tumulus gangs'? That would smack of pure colonialism. But it is not only the power of work that moves mountains, there is faith, too, so they say. So did they introduce the Neolithics, or some of them, to the cult of the individual? In that case they would all have joyfully co-ordinated their efforts to build for the divine prince the tumulus that his prestige demanded. It is very difficult to answer these questions, but meticulous analysis of the soil from the tumuli reveals a great many details about social and everyday life. A study of the marks made in the soil when the mounds were being built, for example, tells us what domestic tools were used: they were still the same as in the Neolithic. Moreover, though earth was taken from the sub-soil to build funeral mounds, it also came from the soil surrounding the settlements. Hence the abundance of potsherds and lithic rubbish which tells us about domestic equipment, which had not changed much either since the Neolithic – small flint scrapers, granite querns, schist polishers and quartz. Only the pottery shows some development with a greater quantity of cordon or fingerprint decoration. There was no revolution, it seems, in everyday life styles.

To sum up, domestic equipment is still essentially based on flint or polished stone. The fine bronze weapons or the ornaments of precious metal remain the prerogative of the chieftains who jealously take them to the grave with them. It is certainly a society with classes. A small aristocracy has exclusive access to the new wealth. The common man is satisfied with very little, even in death: a few burial mounds or tumuli with no grave goods of consequence except, occasionally, a few sherds of pot.

Certain large tumuli, however, raise other problems. At Saint-Jude, in the Guingamp region, two enormous mounds contained only a few decorated sherds and some copper fragments. Were they women's tombs – this would explain the absence of weapons – or perhaps tombs of minor native chiefs who had risen to 'tumulus status' but had not managed to acquire costly bronze weapons? These monuments have been dated by radio-carbon to 1850 BC, or the same period as all the early Bronze Age burials.

Decline in the middle Bronze Age

The Armorican Barrow culture of the early Bronze Age had its moment of glory from 1900 to 1600 and then slowly declined until the beginning of the middle Bronze Age. This was the period when another centre of tumulus burial – independent of and different from the British and Armorican centre – appeared in central Europe: the 'Tumulus culture'.

In Brittany, at this same middle bronze period, funeral mounds were proliferating and moving inland to form tumulus fields in the Monts d'Arée. Hundreds of them are known at Berrien and La Feuillée, for example. The tomb now is usually dug into the ground: it is a funeral pit with walls of stone blocks and a large capstone. But the grave goods become very poor: chiefly pottery, the most classic being four-handled vases. The decoration, however, is often very fine, for example imitation basketry at Lesneven or geometrical motifs, chevrons and triangles on a whole series of small biconical pots. All the pottery differs fundamentally from that of the central European tumuli with its excised decoration, showing decorative motifs in relief.

65 Three-handled vase, middle
Bronze Age, Lannilis (Brittany)

Metal becomes rare: a few axes and daggers, only one of which is decorated with gold nails. Ornaments include a few beads of blue glass, but mostly of bone or shell, and few have survived. The great tumulus of Reuniou at Berrien, which is still imposing, housed a corpse in a shroud of hide, adorned with a necklace of shells and armed with a small dagger. He was lying with his head to the east, and, according to the custom of the time, a four-handled vase had been placed level with his shoulder. The Reuniou tumulus was the biggest in the area but we can say that this king of Berrien was a poor king. However, poverty did not exclude a certain majesty: at Kersaint Plabennec, P. R. Giot excavated a huge tumulus whose occupant proved enigmatic. In the vast burial chamber covered by a great granite block lay a solitary child of about six with a bronze dagger, and the ritual four-handled vases. Was this the son of a prince or a deified child? The mystery persists.

The great menhirs

The Armorican Bronze Age yields few examples of art, apart from the ornaments in the tombs: a few capstones are engraved with cupolas, sometimes joined or arranged in a cross, or simply at random. The good Dr Baudouin, who specialised in esoteric interpretations, thought he saw in them the constellation of the Great Bear and a message from the people of Atlantis, but this is very bold.

But still, it seems that the very large dressed standing stones date from the Bronze Age, too, as for instance the stone at Kerloas en Plouarzel, famous for the two bosses at the base, which make the phallic interpretation, so dear to some, a possibility. Tradition even has it that young newly-weds came by night to rub their bare bellies against it in order to have beautiful children. Fortunately the local clergy were tolerant enough not to destroy this relic of a pagan, not to say debauched cult, as was often the case. This Kerloas stone probably dates from the Bronze Age, for under its stone chocks, which were thrown down by stupid treasure hunters, lay fragments of a bi-conical pot, a propitiatory vase which is undeniably Bronze Age. Here is a precious piece of evidence showing that standing stones were still being erected in the middle of the second millennium. We find the same phenomenon in the British Isles where the most notable circle of standing stones, Stonehenge, dates its finest phase to the Bronze Age.

The religious purpose of these standing stones has frequently been mooted: a phallic cult, a water cult in the case of some examples by springs, but also a cult of the stars; the work of Professor Alexander Thom on Stonehenge and Carnac has revived interest in the latter. The 'Grand Menhir Brisé' at Locmariaguer could, according to this view, have played a key role in the whole system of possible astronomical observations at Carnac: it would have allowed many observations of the setting moon and sun. The alignments at Carnac and the Crozon peninsula, or the numerous rows of stones inland in Brittany, testify to very persistent cults or astronomical work. Early works by A. Devoir in Finistère or R. Merlet in Morbihan agree with the recent researches of Alexander Thom in seeing them as observatories intended primarily for working out the solstices. Little accurate information is available as to the end to which these great monuments were used, but probably they, too, were in use in the heyday of the Bronze Age.

This religious or astronomical purpose may have been backed up by a more practical one. The astronomical marker may have been used as a landmark or lighthouse to guide travellers and sailors. It has been noticed, for instance, that the great stones at Léon were placed near Saint Renan, rich in alluvial tin. It may seem surprising, but it has even been

66 'Irish' lunulae, found at Kerivoa (Brittany)

suggested that these noble monuments could simply be beacons marking mineral deposits and serving as signposts to foreign prospectors. From there to making all the megalithic monuments into motels or milestones for Phoenician travellers is a step that has been taken by some, but we cannot follow their lead.

We will cross the Channel now to visit the princes of Wessex.

The Wessex aristocrats: the barrows

The Wessex culture, a twin of the Armorican, was defined by Professor Stuart Piggott in 1938 from a series of princely tombs in Wiltshire and the neighbouring counties. Gold weapons adorned with gold nails and amber beads testify to a definite kinship with Brittany. But in Wessex the situation has other complications. First, when the princes of the tumuli landed they found not only the descendants of the Neolithic populations in occupation, but also a very strong element of Bell Beaker people, the Beaker people whose many individual burials containing beakers are scattered over the area. This is in contrast with Armorica, where, as we have seen, a Bell Beaker presence in the early Bronze Age, though not unknown, is still exceptional. The copper and tin deposits in nearby Cornwall have some bearing on the density of population in the area. English Bell Beaker influence in the early days of the Wessex civilisation was very strong, much more so than in Brittany. Moreover a whole native population was living in southern England, and even in the early Bronze Age depositing the ashes of its dead in funeral urns – a great technical innovation in funeral rites, which, during the middle and especially the late Bronze Age, steadily replaced inhumation. These agriculturalists, growing barley and wheat and raising sheep and cattle, took shelter in small circular huts with low stone walls and roofs of thatch. This is the population that was dominated or 'colonised' by the Wessex aristocrats, whose funeral customs they sometimes adopted.

As in Brittany, these princely tombs were covered with a tumulus or barrow (to quote English authors). In the chalky soil of Wessex they built various types whose shapes are evoked by the old terms 'bell-barrow', 'bowl-barrow', 'saucer-barrow', 'disc-barrow' or 'pond-barrow'. These last are unique in the annals of the tumuli, for they are hollow barrows: the centre, which is flat or slightly rounded, is surrounded by a bank of earth to give it a pond shape, leaving the central part on a lower level. But whatever the variations, the principle remains the same: burials must be surrounded by a magic circle which is given concrete expression by a ditch, a bank and surrounding stones or wooden stakes. No doubt it was taboo to profane the sacred enclosure, except for another burial; excavations have in fact shown that the same mound could be re-used – sometimes after a lapse of centuries. There must have been urgent cases, or people who were not disposed to take on the heavy navvying involved in making a funeral mound, which certainly represented thousands of blows with antler picks, thousands of shovelfuls of earth, using a cow's shoulder blade, and thousands of linen bags or wicker baskets to be filled and transported.

67 Round-barrows, Winterbourne Stoke Down (near Stonehenge)

68 Cemetery of disc-barrows, Wimborne St Giles (Dorset)

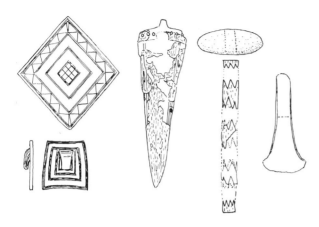

69 'Mycenaean' objects from the Bush Barrow (Wessex), gold ornaments, bronze dagger and axe, 'sceptre' ending in a lump of stone

In Wessex two main phases can be distinguished, one in the early Bronze Age, very close to the Armorican Barrow culture about 1800–1600; the other, more sophisticated, nearer the beginning of the middle Bronze Age and the decline of the Armorican culture, had ogival daggers, and would be dated by calibrated radio-carbon to about 1400 BC.

A typical example of the early phase, the Bush Barrow tumulus, was to yield two bronze daggers, one decorated, as in Brittany, with tiny gold nails arranged in chevrons on the wooden handle, a bronze axe and finely engraved gold appliqué. One of the most important pieces is the famous sceptre: a wooden rod decorated with bands and tips of bone carved in chevrons, the whole thing topped with a mass of perforated stone. The sceptre! For anyone who doubted the princely nature of the Wessex tomb, its presence would be inappropriate, to say the least. Indeed it has affinities with the gold-decorated sceptre of Mycenae and the great 'rods of command' in polished stone from the Breton tumuli.

Gold and amber: the Irish lunulae

Gold and amber abound in these tombs, often in association. At Hameldon, near Dartmoor, an amber pommel was decorated with a cruciform motif of small gold nails. For anyone familiar with the difficulty of working amber, to drive in several hundred gold nails, a third of a millimetre in diameter, in three close rows, is something of an exploit. But for the Wessex goldsmiths, who sculpted the delightful jet cups of Farway Down, this was nothing exceptional. They did not hesitate to work for the great ladies who, it seems, enjoyed princely privileges at times: one of the tumuli at Normanton sheltered the body of a rich lady in woollen garments with bronze weapons and amber discs set in gold, as well as a small amber replica of a halberd, a copy of the shafted halberd of central Germany – a feminine whim, or perhaps an ornamental copy of his weapons presented by her lord or her vassal.

70 Late Bell Beaker (Lambourn, Berks)

71 Incense cup, 'Aldbourne cup' type (Wilts)

We must also mention tiny funerary cups called incense cups – no doubt for burning perfumes – decorated sometimes either with small geometric motifs in the normal style of the contemporary pottery, sometimes in a more original style with little clay blobs suggesting bunches of grapes (grape cups). Curiously, this form had predecessors at Er-Mar, in the Breton Neolithic of Morbihan.

If the Bell Beaker influence played a part in the rise of Wessex, so, too, did the Corded Ware people with their battle axes, marked by a few fine stone shaft-hole hammer axes. Many ancient traditions have come together in the new civilisations of the early Bronze Age, as we can see. From central Europe (and no doubt from Únětice) bronze or bone ring- or crutch-headed pins were imported. For there was a minor revolution in the dressmaking world: clothing was no longer fastened with the disc-shaped bone buttons or toggles, often with V-perforations, like the ones found in the Beaker burials; the linen or woollen peplum-style garments were fastened with real pins, copper, bronze, sometimes even silver for the wealthiest, and bone imitations for the poorer people.

Wessex owed its prosperity partly to the commercial talents of its chiefs, indeed it has even been thought that they played a major part in the spread of gold from that Garden of the Hesperides which was the Ireland of those days, where, starting from the grains in the little coastal rivers, the famous lunulae were being beaten out. The lunula is the magnificent gold crescent glittering on the chest of the great of those days, a fine gold leaf, obtained by hammering out a plain ring, and ending in a small chain or two palettes which fastened together at right angles. But no doubt the lunula was a symbol as well.

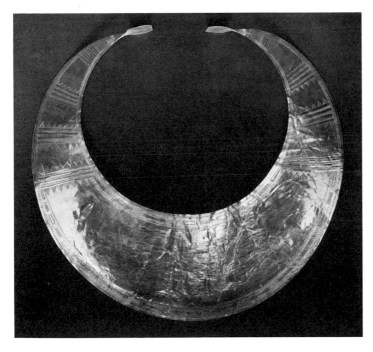

72 Irish gold lunula, Kerry (Ireland)

Had not some goldsmiths of genius captured a crescent moon, at its most brilliant, for man? This would tie in with all the cults of sun and moon suggested by the stone circles and countless other indications. Artistic images, for instance, show solar discs – as in Denmark, with the famous Trundholm chariot. In Brittany, no doubt in the late Bronze Age, a large copper ingot and a gold disc-ring were thrown into the peat bog at Maël Pestivien, to win the favour of the gods. This is interpreted as a sun – but why not a moon? These crescent-shaped ornaments enjoyed a great vogue. They were even copied using cunningly assembled beads of amber, limestone or jet. The spacer beads, pierced obliquely, made it possible to space the threads more and more widely towards the centre of the crescent.

Gold lunulae were exported in large quantities from Ireland to Great Britain and the Continent. One fine series comes from Brittany, with the Kerivoa treasure at Bourbriac, in a zone of early Bronze Age tumuli. At Kerivoa the lunulae are accompanied by a gold tool ending in a palette – palette-torcs according to some, unfinished lunulae say others. All that was required was to hammer the rod in order to obtain the gold crescent. It is difficult to judge. This Bourbriac treasure, found in a farmyard, was saved by a miracle: it lay in a stone chest and the children who found it, encrusted with earth and the dust of the ages, played with it for some time until a local archaeologist, as competent as he was modest, had the whole thing removed to the Musée des Antiquités Nationales. It is a fact that the famous lunulae, instead of being presented in all their glory, had been rolled up like common cigars. No doubt when they were placed there, they had gone out of fashion and their magic or ceremonial function was already forgotten. The bracelet of Besné is often quoted as another example of a Breton object miraculously saved; found in a very dirty state in the ground, it is said to have hung on the branch of an apple tree for nearly a year, until one day it was seen, washed by the rain and glittering in all its glory in the sunshine. The quirks of fate in discoveries!

Stonehenge: the temple of the sun

The time has come to tackle the 'sacred monster' of Salisbury Plain, rising in the midst of the burials of the lords of Wessex. A huge library would be needed to house the mass of legends, flights of fancy of Celtomanes and theoreticians of every kind, soliloquisings of romantic poets, and scientific or pseudo-scientific works dealing with a monument which fascinates astronomers as much as archaeologists. We will leave the legends to one side – almost. . . .

About AD 1100, Geoffrey of Monmouth stated that the stones of Stonehenge were brought from Ireland by the magic powers of the wizard Merlin, at the request of King Ambrosius. It is strange to see here the foreign origin of some of the stones of Stonehenge – the 'blue' stones – appearing in Arthurian legend and being given, as is only right, a supernatural explanation. There is talk of the devil; he almost crushed a poor monk who left the mark of his heel on the stone as he fled – since known as the Heel Stone.

Serious studies began with one of a number of royal visitors to Stonehenge, the most renowned of them, James I, who fell in love with the place around 1620. As King he felt entitled to a kingly and unassailable explanation of it and the best architect at his court, the famous Inigo Jones, who introduced the Palladian style to Great Britain, was charged with the task of clearing up the mystery. His reconstruction reflects his enthusiasm for antique art and we are fortunate that we have it on paper. For his plans show a great temple of circular structure, including the famous trilithons, which however are clearly arranged in a horse-shoe shape. The dissertation concludes: Stonehenge was a temple of the Tuscan order constructed by the Romans and dedicated to the god Coelus shortly after the Roman conquest of the island. The savages had to be civilised by being taught architecture and leaving to the astonished world this grandiose evidence of the conquerors' skill.

This explanation had the misfortune to displease Dr Walter Charleton, apothecary in turn to Charles I and Charles II, who corresponded on scientific matters with the honourable Danish antiquarians of the period, and he suggested that the temple, this *Chorea Gigantum*, or Giants' Dance, could not have been other than a place where the election of the Danish kings took place in the ninth century – AD of course! This was enough to turn to water the blood of Inigo Jones's descendants, he having died meantime. His nephew by marriage, John Webb, who had also been his publisher, launched a vigorous *Vindication* which restored Stonehenge and the Romans to their rightful place: *Stonehenge, a Roman Work and Temple.* . . .

All this shows clearly the passions that were aroused by the famous monument and the fascination it exercised. Ideas progressed as everywhere in Europe and now prehistoric monuments were attributed not to the Romans but – taking a small step back into the past – to the Druids of Gaul. This was the thesis of John Aubrey, for example, the author of an interesting plan of Stonehenge published in 1666, which enables us to see that some of the stones have since disappeared. He it was who revealed the existence of 'cavities' dug all along the outer ditch round the monument and called, after him, the Aubrey Holes. Among the great Celtomanes of the period, we are indebted to William Stukeley for some pertinent observations and a reconstruction of the building method. In particular, he was one of the first to advance the idea of an astronomical function for the temple, by calculating that the axis of the monument was directed towards the sunrise at the time of the summer solstice.

What are the modern views of the monument? It is quite clear that there is a long tradition of stone circles in the British Isles, from the Neolithic to the Bronze Age, and Stonehenge has its place in it. The tradition was particularly strong in Cornwall, Scotland and Ireland, whose many stone circles have been interpreted by Professor Alexander Thom as a means of working out the rising and setting of the sun and the moon, a further support for his theory. What is their origin? These sacred circles have much in common with the wooden stakes that have been found surrounding the Beaker tumuli of the Netherlands, which in turn have parallels with the English Beaker round-barrows and which have yielded a great many beakers, both Bell Beaker and Corded Ware, also dating

73 Part of a circle of standing stones, surrounding a coffer of stone slabs, Cairn Holy, Galloway (Scotland)

to the Chalcolithic. The transfer of this burial practice to religious monuments led first to the henge monuments. These consisted of a large circular ditch with a bank and of one or more belts of stone stelae or wooden stakes. The most famous is at Avebury, near Stonehenge, with its many concentric circles of stones and its great circular ditch, 425m in diameter. These assemblages were not built in one go, but were progressively re-modelled and completed over many years. The first phases are Neolithic, then 'beaker' (that is Chalcolithic) and the final phases are coeval with the Wessex culture (early or middle Bronze Age).

It is this kind of development that is found at Stonehenge and illustrated in the scholarly works of Professor R. J. C. Atkinson. In his very complex history, he distinguishes three main phases which we can only summarise briefly here.

Stonehenge I. This is the first phase around 2000 b.c. (by radio-carbon) or 2500 BC after calibration. It includes the demarcation of the sacred area, which was immediately isolated from the world of the profane by a gigantic ditch backed by a bank, 90m in diameter. Inside, the 56 'Aubrey Holes' were dug in the ground: they are either post-holes or ritual shafts which were sometimes later overlaid by cremation burials. There do not seem to have been human sacrifices here, analogous with those at Woodhenge – an older henge monument near by with wooden posts, in the centre of which the remains of a child were discovered, its head split by an axe. According to Atkinson the Heel Stone was erected at the same time as the first circle, but outside it. It plays a key role at Stonehenge as an essential landmark in the orientation of the monument. Near the Heel Stone traces of post-holes indicate the existence of a triple wooden portico.

Stonehenge II. Around 1700 b.c. – 2100 BC – a double circle of 'bluestones' was built. These stones pose an amazing problem of transport over some 300km, for they came from quarries in Pembrokeshire in south Wales. Much ink has flowed on this topic and various routes have been proposed. It seems that sea, river and land transport were used in succession and this implies the use of huge rafts and wooden sledges pulled by a perfectly co-ordinated team of men.

Stonehenge III. This is the phase that can be assigned to the Wessex culture. Three subdivisions, A, B and C, correspond to modifications in the 'bluestone' structures, but the main thing in Stonehenge III is the building of the great circle of sarsen stones with lintels and the great horseshoe of trilithons. This is yet another exploit, for huge blocks of sarsen, a tertiary sandstone, were used and the nearest deposits are in the Marlborough Downs, 30km to the north of Stonehenge. Here again the faith that moves mountains was needed to extract and transport these tons of stones. Precision techniques were required to quarry the stones and make the mortice and tenon joints and finally a complete knowledge of lifting methods was needed for the ultimate assembly, the hammering into shape of the upright elements and the laying of the heavy transverse lintels. This work was completed around 1500 BC in classical chronology, some centuries earlier if we follow the supporters of a longer chronology; that is in the early Bronze Age. Stonehenge, constantly refurbished and constantly embellished, is the ultimate example of the continuous modification of the

74 Stonehenge: part of the great outer circle of sarsens and the inner circle of small 'bluestones'

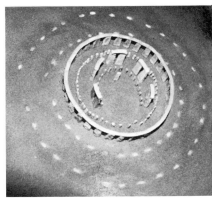

75 Model of Stonehenge in the final phase III

great monuments of faith. The historians of the great cathedrals will not wish to contradict us.

When completed, Stonehenge comprised essentially: a great avenue with the Heel Stone; a great ditch with the 'sacrificial stone' at the entrance; the fifty-six Aubrey Holes; two intermediate series of holes, called circles Y and Z; the great circle of sarsen stones with lintels; a circle of 'bluestones'; the great horseshoe of sarsen trilithons; a horseshoe of 'bluestones'; an altar stone.

The megalithic units of measurement

It is understandable that a monument as complex as Stonehenge should lend itself to the most diverse series of measurements, and so to the establishment of the most daring theories. The eternal search for the Golden Number, the calculation of equivalents to the dimensions of our globe, are so many habitual esoteric speculations which we find in like-minded literature about the Egyptian Pyramids, the Inca Temples or the cathedrals of the Middle Ages.

Without going to such lengths, we may postulate an architect of genius, perhaps several of them, behind the project, men capable of drawing up plans and seeing that they were followed. Will the blueprints of Stonehenge be found one day engraved with flint or a copper stylus on a fragment of schist? Perhaps not: for it is possible that the monument was raised in a flash of empirical genius with no preconceived plan. Such a procedure might shock our modern builders, collapsing under the weight of technical and administrative paperwork, but it need hardly have bothered the builders of peoples with no writing.

Even so they would have needed some mathematical data to start with. Circles were frequently drawn and triangles too. Numerous sitings, close up or at long range, made precision possible in building. These observers of the heavens were past masters at it. Last of all a basic unit was needed and many archaeologists have tried to find it. In a recent study Professor P. R. Giot recalls that as long ago as last century the scholar René Kerviler had worked out a whole system of megalithic measurements. The basic unit was the megalithic foot, equivalent to 0.3m. The megalithic pace was 3ft and the megalithic chain 30 paces. René Merlet, the archivist, a great observer of the stone circles of Morbihan, worked out the megalithic foot more accurately: 0.3175m, a value which was still very close to Kerviler's and was accepted by another researcher from Finistère, the naval officer and prehistorian Commandant A. Devoir. More recently Professor Alexander Thom defined the megalithic yard, equivalent to 0.829m and a megalithic fathom equivalent to two and a half yards. These values are slightly different but on the whole it seems likely that there was a basic unit of around 30cm and multiples equivalent to treble values. The state of the monuments, partially destroyed as they are, often modified or even restored, makes a rigorous calculation of the measurements impossible. But the agreement of researchers of different periods and backgrounds on the length of the basic unit is a positive result for a start. This system of measurement, invented in the Neolithic, was still used by the builders of the later phases of Stonehenge.

Place of worship or astronomical observatory?

Finally the great problem: what was Stonehenge for? An astronomical temple – that much is certain now – but to what extent? In the first place it is a monument on the axis of the sunrise at the summer solstice. At that time there may have been great ceremonies, linked with a worship of the seasons and with agriculture, of which the high point was the awaited gleam of the golden day-star through the stones of the trilithons. The layout of the monument suggests a whole ritual; the arrival in procession along the avenue, the crossing of the sacred ditch and the separation of the faithful into different areas, only the initiated, the officiators at the ceremony or perhaps the princes of Wessex as well, being allowed to pass under the giant trilithons. Shall we succumb to Celtomania and conjure up archdruids, druids or ovates in robes of multi-coloured linen?

The temple may also be more than simply a building destined to follow passively the movements of the sun. The American astronomer, Gerald Hawkins, working with a computer, proves in his *Stonehenge Decoded* that the monument could have been used to observe the rising and setting of the sun and also of the moon. This theory, if carried to its logical conclusion, would imply the prediction of eclipses by repeated observations of the related movements of the moon and the sun. It is easy to imagine the power wielded by a priest who could announce to the faithful that, on a certain date, he would command the stars to disappear. However, R. J. C. Atkinson, the expert on Stonehenge, who has analysed the monument more than once, refutes Hawkins's theories in a competent article humorously entitled 'Moonshine over Stonehenge'. The controversy is far from closed, as Colin Renfrew has foretold, and we have several centuries left to pursue it in. But in all fairness, the monument's state of partial destruction hardly lends itself to checking over-complicated theories.

Stonehenge shows the magnificent transformation and adaptation in the early Bronze Age of a ritual originating in the Neolithic. When a new civilisation is unfolding, complex phenomena of social adaptation often accompany the change.

'Wessex without Mycenae'?

The great debate that we have already mentioned in other connections has been recurring periodically for some forty years: is the flourishing of early Bronze Age Atlantic cultures linked with Mediterranean influences or not? Latterly there was a tendency to favour a strong impulse from the East, when, in 1968, Colin Renfrew launched his vigorous 'Wessex without Mycenae' which disturbed the gentle purring of the usual theories.

What are the facts? The proof of Aegean influences is based mainly on the discovery of exceptional oriental objects which were thought to be imported into the west in the early Bronze Age. The most famous is the gold cup from the barrow at Rillaton in eastern Cornwall. Its bell shape could be imitated from the beakers; on the other hand the corrugation of the gold leaf and the flat handle are characteristic of Mycenaean gold work, and are found at Mycenae in Grave 4 of the circle of shaft graves, where Heinrich Schliemann thought he had uncovered the heroes of Homer. This gold cup has often been interpreted as a gift from an Aegean prospector to his English clients in Cornwall. In the

76 The Rillaton gold cup (Cornwall) – Mycenaean perhaps?

same region, a Mediterranean trading point, the barrow at Pelynt contained a typical 'Mycenaean' dagger, similar to the ones in the tombs at Diakata in Cephalonia, for example. Another example of a 'characteristic' Mediterranean import is the fine double-edged copper axe from Topsham, Devon; it is said to have no exact replica outside the Acropolis in Athens or a nearby Aegean site. At Stonehenge itself, were not two engravings of 'Mycenaean' daggers interpreted as the signature of one of the master builders of the famous monument?

The last bits of merchandise intended to win over the barbarians are the famous beads of 'blue glass', 'faïence' or 'frit' – vague terms indicating small beads of silicate, coloured blue or green by salts of copper. Their shape was very characteristic, tubular rings like the pipe of a gas mask, circles, discs, stars or bi-conical beads. The workshops where this jewellery was made were well known in the Mediterranean zone, particularly in Egypt at Tell-el-Amarna, but also at Mycenae in contexts from 1800 to 1400 BC. The itinerary of their journey west, ending in the British Isles, which has yielded many series, can be traced by the finds dotted along it in the Lipari Isles, Sicily, the South of France, Aquitaine and the coasts of Brittany.

All this inspired dreams. Our ancestors were almost cousins of the Achaeans. The intrepid heroes of the *Iliad* and the *Odyssey*, who were skilled navigators, had sailed as far as Brittany bearing magnificent gifts and the germs of civilisation. Better still, Stonehenge owed its grandeur solely to the collaboration of Aegean architects whose genius had fused classical rigour with rustic barbarity.

The radio-carbon 'revolution'

What are the arguments, on the other side, that militate against acceptance of the Mycenaeans? The most decisive rest on radio-carbon datings. We have already seen that the great tholos tombs in Brittany had been built as early as Neolithic times, almost 3500 years before Christ. They demonstrated that western Neolithic architects had reached a high technical level. So the assistance of Aegean architects was not needed for the building of Stonehenge. What, then, of the 'Mycenaean' daggers carved on one of the sarsen trilithons? They are of no more value chronologically, Colin Renfrew would tell us, than, for instance, Lord Byron's signature on the stones of the Acropolis!

Moreover recent 'calibrations' of radio-carbon dates were pushing the European Bronze Age further back. The dates for the appearance of the first Armorican and Wessex barrows were moved back to 2000 or 1800 BC or even earlier, dates which are incompatible with those of 1500–1300 BC given for the peak of the Mycenaean civilisation. So, in Brittany, a whole series of tumulus datings ranged from 1900 to 1700 b.c., even before calibration.

However, we must concede to the supporters of Mycenae that there is a weakness in this argument based on early dates; the ^{14}C measurements have generally been made using wood from coffins, thus from tree trunks that had perhaps been felled a long time before. Carbon 14 only measures the date of the 'death' of the vegetable matter, not of its use. So some of the very early dates should perhaps be brought forward a little. We must also concede that some datings from the second phase of the Wessex culture, near the middle Bronze Age, with more sophisticated daggers could coincide with those of Mycenae.

The problem of the blue faïence beads has evolved too. Recent series of spectrographic analysis have shown that there were several workshops making them, some Egyptian, others British in Cornwall or Scotland. The 'savages' had managed to imitate, or equal, the ancients in this field. By melting clayey sand, rich in silicate content, with salts of copper at a very high temperature, they obtained products which, at first sight, were indistinguishable from the production of Tell-el-Amarna.

And the Rillaton gold cup? We have pointed out its hybrid nature: a shape strangely reminiscent of the beakers but with corrugation of the gold leaf which has almost no equivalent outside Mycenae. Now the discovery of another gold cup, also with a Bell Beaker shape and corrugated gold leaf has been reported at Eschenz in Switzerland. So Rillaton is no longer an isolated case. This is becoming disturbing and we may wonder whether the ingenious Bell Beaker folk, or their immediate successors, had not already learnt to make fine gold vessels some centuries before Mycenae.

To conclude, the idea that is emerging from all this is that the early Bronze Age Atlantic cultures flourished probably before Mycenae. There certainly were contacts with the Aegean, no doubt due to the quest for tin on the part of the Mediterranean peoples. But the need is no longer felt to refer continually to the Mycenaeans in order to explain the origins of the finest artistic manifestations of the west. It is probable that, like the splendid Armorican arrowheads, or the dazzling Irish lunulae, the amber set in gold, or the daggers decorated with thousands of gold studs, they are native creations and perhaps were even imitated by the 'civilised' peoples. And why should we not leave with the good barbarian princes of Wessex the architectural genius that conceived Stonehenge?

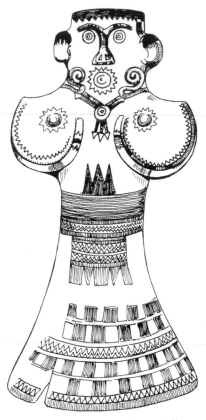

77 The bell-skirted goddess, clay, from Kličevac (Yugoslavia)

After the period of the nascent metal civilisations, the world of Bronze Age man was to diversify. In the heart of Europe, the Tumulus culture showed classic features continuing the traditions outlined in the early Bronze Age. In the Nordic countries, we find the awakening of the first metal cultures which, although late – they are only beginning at the start of the middle Bronze Age – were among the most brilliant and were to last uninterruptedly until well into the European Iron Age. In the south, too, the great islands of the western Mediterranean display civilisations which lie outside the classic chronological framework. Similarly, the marvellous centres of cave art, hidden in the Alpine valleys cover periods ranging from early Bronze Age down to historic times.

Chapter 6

The Protoceltic Tumuli

In the middle of the second millennium, which corresponds to the middle Bronze Age, there was a tendency to a certain stability in barbarian Europe. After the great disturbances of the early Bronze Age, a breathing-space was needed. Everything was certainly not calm in that mosaic of small tribes, but, through the archaeological record, it is possible to sense the establishment of a kind of equilibrium between great areas in which the same funeral rites, the same production of metal objects – in short the same kinds of society – were to be found.

The great event is the covering of the central area of Europe in the middle Bronze Age, with the Tumulus culture, the *Hügelgräberkultur*.

By their shape, these tumuli are certainly reminiscent of the early Bronze Age, Únětician tumuli (Leubingen) or the tumuli of western Europe (Wessex and Armorica). But by their furnishings, their great numbers and their geographic distribution, they form a new cultural whole which was to continue developing throughout the middle Bronze Age. The Nordic, Atlantic and Mediterranean zones remained partially outside this phenomenon, preserving a separate development.

The 'protoceltic invasions'

In their time, the Corded Ware peoples had popularised the rite of individual burial throughout northern and central Europe. The tribes of Únětice and their successors at Straubing had adopted it 'en masse'. The potentates of Leubingen had, exceptionally, given it 'princely' attributes. The Tumulus culture was to give it a new dimension and extend it to an unusual degree by adding the funeral mound. Under this impetus 'tumulus fields' were to appear on many a plain and hill of barbarian Europe, from the Alps to the Baltic and from Alsace to the Balkans.

The phenomenon was on such a large scale that, at the time when the myth of folk migrations was in fashion, it was readily seen as one of the first Celtic invasions. We must acknowledge the rather daring quality of this thesis; first of all we have no linguistic evidence from these peoples, other than a few risky arguments comparing their geographic distribution and the corresponding toponymy. Then two great cycles of civilisations separate the tumulus people chronologically from the Celts: these are the Urnfield culture of the late Bronze Age and the Hallstatt culture of the early Iron Age. The Tumulus people were not necessarily of the same ethnic strain as the Urnfield people, still less the Celts. History has often shown successive invasions covering the same areas of Europe but varying greatly in origin. It is very probable that the Tumulus people were Indo-Europeans, but the label 'protoceltic' should be handled with great caution.

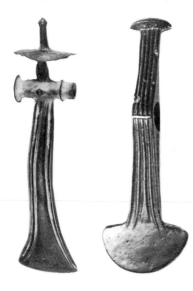

78 (*far left*) Bronze axe, Tumulus culture, Steinamanger (Hungary)
79 (*left*) Bronze axe, Tumulus culture, Lüneburg (north Germany)

Finally, we are beginning to move away from all these great migrations, the great severers of ancient civilisations. Movements of peoples who are easily identified by a type of pottery which cannot be disputed – like the Bell Beakers – are rare. The Tumulus culture, with one and the same funeral rite, included a host of regional groups. There were confrontations, however, as witness the abundance of weapons, which were not all status symbols, and the fortified villages, known in many districts. The most frequent clashes must have taken place at the edges of territories; the countless finds of swords in rivers, at crossing places or fords, frequent in the late Bronze Age, seem to support this notion. Combat at the ford was long a vivid memory in Irish Celtic tradition. It was on or beside water that the heroes fought and the arms of the vanquished were lost in the blood-stained stream, for, as natural frontiers, rivers and streams played a major part in separating different ethnic groups.

The Tumulus culture included a multitude of small regional groups, identified by F. Holste from inventories of grave goods, supplemented by studying hoards of bronze objects and settlements. A swift bird's-eye view gives some idea of the variety which is not compatible with the idea of a great 'protoceltic' folk movement.

80 (*above left*) *Vollgriffschwert*, Meckelfeld (north Germany)

81 (*above right*) Spiral motif, middle Bronze Age (Hungary)

82 (*right*) Fibula, Lüneburg region (north Germany)

The tumuli of the Danube region yield large sickle-shaped dress pins and maintain the Hungarian battle-axe tradition with elegant, often decorated hafted weapons. On the Austrian side, leather or wooden bucklers were reinforced with an enormous Maltese cross in bronze. This 'umbo' on the buckler, moreover, was fitted with a central spike. The many bronze sickles in the deposits testify to an innovation, the use of bronze for agricultural purposes. Pottery has one peculiar feature: it is deposited in hoards, which is exceptional and suggests a caste of specialist potters or pot merchants.

The Bavarian group specialised in making bronze swords with solid hilts, the *Vollgriffschwerter*, by the development of which a chronology has been established. The models become more and more complicated both in the shape of the hilt – straight at first and then octagonal – and in the often very fine geometric decoration based, as always, on triangles, circles or spirals – the spiral which came from the Aegean via the Danube.

In north Germany the groups are more hybrid and the influence of the fine Nordic Bronze Age is felt, especially in the distinctive group from the Lüneburg region. The women's tombs exhibit an opulence in the bronze jewellery, as in the tomb at Hengstberg where a young girl lay, lavishly adorned: there were small bronze discs in her hair, spiral rings in her ears, round her neck a necklace of bronze beads, a bronze collar, a bronze disc with repoussé decoration – but this should be worn lower down, on the belt – and a huge paletted pin to fasten the garment. Finally on her arms and legs were heavy spiral bracelets – not to mention the finger rings. In this way the young girl had taken with her all her bronze jewellery whose massive quality was offset by the elegant delicacy of the geometric decoration. The wooden furnishings are well known and one of the prides of Harburg Museum is the little, reconstructed, folding fisherman's – I should say minor chieftain's – stool, made of wooden uprights arranged cross-wise and capable of being folded, thanks to a bronze pin. The seat is leather. This stool was adorned with bronze ends, decorated with circles and fitted with small, jingling pendants. This is the *Klappstuhl* found at Daense, the luxury stool reserved for noble visitors or the old patriarch, a model inspired by the Near East or Egypt.

83 Short sword, imported into north Germany, middle Bronze Age

The Hercynian group from the Palatinate and Franconia used daggers, trapezoidal-tanged swords, and Hungarian palstaves with a stop ridge with triangular indentations and perforated, heart-shaped pendants. The Würtemberg, Alsatian and Rhine groups are identified by spiral leg-pieces and pottery with excised decoration – in other words the clay was removed from around the design while still soft. So each group has its own particular weapons, pots and items of adornment. A detailed account of the types of pot or of pins, of which the variations are legion, would only confirm this proliferation of local differentiations within the same broad pattern of civilisation.

In France the Tumulus culture got as far as the eastern region and is well represented in Alsace by the necropolis at Haguenau.

The mounds of Haguenau Forest

The charming little town of Haguenau, a favourite residence of the Holy Roman Emperors, played an important part in Alsatian history. But in the shade of Haguenau Forest lay hidden traces of a much more ancient occupation in the form of thousands of mounds, some dating from the Bronze Age. Since the beginning of the study of prehistory in the mid-nineteenth century these have attracted archaeologists. In about 1860 Max de Ring was there, at the request of Henri de Quatrefage, the great anthropologist, looking mainly for skeletons. To this end the Celtic tombs were ransacked – there is no other word for it – in a matter of a few hours, and a few potsherds and bits of bronze were picked up at random. But we must not be too hard on these pioneers. At that time prehistory was just an entertaining pastime and excavation techniques were mainly those of the treasure-hunter or body-snatcher.

Serious work began with Xavier-Joseph Nessel, an administrator, who took matters in hand methodically and consistently. In some thirty summer excavation seasons he explored about 500 tombs, a record which could hardly be equalled nowadays when archaeologists are in much less of a hurry. His team of about ten labourers was highly organised and if by misfortune a spade shattered a piece of pottery, it was not an irreparable disaster. M. Nessel had invented and perfected a kind of fish glue with which the damage could be repaired. The series of pots at present in the museum at Haguenau bear witness to his undoubted talents as a restorer.

Nessel assembled an amazing yield of finds which makes the Haguenau collections among the most valuable in Europe. They lie cheek by jowl with an appetising ethnographic and historical collection. Nessel, absorbed as he was in his administrative responsibilities, published only brief notes. But he allowed others to study his collection and the Haguenau bronzes were repeatedly referred to. Starting in 1905, A.-W. Naue published a series in which the famous spiral leg-pieces appeared. But it was Professor C. F. A. Schaeffer's celebrated monograph in 1926 which was to reveal to the archaeological world in Europe the riches of the Haguenau mounds. This work was often quoted as an example but was rarely imitated, unfortunately for French prehistory.

84 Fibula, Lüneburg region (north Germany)

C. F. A. Schaeffer was a scholarly and methodical man who brought order to the tumuli. It was a Herculean task but Nessel, who was a meticulous man, had kept a log of his excavations, which remained unpublished, and in which the essentials of his observations were recorded. Better still, he had labelled his material conscientiously ensuring that its provenance should not be lost beyond recall. This was an elementary precaution, which was considered unimportant by many of the great names of nineteenth-century prehistory, who thus contributed to the reject pieces in collections and small museums.

The first great surprise was the continuity of occupation in the Haguenau region. The first traces were Neolithic. Then came a few early Bronze Age tombs like the one at Donauberg, with triangular daggers and a rolled torc imported from Únětice or Straubing. A great proliferation of tombs was associated with the middle Bronze Age Tumulus culture and later some new late Bronze Age strains were introduced, before a new wave of burials in the Iron Age. So, in the same place, people had quietly gone on burying their dead despite the invasions, folk migrations and wars which, according to some theories, had been devastating Europe. Only the climate, it seems, had brought about a modification of the occupation pattern. In the Neolithic period the forest was so damp and marshy as to be hardly habitable, and settlements were sited on its fringes. It was intensively settled as the climate grew warmer in the Bronze Age, but at the dawn of the Iron Age a new deterioration again made the climate under the forest canopy unhealthy and the Iron Age burials, like the settlements, returned once more to the edges of the forest.

Not much is known of the funeral rites of Haguenau Forest. In the heroic period when he was digging, X.-J. Nessel collected neither detailed observations nor stratigraphical sections and was content to indicate briefly the depth of the various finds. But even so a few revealing facts can be ascertained, according to C. F. A. Schaeffer.

In the first place rites involving funerary mounds had never before been so widespread in Alsace. And though nowadays it would not be surprising to find pottery with the characteristic goblet shape and cord decoration of Corded ware amongst the most ancient barrows at Donauberg, in 1926 it was startling. So here once more it was a branch of the Corded Ware culture that introduced the rite of individual burial, which became generalised later.

The skeletons were generally lying on their backs. This was the rule in the middle Bronze Age, and the custom of crouched burials was abandoned – a slight change of mind. The size of the mounds allowed the corpse to be laid directly on to the ground without digging a trench and its position was not important. If there was religious significance in the crouched burial, the so-called embryo position, there was also a practical reason: the more the corpse was folded in on itself, the quicker the trench could be dug. But we must not be unkind. . . . The alignment of the bodies varied somewhat and the preferred east–west direction with the head towards the rising sun was no longer so rigorously adhered to. Besides the dead were soon to be cremated, at first mainly the women and children, but by the end of the Bronze Age all sections of the population.

Animal offerings included pig, and the head of one young girl was laid delicately on a pig's head; at that time it showed no lack of respect: it was simply a natural gesture, when animal husbandry was an honoured occupation, to furnish a young swineherd's tomb with an offering recalling her past occupation and providing a symbolic repast for the after life.

The grave goods commonly included pottery. The small corded vase was succeeded by a whole series of pitchers, cups, beakers and bowls. The little cups with handles of the early Bronze Age were followed by the fine pottery of the Tumulus culture, decorated with incisions, by impressing cords into the surface, and, in particular, with the fine 'excised' decoration known as *Kerbschnitt*: simple zigzag or chevron motifs were 'raised' on the vase by removing the soft clay before firing. This technique is derived from wood-carving and even the shape of the little cups or beakers is the same as that of the wooden receptacles preserved in the peat-bogs of northern Europe or the Swiss lake-dwellings. This implies

85 Polypod with excised decoration, Haguenau tumulus

86 Jug, Haguenau tumulus

that we have lost a whole range of wooden domestic ware in this as in other regions. The designs of the Haguenau decoration are among the finest of the whole *Kerbschnitt* series. The firing of the pots and the fineness of the decoration combine to produce perfect specimens. Sometimes the potters cheated a little and made 'impressed' ware; instead of removing the unfired clay they pressed it back using some form of punch and the motif still appeared in relief. We find this technique again in the Iron Age. In the late Bronze Age large beakers and grooved pottery, copied from the new Urnfield culture, are found in association with 'excised' ware.

Metal offerings are plentiful at Haguenau. For the men there are weapons, axes, a few items of adornment, a few bracelets and, of course, the indispensable pins to hold the clothing together. For the women there are, very occasionally, knives in the later period, but above all items of adornment and pins. The people of Haguenau were not particularly war-like: the weapons are confined to small trapezoidal-tanged daggers fitted with four, and later two, rivets. Sometimes the blade is extended to give a large tongued sword with two rivets, but that is all. There are none of the fine *Vollgriffschwerter* which were the glory of their Bavarian cousins. The range of tools evolved slowly, starting with the early flat axes, and they even had their own peculiar type of palstave, the 'Haguenau type', an imitation, though more solid, of the Atlantic models.

87. Atlantic palstave, middle Bronze Age

105

88 Leg-ring with spiral decoration, Haguenau tumulus

Pins show the wide variety that was usual in tumuli of various periods. In the early Bronze Age there are derivatives of distant Anatolian models with palettes or rolls of wire. Then there are imitations of ring- or wheel-headed pins from Straubing – the sun symbol again. In the middle Bronze Age the pins of the Tumulus culture proliferate, bulb-headed with small perforations through which a thread could pass, trumpet-headed, etc. All of them are decorated with little incisions or chevrons. The bracelets are still simple with geometric decoration. The finest product of the Haguenau smiths was to be the spiral leg-piece. Here, too, the idea came from Straubing. At first a bronze wire ending in two spiral twists was placed around the calf. Later on the wire was replaced by a flat band of metal decorated with a few chevrons. In the end the most highly developed model had a broad band, richly decorated with geometric motifs and edged with a substantial bronze wire, while the spiral terminals were much bigger, with a dozen turns. These leg-pieces seem to have been worn by the women, anxious to draw attention to their shapely legs. But at times it had been thought that they could have been variations on the cnemid, the bronze shin-protector worn by Greek warriors in combat. These Greek cnemids were made from a lozenge-shaped plaque attached to the front of the leg. One of them – Mycenaean no less – was imported into France and found as far inland as Seine-et-Marne, at Cannes-Ecluse in a middle Bronze Age hoard which included axes, bracelets and sickles of a western type. Its Mycenaean origin is confirmed by the characteristic shape and the spiral decoration which is unusual in the west, as G. Gaucher observes in the report of the find.

What was the source of the evident prosperity of the prehistoric populations of Haguenau Forest? If we accept the view of C. F. A. Schaeffer it was mainly pig breeding. However unexpected this conclusion may be, there are a number of arguments to support it. First of all the presence of bones belonging to the pig family in the graves and even of whole pigs' heads clearly in place of honour in the burials. Then there is historic confirmation: G. Hüffel, relating *The History of the Holy Forest of Haguenau in Alsace*, records that, in the Middle Ages, Haguenau Forest was renowned for its acorns. In a year when the oaks were producing well, as many as 10,000 pigs were brought there, some of them from a considerable distance, since, in 1581 a herd of 300 head was brought from a place more than 80km away! The pigs remained in the forest, in the care of swineherds who had taken an oath of loyalty, housed in wooden huts throughout the acorn season and beyond, from August till April. An example like that from history may be part of a very long tradition. Pollen studies which could identify the plant population of the period would give added confirmation. In any case pigs there were – and no doubt oak trees as well.

So Haguenau is an example of a peaceable population of pig breeders, who, in addition, were acquainted with the finest art production of the Bronze Age. But there do not seem to be traces of any foundries and we may wonder at times whether the fine pins and leg-pieces were not obtained simply by bartering livestock at a neighbouring centre of metallurgy which we have yet to identify.

Haguenau remains an exception in the Tumulus culture in France. Elsewhere, in Haut Rhin as well as in the Jura and the Rhône valley, middle Bronze Age tumuli are more scattered and also more mixed. The influence of metal types common at this period can be found again in the Alps and the South of France. Excised pottery was to be exported far into the west; derivatives can be found in settlements like Videlles in Seine-et-Oise and Vilhonneur in Charente. Similarly in the South of France the *Kerbschnitt* technique was to appear in the local style of Saint-Véredème. These excised vases were to compete with the handled vases from Italy. The South of France remained a point of contact between the Mediterranean and central European worlds. The symbolic fusion of these influences is seen in the vases with continental excised decoration and Italianate thumb-grip handles. These are as common in southern France as in the Iberian peninsula.

Fire and sun worship

The funeral rite of the middle Bronze Age Tumulus culture involved a mound, covering the corpse and the offerings for its use in the next world. Gradually inhumation was to be superseded by cremation and this reflects an important change in religious ideas. Outside the tombs we have little information about social and religious life. However, graves have been found in the Danube region, with offerings in which pots, bones and even human skulls are mingled together. It was possible, then, to make both human and animal sacrifices to win divine favour. A few baked clay altars have been found in Danubian settlements, with a raised decoration in which horns, boats and triangles are vaguely outlined.

In northern Europe some golden solar discs have been found like the one at Moordorf near Aurich in Lower Saxony; no doubt the influence of the Nordic Bronze Age is at work here. But the decoration is less finished than on the Danish sun chariot from Trundholm. The sun cult is reflected too in engravings on rocks, concentric circles engraved on morainic blocks, at Sonnenstein and Beckstedt. These solar symbols are sometimes coupled with wheels and even small chariots, foreshadowing the cave art of Scandinavia. 'Cup marks' and sun symbols were to be found in large numbers in Europe and are often difficult to date, since they were still lingering on in the Iron Age.

Another religious symbol of the late middle Bronze Age is the cone. In France the most famous is the one from Avanton, a small township in the Poitiers area. It was discovered in 1844 and has often been held to be a ceremonial quiver. It is a conical object in gold leaf, 46cm high but incomplete, and decorated with concentric circles. The quiver hypothesis is doubtful – another suggestion was that it was a mitre, by analogy with some statuettes from the Near East. If it is turned upside down it could well be a rhyton or long libation vessel. But another gold cone, found around the same period at Schifferstadt in the Palatinate, was more complete, with a broad base. It was clear that the vessel should be placed with the point upwards; it might even have covered a wooden or stone armature. No doubt it was a small baetyl, a cult object intended for display in the temples or in processions. But the finest example of the series is the one at Etzelsdorf near Nuremberg, 95cm high and 13.5cm wide. In the decoration wheels, linked rings, circles and small bosses are combined: sun symbols again. The cone is very slender and has something of the modern space rocket in its shape. It is only a short step from the sun to fire and Professor H. Muller-Karpe saw in these gold symbols the image of a flame, a burning fire rising

89 (*left*) The Avanton Cone (Poitou)
90 (*above*) Wheel-headed pins, middle Bronze Age (north Germany)
91 (*right*) Funeral stela, Urnfield period, Illmitz (Austria)

heavenwards analogous to the column of fire which guided the Children of Israel by night in the Sinai wilderness. Flame or sun symbol, these masterpieces must have been guarded closely in the depth of the temples, which were no doubt built of wood and have disappeared. They could also be carried in procession on ceremonial occasions. The Schifferstadt cone is said to have been associated with palstaves, a valuable chronological indication which makes it possible to date the cone to the late middle Bronze Age period.

To sum up, the religious art of the tumuli is still often abstract with a symbol replacing the image of the god. Wheels, large and small, suggest the sun. The same abstract quality informs the decoration of everyday objects, still based on the everlasting 'ancient European geometric style'.

Danubian gods and rites

We must go back to the world of the Danube to find a more alluring representation of gods or goddesses. A whole series of clay figurines continues from the early to the late middle Bronze Age there – in other words from 1700 to 1000 BC according to the distinguished Yugoslavian expert in that field, Zagorka Letiča. The origins of these statuettes go right back to Chalcolithic times. Did Creto-Mycenaean influences play a part in the birth of this art? More precisely, did the skirt worn by many of these ladies not come from Crete or Mycenae? Zagorka Letiča observes that typical Aegean imports have been found in the area in which these Danubian statuettes are distributed. And the Danubian style, which is in fact very varied, differs markedly from the Aegean. There has been influence from the Aegean but only at a certain stage of development.

The ancient statues from Kličevac represent goddesses with bell-shaped skirts decorated with pretty geometric motifs. The eyes are indicated by concentric circles, somewhat in the manner of the El Argar idols. The arms are cupped just under the breasts, a frequent feature of this Danubian art. In this host of female images a trend towards the abstract, or at least the schematic can be observed. At Glamija the statue has become a cylinder topped with an inverted heart, charmingly decorated with spirals; there is even a violin-shaped idol reminiscent of the Cyclades. The varied decoration of the skirts or dresses suggests that Bronze Age ladies wore embroidered garments, perhaps multi-coloured. Can it be that the long tradition of the national costumes still worn in the Balkans goes right back to the Bronze Age goddesses?

Goddesses . . . or gods? It is not always easy to tell the sex under the dress. Sometimes the breasts are strongly marked, but some flat-chested frocked figures could be priests or gods in ceremonial dress.

The tradition of making statuettes of gods and goddesses was persistent in the Danube region. In the Neolithic the idols at Vinča were linked with the fertility cult of the Mother Goddess, dear to essentially agricultural peoples. In the Bronze Age the deities evolved too. They modernised themselves and at times even travelled. Little votive chariots appeared.

92 The Dupljaja chariot, drawn by sacred ducks (Yugoslavia)

In the province of Voïvodine on the Romanian frontier, baked clay chariots from Dupljaja provide valuable information on Bronze Age mythology.

One of the chariots is carrying a deity. It has only two wheels, but the front part or shaft may be incomplete. The god has a curious face with a pointed nose, perhaps a mask, and is marked with a swastika, the crooked cross of the Indo-Europeans which was to spread from India into Europe.

The second chariot from Dupljaja, also of baked clay, is one of the glories of the National Museum in Belgrade. This little votive chariot holds a key position in the study of the evolution of cult chariots. It has three wheels, two at the back and one in front, along the axis. It carries one figure and is pulled by three ducks. A little cup of decorated clay was with it and was thought to be a small parasol or canopy for the travelling god. A. Forrer thought that it might be some sort of bell. The figure's small, owl-like head, typical of Bronze Age Danubian idols, is held high, with its large, ingenuous eyes and pointed beak-like nose. The arms, in the classic cupped position, end in tentative fingers which are no more than simple little sticks. The bust is decorated with spirals, two of which imitate a torc round the neck. The dress is adorned in the middle and towards the hem with two bands of hatched triangles, with concentric circles between the bands. Those who have been sufficiently impertinent to peep under the skirt have seen a small phallus; so it really is a god, as may have been assumed from the absence of breasts. In his chariot with its spoked wheels, this god is driving a team of water fowl, either ducks or swans. No clearer symbolism could be hoped for in a cult chariot. On earth, and in the after life, it can make light of every obstacle: the wheels carry it along the long trails of the steppes, the birds can fly and carry it off over mountains and the ducks can swim with it across rivers and oceans. But the most important symbol must have been the ability to take to the air, leaving earth behind, and return to the realm of the sun. The concentric circles on the statuette are classic sun signs. Moreover it is a god: Graeco-Latin mythology was to maintain the principle of a male to evoke the Sun God: Helios, Phoebus or Apollo. To find the first traces of this firmly in the Bronze Age is indeed a revelation, even if the famous Trundholm sun chariot from further north is well known.

In the past the Dupljaja chariot was sometimes attributed to the Iron Age, because of its ducks which are strangely reminiscent of many representations in bronze or pottery from the Hallstatt cultures. But recent studies have settled the question: the style of the figure in the chariot is not isolated and has links with the whole series studied by Zagorka Letiča. The Dupljaja ducks are not pale and clumsy clay imitations of the fine Hallstatt bronzes, but they herald them almost a thousand years earlier. The eternal creative genius of the Danube civilisations never ceased to contribute, with the other barbarian cultures, to the rise of the European world!

Atlantic worlds in the middle Bronze Age

In the west the Atlantic world in its widest sense – that is from Spain to the North Sea – evolved along lines which are only partly similar. The heyday of Wessex and Armorica, in the early Bronze Age, was only a memory. The heroic epic of princelings with gold nails and of builders of sun temples gradually lost its edge. In the middle Bronze Age, the rich princely tombs are replaced by poorer tumuli with more nondescript pottery and then, quite quickly in Brittany, by meagrely furnished smaller mounds from which an occasional radio-carbon date may, by good fortune, be obtainable to identify a burial containing a very few potsherds or pieces of carbonised wood.

But not all the Atlantic peoples became, so to speak, 'unbelievers' with no care for their dead. On the contrary, in the north-west of the British Isles a strong tradition of funeral urns was becoming established. For the dead were cremated henceforth and the ashes deposited in large, rather crude urns. These had rolled edges and are known as 'overhanging urns', with thick, decorated rims. Later they were succeeded by the Deverel urns of south-west England, cordoned vessels with fingerprint decoration on the cordons. The phenomenon spread to Belgium and the Netherlands where there is talk of Hilversum urns, frequently with impressed cord decoration, a tradition which had persisted in these regions from the first arrivals of Corded Ware peoples. Later there would be the Drakenstein urns decorated with a relief of small horseshoes. Some urns strayed into northern France and even as far as the Aisne valley. In Brittany a few years ago Tourony beach at Tregastel brought to light two large pots sticking up from the old soil level. With their big cordons under the rim they were close to the British overhanging urns in style. No doubt some British tourists had come to end their days on the Breton coast around 1200 BC.

The period of the menhirs was over now, although from time to time we may suspect that a few small blocks associated with bronzes are a debased version of them. The absence of stone monuments need not imply an absence of religious monuments, however, and a Dutch find provides striking proof of this. At Bargeroosterveld we find the exceptional case of a small oak temple being preserved in a peat-bog. It consisted of a quadrangular construction surmounted by lintels in the shape of horns. As was fitting, the sanctuary was isolated by means of a sacred circle, given concrete form by a ring of stones. The wooden pieces, which were simply lying in the peat, were still sufficiently well preserved to permit a reconstruction of the building which looked something like a small Asian temple. By radio-carbon it was possible to date the monument to 1290 BC. The horns crowning the temple no doubt reflected by their presence the cult of the bull or of cattle raising which is attested all through the Bronze Age, especially by horns of clay right down to the late Bronze Age period. These western barbarians were both herdsmen and metallurgists.

93 Flanged axe, Tréboul group (Brittany)

94 Palstave, Languénan (Brittany)

Increasingly, though, they were becoming metallurgists and new schools of metalwork were opening on all sides. In France Medoc was the first district to launch itself on the industrial venture. Were these the successors of a group of flat-axe manufacturers who were practising their craft back in the Chalcolithic in Vendée? The time lag is not easy to fill. There, as often elsewhere, certain remote Únětician influences have been observed. Be that as it may, the fortune of these people of the Gironde stemmed in the first place from bronze, long before the vineyards. Their massive, laterally flanged axes, which have been found in hundreds in the Pauillac area, were exported to southern and south-western France.

In Brittany, the peoples of the coasts created their own distinctive products in the middle Bronze Age: spear heads, Saint-Brandan rapiers with bronze hilts, exported as far as Holland, and curious ceremonial blades like the one from Plougrescant which weighed more than 2kg. We find them again at Beaune in Côte d'Or but also at Ommerschans in the Netherlands. Ceremonial weapons, masterpieces of the smith's craft, symbolic weapons exchanged on the occasion of exceptional pacts – we may opt for any of these interpretations but not for that of a functional weapon, even though certain 'two-handed'

95 Bronze sword from Saint-Brandan (Brittany)

swords from the Crusades, or used by the executioner at the Tower of London, show something of the same lineage as these impressive blades.

Palstaves are about to appear. They were equipped with stop ridges, allowing better control of the handle. They were soon to be made in hundreds and are found exclusively in hoards of axes. This is the beginning of specialisation, the transition from the individual craftsman to a semi-industrial stage, with the need for well organised trading outlets. By studying shape and decoration we are able to distinguish the main production centres: the one in upper Brittany had a very active rival in the one in Normandy which was concentrated mainly around the lower Seine. Competition was tough, but mergers between centres suggest that the *entente* was *cordiale* on the whole.

96 (*above left*) Spearhead with eyelets, Antrim (Ireland)
97 (*above right*) gold torc, Boyton (Suffolk)

98 and 99 Decorated bronze axes (Great Britain)

The British Isles were exporting, too: spear heads with loops at the base, long rapiers and gold. Indeed Ireland had not yet exhausted its alluvial gold. The early Bronze Age lunulae had disappeared but the new products were no less amazing: great twisted ropes, a metre long, which could be entwined spirally and worn round the neck. These are the Tara–Yeovil torcs, found on the Continent in north-west France at Saint-Leu-d'Esserent in Oise, or at Cesson in Ille-et-Vilaine, one of the glories of the Musée de Cluny in Paris.

As for the Nordic world, which must be treated at greater length, it was awakening belatedly, but with such vigour, such consummate art in bronze that it was to produce the most distinctive barbarian cultures of all.

Mediterranean worlds

Mediterranean evolution in the middle Bronze Age is very complex and difficult to grasp in its entirety. The South of France remained a zone in which the central European influences filtering down the Rhône valley came into contact with those of the Mediterranean. Local styles derive from the Rhône culture. The world of the western Mediterranean islands remained closed and produced highly insular cultures, a little outside the times, centred on Sardinia, Corsica and the Balearics. We shall come back to them.

Northern Italy witnessed the development of its most distinctive cultures, in the zone which was to give birth to the Iron Age of Villa Nova. In Aemilia there was the Terramares culture, heaps of black earth used down the centuries by peasants who were wrong to care so little that they were destroying venerable remains. These 'terramares' are artificial mounds resulting from rebuilding villages on the same spot, a phenomenon which has its counterpart in the Near East with the formation of the tells, which are known too in Hungary. It has even been suggested that some of the inhabitants of the terramares could have come from the Danubian plains. They were a people of herdsmen and tillers of the soil who, at the same time, practised a simple local metallurgy. In Lombardy and the Venetian region, villages were protected from flooding by dykes. At first the metalworkers copied products from north of the Alps, but soon an original school was to create dagger and sword types that were to undergo a significant development later. In particular it was in this region that razors were to be made and, most important of all, at Peschiera around 1250, the first fibulae, or 'safety pins', which were more practical than the straight Bronze Age pins for holding clothes together. The fibula appeared very early in northern Italy but was not to be in general use until the Iron Age of which it was to become the 'type' fossil and was to live on long into the Roman world.

At the other end of the Mediterranean was Mycenae, which after 1500 was to reign supreme over the Aegean world. The Mycenaean world hardly concerns us any more. It entered history when its script, the Linear B, was deciphered and found to be close to archaic Greek, which proved beyond all possible doubt that the Achaeans really were

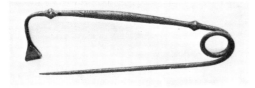

100 Fibula, Bacino Marina, Verona (Italy)

101 Razor, lake-settlement of Peschiera, Verona (Italy)

Indo-Europeans. Mycenae had abandoned its ancient shaft graves, destined for its early princes, those gold-masked heroes, noble, bearded ancestors of Agamemnon. Now the magnificent tholos tombs were being raised, christened 'Treasures of Atreus or Clytemnestra' by unassailable Homeric tradition. Mycenae cultivated trade relations with the barbarians, chiefly because of amber and tin, and this gave rise to small gifts and bartering between the two worlds. These trifles are sometimes useful, giving 'cross-datings' which enable us to establish chronological synchronisms. Even if a radio-carbon date – and worse still its calibration – comes along from time to time to overthrow these synchronisms by making the objects several centuries older, enough remains to command attention.

Of course, the ageing of the early Bronze Age civilisations in the west has robbed Mycenae of the honour of having, perhaps, sent one of its architects to Stonehenge, and of a few gold vessels which are now attributed to the creative genius of barbarian goldsmiths. What then? Mycenaean influence was profound throughout the Mediterranean world and

102 Cup with excised decoration, Cueva dels Encantats, Gerona (Spain)

103 Sword with Mycenae-type decoration, Castions di Strada, near Trieste (Italy)

the Balkans. Further north, further west, it is difficult to measure the exact part played by Aegean contributions, which are often restricted to exceptional imports, which no doubt suffered many vicissitudes on the way. Some series of objects are an exception by their regular occurrence. We have already seen that rings or discs made from antler and decorated with Mycenaean spirals enabled us to date the end of the Únětician world. Similarly amber spacer-beads found in the early tumuli of southern Germany can be dated to around 1450 by analogy with the same jewels found at Kakovatos in the Mycenaean area.

Chapter 7

The Fine Bronze of the Amber Countries

Amber, a wonderful material, was one of the most highly prized substances among the peoples of prehistory and antiquity. From as far back as Paleolithic times, it exercised its fascination over the barbarians, who shaped it into amulets or jewels, the most famous of which are the small amber animals of the Baltic. Its charm lay in its lustrous russet colouring, like honey, and its translucent glass-like fissures, and it could be married most successfully with that other 'monstre sacré', gold. The ancients pursued it avidly for its magic and medical properties, and named it 'electrum'. It gave its name to electricity, for when rubbed it becomes negatively charged. The word 'amber' came later from the Arabic 'ambar' meaning the sperm whale, by confusion with ambergris, a pungent organic secretion produced by that creature. For a long time it was used for its medicinal powers and in the seventeenth century was recommended both for brain disorders and venereal diseases.

The 'amber roads'

But where did amber come from? Mineralogists classify it among the fossil resins, succinite and retinite. These are found in all brown coal formations of the Carboniferous period in the primary era of the present epoch (Upper Palaeozoic) but the purest amber is found most abundantly in formations of the Oligocene in northern Europe where the great pine forests (*Pinus succinifer*) developed. Amber is still called 'succin' in French, from the Latin word for sap. It is often trapped in later geological formations but is released by the erosion of rivers and seas: this is why lumps of amber can often be picked up at the foot of cliffs, for they have the property of floating in salt water. It is on this that the fortunes of the Baltic shores are based.

However, not all amber was Nordic. The great mineralogist A. Lacroix produced a whole list of small deposits of fossil resin in France, but he thought these ambers were unsuitable for cutting. This is not always so and we have managed to cut small pendants from a lump of amber-coloured fossil resin, found by a geologist from Rennes in the area

104 Carved rock, ritual scene with boats, Denmark

round Dax in the Landes. Amber was of economic importance on occasions even in historic times, in the Gironde, for example, as A. Coffyn reports. So we should not underestimate these secondary deposits which may have played a part locally. Last, besides true amber, there is a whole range of more or less pure resins, jets or lignites, which have been used as substitutes. As they have often deteriorated in tombs or prehistoric deposits, it has sometimes been difficult to recognise them, and Breton jet bead, for example, has been described as tortoiseshell.

But despite this variety of possible sources, the greater part of prehistoric amber was supplied by the Baltic and the Mediterranean, more particularly the Adriatic, with the Baltic as the main source; for the need for amber in the Mediterranean world became so great that they began to import it from northern Europe. This was a cause of great

105 Great ceremonial axe, first period of Danish Bronze Age

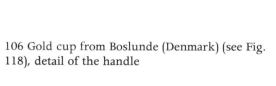

106 Gold cup from Boslunde (Denmark) (see Fig. 118), detail of the handle

excitement among archaeologists for a long time. We have lost count of the multitude of 'amber roads' which have been recognised and, at times, imagined – the more so since old chemical analyses claimed to be able to distinguish easily between Mediterranean and Nordic ambers. Recent analyses are much less dogmatic. The interplay of patina and deterioration often makes identification difficult, and studies carried out by X-ray diffraction methods seem to show that many people had been deluded by the famous succinic acid method, as far as finds from digs are concerned.

Despite these reservations, the study of archaeological material shows that an amber trade existed between the Baltic and the Mediterranean. The principal exchange routes – the 'amber roads' – can reasonably be restricted to two or three main transit roads along the northern rivers. Some reached the northern Adriatic via the Alpine passes and then followed the Dalmatian coast to finish in Greece. Others, more easterly, started from the Vistula or the north of European Russia, headed down towards the Danube area and then cut across to end in the Adriatic as well. Finally we are left with the amber from Brittany and Wessex; no doubt it travelled down the North Sea and the Channel.

107 Trundholm sun chariot, detail of the horse's head

But things might be much more complex: there could have been a trade in raw amber from the north, and why not a return current, an amber *Rückstrom*, as E. Sangmeister might have suggested? Aegean workshops could have sent finished jewels to Europe, like the amber bubbles set in gold which have been found in Wessex, or the spacer-beads with their complex holes for making composite crescent-shaped necklaces, which are found in south Germany, Alsace and in the west, but which were also in use, as we have seen, in the Mycenaean world at Kakovatos. They date from 1450 BC in classical chronology: this is equally valid for the beads of the Tumulus culture of central Europe.

On the other hand for the tumuli of early Bronze Age Brittany or Wessex things become more difficult. A tumulus in Morbihan, at Saint-Fiacre, contained such a spacer-bead in amber, with bronze daggers, axes, arrow-heads and a damaged silver cup. Now the date obtained from the wood of the burial chamber takes us back to around 1900 BC even without 'calibrating' the date : at least some 400 years before Mycenae! These beads, then, were in use in the 'barbarian' world well before the ones at Kakovatos, and, rather like the blue glass beads, they remained in use a very long time, almost half a millennium. This is what put two of the 'amber roads' out of the running, and indeed the most complicated of those the old writers revelled in describing : the one which is said to have run along the Adriatic, through Austria and Germany and that was made to turn back westwards via the North Sea and the Channel ; and the other which took in the Mediterranean, the South of France, where spacer-beads are known, the Carcassonne gap, the Atlantic, Brittany and, finally, Wessex.

So, it can be seen that some of the famous 'amber roads' should often be treated with caution in their remoter wanderings. On the other hand the one from the Adriatic to Denmark and the Baltic seems more reliable. It took in the Brenner Pass, the Inn, the Danube, the Saale and the Elbe. Indeed there are so many striking connections between the Nordic world and the Aegean that they cannot all be reduced to an intermittent exchange of a few jewels. There is the whole Aegean geometric style of decoration in particular, based on single or double spirals and concentric circles, which is found on Danish or Scandinavian bronzes. Not a contribution but a transposition! We are left with a few imported or copied objects of which the most unexpected are the little wooden folding stools of North Germany (like the *Klappstuhl* in the Museum at Harburg, already described) and Denmark, prototypes of which are found only in Egypt, Crete or the Near East.

108 Razor with the likeness of a boat (Denmark)

We must underline, too, one of the paradoxes of the Nordic Bronze Age : its flowering in a region which possessed practically no mineable deposits of copper or tin, so much so that for a long time the north had to be content with a few imports from Únětice or the Balkans, like the short-bladed Jutland sabres. Imitations were made, to perfection, of the first bronze daggers, by an extraordinary use of flint. Then, suddenly, there is an explosion of bronze metallurgy. Yet the tin had to be brought from Brittany, Cornwall or

Bohemia, and the copper from the Alps. What was the currency of exchange if not amber – fascinating and probably commercially very valuable? Of course we can only judge, unfortunately, from the material that has reached us down the millennia. No one will ever know, for example, the precise part played by trade in livestock, although we know how important it was at that period, in the complex circuit of prehistoric commercial exchanges.

Nordic bronze

Some of the first objects from the remote past to be studied in Europe were those from Denmark. As early as 1807 King Christian VII of Denmark nominated a Royal Commission for the Preservation of Ancient Remains. Then he appointed a brilliant young man, Christian Jurgensen Thomsen, to classify a whole series of objects discovered by chance in Danish mounds in the course of ploughing or other work. Thomsen set to work with enthusiasm and soon earned the title 'Father of the Bronze Age'. Indeed he observed that, among the objects he had to classify, the most ancient were basically flint or polished stone, the most recent were iron and in between was a whole category of bronzes, associated with stone at the start and with iron at the end. Starting from the collections of the 'Old Nordic Museum', he had just set up the system of the three ages: Stone Age, Bronze Age and Iron Age. This unleashed passionate polemics in the mid-nineteenth century and ultimately the three prehistoric ages in Europe were recognised. Moreover C. J. Thomsen inaugurated the first site work and was a wonderful lecturer when occasion demanded. It is said that he did not hesitate to open one of the precious museum cases and place the most handsome torc in the collection round the neck of one of the visiting ladies, who was suitably overwhelmed – a custom that has been totally lost in our museums, where the slightest move of that nature would set off the alarm sirens.

C. J. Thomsen, with his genius for innovation, was succeeded by A. Worsae, who distinguished two broad phases in Danish tumuli, one characterised by the rite of inhumation and the other by cremation. But it was the great scholar Oscar Montelius who put the Nordic Bronze Age in order with his famous classification into six periods: Montelius I to VI, stretching from 1800 to 450 BC. This already reveals the extraordinary longevity and power of survival of bronze in the Nordic zone, since periods V and VI are contemporary with the early Iron Ages in the rest of Europe.

The traditional Nordic bronze area includes Denmark, Schleswig-Holstein and the south of the Scandinavian peninsula. In addition it exercised a strong influence on the Tumulus culture in north Germany, and the Lüneburg region in particular. The glory of this northern culture lies in the beauty of its ornamental bronzes, the cultural, religious and musical aspects which it has handed down to us and, above all, the preservation of objects of organic matter, which have allowed us a clearer knowledge of the dress and many customs of these populations.

The wonderful tombs of Jutland

At the beginning of the Danish Bronze Age in Montelius II, about 1400, the tombs were enormous tumuli covering inhumations in stone coffers or oak coffins. The addition of a vast quantity of turves and the use of tree trunks rich in tannin have often led to an extraordinary degree of preservation of the funeral deposits. The tumuli reached an average height of 3 to 4m and a diameter of some 20m, but some were even bigger. Frequently the soil was tilled before they were built. Traces of ploughing are still visible to the excavators, and as they stop at the edge of the tumulus area and furthermore the tumuli are often set up in zones that are hardly suitable for agriculture, it is easy to conclude that this was a ritual gesture. The earth had to be symbolically prepared so that the dead, laid thus in the friendly glebe, might germinate to a new life in the world beyond. Tumuli had to be conspicuous to remind the living of the existence of the dead, and their alignment on hilltops or along trackways is an early hint of a rite which survived a great while – we may think of the tombs aligned along the Appian Way, leading to Rome.

109 Gold bracelet (Denmark)

Under the tumulus, sometimes surrounded by a circle of stones or wooden stakes in the old tradition which started with the Corded Ware people, the dead rested in the centre, sometimes in a stone burial chamber, but more often in a wooden coffin. A fairly large oak trunk, some 80cm in diameter at least, had to be chopped down to be hollowed out as a coffin. The trunk was split in two, using the axe again, and then no doubt by means of ropes and sand or by carving patiently with a knife. Fire may have been used too. The inside was always burnt away and then painstakingly chipped with an adze. Once it had been filled with the funeral deposit and the offerings it was closed and wedged with stones to stop it rolling. In tumuli where conditions were not favourable for the preservation of wood, the wedging stones are often left, showing the 'ghost' of the trunk in the centre. At times several inhumations took place in the same tumulus, but it is mainly in the later phases of the Bronze Age that cremation urns were inserted inside older tumuli.

The work of the Danes H. C. Broholm, J. Broendsted and O. Klindt-Jensen has publicised some of the wonderfully preserved burials of Jutland. The most famous is perhaps that of the young girl from Egtved found somewhere in east Jutland in 1921, thanks to the diligence of the conservators of the National Museum at Copenhagen. In fact the coffin was removed whole and patiently studied in the laboratory. The body was lying in a huge oxhide. As a last delicate farewell a branch of milfoil in flower has been placed in the coffin before it was closed. The girl had passed away at the height of summer. She was sleeping, magnificently intact, under the leather shroud, her long hair floating around her head that was inclined towards the right shoulder. Despite being a little crumpled, the skin outlined her long, slender body in the splendour of her twenty years. She was smiling, showing the enamel of her teeth, and her fingers still bore their delicate fingernails. The skeleton had stood up less well to the test of time. For once the factors of deterioration had acted inversely: the acidity of the soils and the tannins had preserved the skin, the hair, the enamel of the teeth and the fingernails, but dissolved the calcareous parts.

For the greater delight of archaeologists the female costume was preserved too: the young woman was wearing a woollen jumper with sleeves to the elbows. The skirt was made from small woollen bands hanging from a belt wound twice round the waist; in the middle of the abdomen was a disc of engraved bronze armed with a spike; Ole Klindt-Jensen tells us that its purpose was to keep over-ardent admirers at a distance. Her feet were hidden in two little woollen socks. On her arms were a few bronze bracelets, her only jewels. Little boxes made of birch bark in the coffin contained many surprises. In one was a woollen cord full of knots, a hair ribbon and an awl. In the other some powder, the remains of a beverage, shown by analysis to contain bilberries and wheat to which honey had been added — a kind of cross between beer and fruit juice. Feminine vanity was acknowledged

110 Belt-discs and choker (Denmark)

111 Reconstruction of woman's costume of the Nordic Bronze Age

with a small comb of horn, hanging from the fair maid's girdle, and somewhat similar to the side combs worn in the early 1900s.

Last, a final strange deposit, in a little bag were the burnt bones of a child about eight. Had the young woman lost a child and preserved the precious bones until her own death? It is possible. Indeed this was not a new tradition for the cemeteries of Únětice already included tombs in which the skeleton of a young woman was accompanied by the cremated bones of children.

Another remarkable tomb completes our knowledge of female costume; this is the one at Skrydstrup, in the south of Jutland this time. It shows that women, even when still young, did not always wear the cheeky little fringed skirt of Egtved, but large austere pieces of woollen materials as well, tied at the waist and falling over the belt. These garments reached to the feet. But the tall lady of Skrydstrup (she was about 1m 70) was concerned with elegance, too; she was wearing small earrings of fine gold spirals and on her hair an elegant woollen bonnet over a snood made of plaited woollen mesh.

Other tombs have yielded traces of these women's clothes which must have been worn all over northern Europe; and on a few bronze statuettes from the Danish late Bronze Age a representation of skirts made of short woollen straps has been found. As for the heavy ankle-length dress, another almost complete example associated with a cloak comes from Borum Eshoej, still in Jutland. It has sometimes been thought that these garments could be shrouds rather than everyday garments, but we should add that quantities of small bronze tubes or spirals could be sewn into the skirts too.

Male fashion was somewhat different from that of today. Trousers had not yet been invented and the men went about clad in hooded coats made from a large piece of material thrown over the shoulders. They were fastened in front with a pin, later with buttons and towards the end with very fine bronze fibulae. Underneath, a peplum was pulled in at the waist by a belt and sometimes there was a leather strap over the shoulder. Thus was the man from Muldbjerg dressed, and he was wearing a small round hat as well. At least two types of hat were being made: one a 'top hat' with a cylindrical framework covered with a spherical skull cap; the other was just a spherical skull cap. These bonnets were substantial, made of several pieces of material sewn together, and some even had a framework of wood or ash bark. This was the beginning of the evolution of the helmet and was a considerable protection against blows or falls. Some underclothes are known: small loincloths held in place by leather or woollen cords. Last leather sandals with laces were worn in addition to woollen socks.

The basic material was black wool. In summer, no doubt, the wool was pulled off the sheep by hand in the absence of clippers or shears. The looms were large wooden constructions on which the vertical threads were kept taut by means of big weights of baked clay, examples of which are found quite frequently all over Europe in the Metal Ages. The spindles must have been wooden with small clay spindle whorls. A whole range of equipment – shuttles, awls, punches, needles etc. – was made, basically of wood, bone, horn or metal. Fibre textiles supplemented the wool, in particular flax, but also other plant species such as aquatic vegetation. Leather and different animal substances as varied as tendons or the skin of certain fishes, like eels, must have provided a by no means negligible addition to the activities of dressmakers and weavers of the period.

Wood, marvellously preserved in the Danish tombs, had an astonishing range of uses. Buckets were made of bark or fine strips of wood, using ash, birch or lime. Numerous bowls and cups were used for food and the tombs indicate that wooden utensils were often preferred to pot. In the middle phase of the Nordic Bronze Age pottery was not very plentiful in the tombs. It only became frequent in the latest phases with the generalisation of the rite of cremation. To dip into the bowls or buckets, spoons or ladles were used; these were also wooden, as at Guldhoej, a tomb which has yielded one of those little wooden folding stools like the one at Harburg. Wood was also used to make scabbards for daggers and swords.

The art of the Danish bronze smiths

The artisans of the north had been magnificent flint knappers. At first they made stone copies of metal weapons like Ùnětician daggers or the famous bronze sabres with curved blades from the Danish island of Fyn, a mysterious import, perhaps from the Balkans. But soon, apparently, it became more economically rewarding to be converted: the flint knapper became a metalworker, as soon as the trading networks could supply him with the raw materials.

'Solid-hilted swords' replaced daggers. At first these too were imported, the

112 Nordic Bronze Age swords (Denmark)

125

Vollgriffschwerter originating in Germany. But the Nordic armourers created their own styles. Their speciality was the composite hilt; discs of various materials, some organic and some metal, alternated along an axis, and this arrangement, when the organic element has disappeared, produces the swords with 'openwork hilts' in our modern museums. The great chieftains took pride in magnificent grips in which bronze, set in gold leaf, alternated with amber rings. The less affluent were content with sober bronze finished with bone, horn or antler.

Decoration remained geometric at first. As the Nordic Bronze Age lingered on and on, the material, bronze, was preserved but the animal or figurative style that was being introduced by contemporary Iron Age civilisations throughout the rest of Europe was adopted. And so horses, stags, anthropomorphic figurines were to appear in the later stages of Nordic Bronze, periods IV and V on Montelius's scale, from 800 to 500, with a final phase in which the style was to become baroque.

Defensive weaponry showed a convergence of two decorative styles: geometric and zoomorphic. The great Scandinavian bronze shields were decorated with delicately engraved double spirals or concentric circles. The helmets were more exuberant. The two Viksö helmets are the most celebrated. The chape was covered with small bosses, but over the forehead two more strongly marked reliefs underlined by arcs of a circle represent two huge eyes on either side of a bronze loop: here is the fascinating stare of a bird of prey. To crown it all, the helmet was fitted with a ribbed crest along the centre, in which an enormous plume of feathers (which have since vanished) could be inserted. Lastly two enormous hollow horns rise up on either side. He must have looked impressive, this Nordic warrior, horned and helmeted, the enormous plume waving over his vulture head in the midst of the fray. Horned helmets were in vogue. They are found again on figures engraved on rocks and also on the heads of small bronze figurines. One of these small figures is depicted kneeling with his hand on his chest, but even in this devout attitude he has kept his fine helmet with its hollow horns on his head.

The art of the Scandinavian bronze workers raises the most modest articles of toilet to

113 Bronze helmets, Viksö
(Denmark)

the rank of masterpieces, particularly the razors. Their small bronze handles are transformed into wheels and spirals and also into the heads of swans, birds, horses or deities. The razor blade becomes a picture of Scandinavian sailing boats or of merry dancers playing lurs, those great bronze horns.

The early spiked discs worn by ladies on the abdomen were replaced by curious belt-boxes, another Danish invention. This is a cup or round box attached to the belt by two strap loops. No doubt the first ones were wooden, but in more recent times progress in metallurgy made it possible to cast these magnificent artefacts, decorated in the proud style of the shields: a complicated interplay of spirals running on for ever in the inspired line of the engraver. In these belt-boxes fair ladies carried their combs, perhaps their razors, their spare jewels and small trifles essential to feminine elegance.

114 Shield with repoussé decoration (Denmark)

115 Nordic bronze fibula, found in Switzerland

Clothing, too, benefited in the more evolved phases from the progress of the metallurgists: there were buttons with double heads like the ones on duffle coats, but there were also Nordic fibulae. These are improved pins. A second stem passes through a hole and is held at the other end by a hook. These northern fibulae lack the spring which is typical of the Italianate ones and gives a better fastening, something like our modern safety pins. But the Nordic fibulae are impressive. They are adorned with double discs and, in the more baroque forms become, in archaeological terminology, spectacle brooches, recalling the pince-nez of our grandmothers.

Funeral deposits, sacred cauldrons and the Trundholm sun chariot

The cult of the dead was gradually modified as the Nordic Bronze Age evolved. The great tumuli of the early period became rarer and rarer. In the advanced phases cremation gradually took over from inhumation as it did everywhere else in Europe. The ashes of the dead are found in urns and were sometimes buried in the tumuli of the earlier period. Very often grave goods were poorer. In some regions there is evidence of local rituals: thus in the island of Gotland in Sweden the tombs are boat-shaped. A great stone structure over the corpse outlined the funeral ship that was to carry the deceased into the everlasting, beyond unknown oceans, a tradition that was to persist in Scandinavia to the time of the Viking lords, buried in their great wooden ships. The funerary urns also displayed some curious features: they became little houses of baked clay as at Roeheck in Denmark, or we find a human face drawn on the body of the urn, another move towards the funeral rites of the south and, in particular, towards those of the early Iron Age in Italy which was contemporary with the final phases of the Nordic Bronze Age. Commercial and cultural links were still as lively along the 'amber roads'.

If the cult of the dead lost something of its grandeur, the rite of making offerings to the gods developed considerably. The new rich of the metal industry prudently gave the gods their due and deliberately sacrificed a substantial share of their treasures to propitiate the angers of the deities. They threw their loveliest gold objects into peat-bogs. At Nors, in Denmark again, it was a whole flotilla of little boats – to repeat the expression used by Professor S. de Laet – that were sacrificed in this way. These little boats of gold leaf, about 10cm long, have their counterpart in Ireland. Gold and bronze vessels, too, were a favourite present to the gods. Little gold cups with rings of repoussé decoration at Lavindsgaard Mose accompany a great bronze cauldron embellished with little ducks, a favourite theme of early Iron Age mythology in Europe. No doubt they were imported. Cauldrons were sometimes hallowed and seemed to be held in as much honour as the cult chariots both in the Nordic districts and elsewhere in Europe in the late Bronze Age. Nordic bronze was in its later phases by this time but the cult of the chariot was known from the Nordic middle Bronze Age, with the most renowned sun symbol in the whole of Europe – the chariot of Trundholm.

It, too, came from a peat-bog. It is 60cm long and consists of a central axis with three pairs of wheels, each with four spokes. The first two are carrying the bronze horse, a thoroughbred. The head is finely chiselled emphasising the mouth and large eyes. The well groomed mane and short tail indicate a horse dressed for parade with plaited or trimmed hair. The splendour of the object is the solar disc: a bronze core overlaid with gold leaf decorated with concentric circles and spirals.

The Trundholm chariot was not the only one of its kind; a similar find in 1895 at Halsingborg in Sweden, has quite simply been lost. And countless representations of the sun – gold discs, very rare indeed, and many engraved concentric circles – are known all over northern Europe, not to mention innumerable bronze wheels, recalling the sacred theme. These little bronzes may have been replicas of real, life-size chariots, drawn by animals which were later sacrificed to the great Sun God. Classical history provides many such examples and Alexander the Great, before setting out in search of adventure, offered some of his finest white horses to the gods; that was after a long procession of cult chariots in which priests, dignitaries and soldiers mingled. The horse–sun association, datable at Trundholm to some 1200 BC in the middle of the Bronze Age, was to continue for centuries,

116 The Trundholm sun chariot (Denmark)

the apotheosis being the chariot of Phoebus-Apollo, dear to the Graeco-Roman world. One of the classical myths thrusts its deepest roots far back into the European Bronze Age, a symbolic image of the cultural and religious contributions made by these 'barbarian' peoples to the old religious storehouse of pagan Europe.

The Trundholm chariot also symbolises the evolution of religious customs. It is fire, the sun that is worshipped by these metal-working peoples; it is also the horse, which makes travel over great distances possible, that is honoured. It is a body of masculine values that has replaced the old Neolithic cults of the Mother Goddesses. Already the Danube had shown the way with the little frocked god of Dupljaja driving his team of divine swans, symbol of a society which had become patriarchal, a world of petty chiefs, powerful through their arms – or through the wealth produced by ever more sophisticated business transactions.

Music: the lurs

The Danish peat-bogs yielded not only wonderful gold vessels but also those extraordinary instruments the lurs, great Bronze Age horns; these, too, were offered to the gods.

129

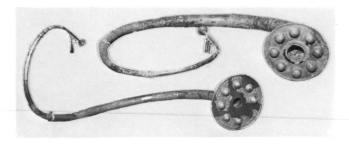

117 Lurs, Nordic Bronze Age (Denmark)

The lurs, or lours, are huge bronze horns, the manufacture of which is an exploit in itself. They were cast by the lost-wax method. A wax model was prepared and then stuffed and surrounded with clay. This was heated and the wax ran off leaving a space for casting the bronze. But a great deal of skill was required to keep the clay walls in place with an even space between them. This was achieved by using small bronze chaplets with a lower tin content than the lurs. These chaplets, having a higher melting point, remained in position without melting during the casting. Lurs were made up of several parts, as many as three or four for the more complex ones. They could even be dismantled, for carrying about, by a system of assembly sleeves. The casting and assembly of the movable parts was perfect, for any defect would have irremediably ruined their pitch. They have often been looked on as the masterpieces of the Nordic foundrymen.

About fifty lurs have been found, mostly in Denmark, but some in north Germany and southern Scandinavia as well. In most instances they were buried in pairs, absolutely identical as regards their form, decoration, attachments and pitch. This was no accident, for these instruments, whose purpose was to accompany religious ceremonies, had remote ancestors in the shape of cattle horns which are among the earliest musical instruments

118 Gold cup from Boslunde (Denmark)

used. Now, as everyone knows, horns normally come in pairs, and moreover, horns used in worship had to be taken from consecrated beasts. The lurs found in pairs are certainly an echo of the ritual horns, still one of the fundamental features of Bronze Age religion.

Lurs vary in shape. Some primitive types have a short, curved tube, something between the hunting horn and the true lur, which was different, too, from the serpent of medieval orchestras. It was held differently with the bell uppermost as in modern tubas. The lur had to be held at arm's length as can be seen in pictures of lur players in Scandinavian rock carvings. These players had to be sturdy fellows with powerful lungs and biceps.

The lur was often fitted with a small chain by which it could be held steady. This chain ran from the bell to the mouthpiece, analogous with that of the modern bugle. The bell was not really functional since it cut the tube at right angles. It was chiefly an embellishment. To begin with it was adorned with incised motifs, then, in the latest models, with bosses. Small pendants which jingled against the tube completed the decoration.

Of some fifty lurs that have been discovered, only a dozen were sufficiently well preserved to allow their musical potential to be tested after reasonable restoration. It proved a great surprise; whereas it had been thought that these were no more than huge hunting horns that were spectacular only for the size of the instrument, it now had to be admitted that they were intended to be heard as well as seen.

119 Large ceremonial axe (Denmark)

Their range is extensive. The most sophisticated allow 22 tones over 4 octaves, but in normal use one could not reasonably expect more than the fundamental and its harmonics over three octaves, similar to the modern bugle. There is, in fact, no device for lengthening the tube and no hole to modify the pitch. There are lurs of various keys, some in C, others in D or F. Nevertheless serious practice is required to be able to play them. Personally all we have got from the lur preserved in the Musée des Antiquités Nationales at Saint Germain-en-Laye is a mighty groan, after a memorable effort of the lungs. But to listen to records of lurs, made in recent years, is to hear something very surprising. Musicians of the Royal Orchestra of Copenhagen are past masters in these curious recordings of the lurs in the Danish National Museum. Of course, Bronze Age scores have 'gone with the wind', more especially since they were handed down from mouth to ear – to coin a phrase! The records are first and foremost a striking demonstration of their musical potential but do not claim to reproduce anything prehistoric. French listeners will be surprised to recognise modern military tunes since the players drew on the bugle repertoire and 'French

120 and 121 Gold bracelet and cup,
Nordic Bronze Age (Denmark)

marches'. Jazz harmonies with the use of counterpoint are no less astonishing, suggesting dawn in the fowl house. Purists and romantics would no doubt prefer a majestic evocation of a Phantom Ship. But these varied possibilities show that these first 'brass' instruments were not simply single-note horns and that they can even be seen as forerunners of modern European orchestras.

Danish lurs are still an exceptional phenomenon. Yet they were not the only metal wind instruments of the Bronze Age. If we turn our gaze to the British Isles, or, more precisely, Ireland, we shall find there a whole series of late Bronze Age horns, also made of metal, which have been studied in detail by J. Coles. They are made in different keys – C, C sharp, D, D sharp – but their potential is more limited than that of the lurs – one note, occasionally two, and the corresponding octaves. Some horns have a hole. The mouthpiece is either at the side or at the end. A few dubious remains of trumpets appear in Atlantic deposits, as in the Jardin des Plantes at Nantes or at Vénat in Charente. The horns are undoubtedly forerunners of the Gaulish and Roman trumpets: they were probably used to call to battle or to mark the stages of ceremonials, rather than as musical instruments.

So metallurgy gave rise to the first copper and bronze instruments, but a whole range of wooden instruments must have existed alongside them. No doubt wooden flutes and pipes were made and bone whistles. Statuettes from the Cyclades show lyres and cithara and other stringed instruments being used in the Mediterranean world, and these may have reached northern Europe, but it seems that no traces have been found so far.

122 (*left*) Horns (Ireland)

123 (*above*) Crotals (Ireland)

124 Clay citharist and flautist
(Cyprus)

For dances percussion certainly played a major part. From the end of the Neolithic, drums were known, made of skins stretched over large pots, particularly in the Baden culture. Other wooden instruments of the tom-tom type may have existed.

The Bronze Age brought a new category of objects which, if not musical, could at least rattle and keep time for marches and dances. Metal provided the 'rattle pendants' which could either be worn on the belt or else adorn chariots or the breast-pieces of horses. They proliferated in the late Bronze Age with great circular or annular pendants – which were sometimes known as tintinnabula – and which are illustrated by some discoveries in the Saar and Lorraine, recently published by Professor J. P. Millotte. A final category is that of the sheep bells, hollow balls with little bits of bronze or small stones inside. They were sometimes called 'crotals'. Those from Dowris in Ireland are enormous olives, fitted with rings; as they were some 15cm long and weighed from 300 to 400gm they could hardly have been worn as pendants and must have been used in religious ceremonies. For J. Coles these instruments, with their unexciting sound, must have served some religious purpose, especially one linked with the worship of the bull whose virile parts they represent. They are often associated with small horns; so we see the horn and the virile attributes of the bull united to his honour in late Bronze Age religious ceremonies.

Chapter 8

The Great Islands of the Western Mediterranean

The islands of the western Mediterranean developed individual cultures which started from a common stock and evolved in peculiar directions due to their enclosed environment. The common stock is first of all the prolonged survival of funeral rites, inherited from Neolithic times, and of megalithic customs – in contrast with the profound changes marking the onset of the Bronze Age in central Europe. The persistence of collective burial and the use for these burials either of grottoes or natural hypogea or of hypogea hollowed out of the ground, especially in the early period, are particularly characteristic. There is also the use of structures of large stones, in the Cyclopean style, for the ramparts and defensive towers of the villages: the talayots of the Balearics, the torre of Corsica and the nuraghi of Sardinia, each with their own particular style. Other things which all these islands have in common are a chronology which is very long but difficult to determine accurately and the absence, very often, of certain traditional features of the Bronze Age.

125 (*left*) Marble idol of Cycladic type, Senorbi (Sardinia)
126 (*above*) Votive boat of stuccoed wood, Thebes, eleventh dynasty

The first seafarers in the Mediterranean

In contrast with the Atlantic zone, the Mediterranean is rich in varied depictions of boats and ships, giving rise to many studies of ancient navigation. The sources are manifold: pictures on the walls of tombs or temples, decoration on pottery, funeral ships – true models reduced in size – children's toy clay boats, not to mention a few traces of actual craft found at the bottom of the sea.

The boats are as diverse as the materials from which they were made. Some representations suggest that the boats used had wooden frames covered with skins or pitched leather, like the Atlantic curraghs. Dug-out canoes, barges and wooden lighters sailed the rivers and were sometimes towed from the banks. Strange skiffs floated along the Nile, made of bundles of papyrus in a crescent shape, a type of craft that still has remote descendants in the Sudan. Sails were known very early, from the fourth millennium in both Mesopotamia and Egypt. Soon vessels became more sturdy, built of wood for preference, choice timber as is only fitting, and very soon the famous cedars of Lebanon were being used. The first Egyptian ships preserved the crescent shape of the papyrus boats, but they soon evolved. The mast could be lowered when there was a head wind and recourse to the oars was necessary. Skiffs were propelled by means of either one or two steering oars placed at the side of the poop. Very soon, too, pictures show that some kind of shelter was attempted on ships. At first rustic huts were improvised amidships, then benches and decks were developed leading to warships in which the oarsmen were separated from the fighting men by a floor. The famous and often-quoted relief in the temple at Medinet-Habu (see Figure 140) celebrates the victory of Rameses III over the Peoples of the Sea around 1200 BC. This extraordinary depiction of a naval battle shows the Egyptian ships with oars and sails clashing victoriously with horned sailors, Sardinians perhaps, whose ships had only sails and carried the emblem of a duck on the poop. So national navies already had distinctive types of vessel.

In the Aegean Bronze Age, the rowing boat was often preferred and about the year 2000 the People of the Cyclades were undertaking both commercial transactions and the piratical raids, of which they were often suspected, in small swift craft with twenty pairs of oars. Their distinguishing mark was a fish, floating aloft on the very high prows. Later, the Minoans and Mycenaeans used sailing boats, as did the Phoenicians, the navigators par excellence who sailed the Mediterranean from East to West.

The wreck at Cape Gelidonya

An extraordinary document on eastern Mediterranean maritime activities was provided by a boat which sank off Cape Gelidonya in the south of what is now Turkey. It was in 1958 that young sponge divers located the wreck in some 30m of water. An American expedition, sent out in 1960, led to the excavation of this valuable relic, which is of interest far beyond the limits of the Aegean Bronze Age. It is an unrivalled example of trade in metal goods, and is now well known, thanks to the excellent report by G. F. Bass.

Remains of the wooden ship were greatly reduced but nevertheless they showed the carcase of a ship some 10m long. In the hold there was still the wooden dunnage, which served both as ballast and to support the merchandise. The beams, squared with an axe had been assembled by means of big wooden pegs. Cypress and oak had been used to build it. The cargo showed clearly that it was a boat belonging to a trader in metal ware. Almost a ton of metal has been successfully recovered, including large ingots in the shape of ox hides with four points, of the normal Cypriot type, weighing some 25kg each. The boat must have called at Cyprus some time before it sank. Other small copper and bronze ingots were in the form of plano-convex plates with the stamp of the crucible in which they had been cast. This shape is not peculiar to the Mediterranean but was found widely in western Europe, from the middle Bronze Age on. Other ingots were of tin.

127 Ingot bearer, bronze, Kourion (Cyprus)

Beside these raw materials a whole variety of tools was found, for the ultimate use of the customers: hoes, adzes, flat or shaft-hole axes, double edged axes, axe-adzes, chisels, punches, etc. It seems that the metallurgist could work to order for he had brought with him a small outfit consisting of a forge, stone hammers, crucibles, anvils and small tools. Table ware and a tripod piece proved that he could produce art metalwork if required. The metal goods were stocked in wicker baskets or between fibre matting made from water plants. For the business of selling, weights made of haematite had been provided as well as a small signet of an archaic type which must have been used to seal bargains. Among the more curious objects was an ankle-bone and some small scarabs, no doubt fetiches, intended to ensure a safe voyage for the vessel. Sadly, for once, their attention wandered for a moment! The meticulous work of G. Bass and his team has revealed even the food of the sailors: fish and olives, the time-honoured Mediterranean menu.

The archaeological goods, pots, etc., as well as radio-carbon dating from the wood of the boat, have enabled the precise date of the shipwreck to be determined. At first G. Bass placed it around 1200 BC. More recently he has emphasised that the craft itself could have been older since a great deal of the material was already being made in Cyprus from 2000 onwards.

Other boats that sank around the fifteenth century have been found in the eastern Mediterranean, also with ingots. So this trade in ingots was intense, and no doubt reached as far as the shores of the western Mediterranean where small trading posts – not colonies – were created. This Aegean or Levantine trade reached southern Italy, Sicily and Sardinia. Further west its limits are often difficult to determine. As the great Fernand Benoit noted in his research into the Hellenisation of southern Gaul, not only is the ancient origin of many pieces still uncertain, but we must be on guard against the activities of forgers who went so far as to stuff the strata of southern France with recent imports from the Aegean or the near East and even to give false attributions to museum pieces.

It is only towards the dawn of the Iron Age that there can be no further doubt about the abundance of imports, and it is known that, in the sixth and seventh centuries, the Phoenicians frequented numerous trading posts in the western Mediterranean and even passed through the Pillars of Hercules to reach the legendary realm of Tartessos. Previously things were much less clearly defined, particularly in southern France. We may recall a few finds of 'Cypriot' daggers in Provence and even in Brittany, but they are still debatable. In north-eastern Iberia Cypriot pottery has been recorded at Ampurias and a little Cycladic jug, found in the Balearics, has been quoted.

The talayots of the Balearics

The charming islands of the Balearic archipelago make a fortune for travel agents nowadays. These little, almost tranquil, paradises sheltered the tempestuous love of George Sand and Chopin, as we are reminded by the prospectuses and postcards which, by contrast, neglect their extraordinary archaeological past. And yet the great Cyclopean constructions of the Balearics attracted tourists from a very early time. At a period when they were even more impressive than they are now, a traveller like Binnelis in 1593 spoke with respect of those grandiose monuments which could only be the work of demons or giants. Popular tradition christened them 'Clapers de Gegant' or again 'talaia' or 'talayot' which means 'watch-tower' in the local dialect, as we are told by Professor L. Pericot Garcia, author of an excellent recent account of the past of the Balearics.

Many travellers waxed enthusiastic about these monuments, which, after being attributed as usual to giants, became Celtic and finally – particularly after the first serious works like that of the Frenchman E. Cartailhac from 1872 on – prehistoric. The chronology of the talayots has been the subject of impassioned argument, the more so since their furnishings included varied elements stretching from the Bronze Age to much more recent periods – including the period of Carthaginian colonisation – and there was a tendency at times to make them too recent.

128 Talayot of Sa Canova (Majorca)

In recent years a whole series of field expeditions, of scale plans and excavations, supported by a long list of radio-carbon dates, have enabled us to penetrate, to some extent, the mystery of these monuments.

The Balearic Islands were occupied from the beginning of the Neolithic around the fourth millennium, but it was only towards 2000 BC that some fairly homogeneous styles appeared. Burials in hypogea, which are found so frequently both in Sardinia and in southern France, proliferated here as they did throughout the Mediterranean world. Some of them, like the one at Cala Sant Vicens in Majorca, are still very well preserved. This one has a short corridor leading through a narrow passage to an antechamber, flanked by two side chambers, and lying in front of the great, rectangular main chamber. It is the classical plan which was to reappear, for example, at the 'Epée de Roland' in the neighbourhood of Arles.

We can place the beginning of these monuments by radio-carbon. A few natural grottoes have been dated to somewhere between 1960 and 1800 BC. The more complex models with multiple chambers are more recent and remained in use down to the first millennium. In fact a persistent tradition of grotto burials was to be found as late as the Punic period with the famous cemetery of Puig des Molins in the little island of Ibiza.

The earliest hypogea produced classical Chalcolithic furnishings: a few copper awls, a few triangular daggers, buttons with V-perforations like the ones that adorned the clothes of the Bell Beaker peoples; can they have visited the Balearics too? It seems, in fact, that they did: a little bowl at Deya is decorated with triangle and 'zip fastener' motifs

138

129 Model of the taula at Telaty de Dalt (Minorca)

130 Model of the rampart and houses of a talayot village (Capocarp Viell, Majorca)

reminiscent of the Bell Beaker ware in the South of France. May we venture a word on the subject of the little Cycladic jug in the museum in Minorca? It is a typical *Schnabelkanne* – a beaked jug – painted, with one handle and the classic raised beak, suggestive of a bird drinking: fragile evidence of links between the Cyclades and the Balearics.

The great event in these islands is the Talayot culture. The talayot is the great fortified tower that dominated the village, serving as both a place of refuge and a watch-tower. It is calculated that the tallest of them probably reached a height of some 12m with a diameter of up to 30m. Not all of them are circular and there are many variations on a square or rectangular plan. The village was organised around this 'keep'; the huts were built of round or rectangular stones, the whole surrounded by those Cyclopean walls that only the Mediterranean peoples knew how to build. It is true that elsewhere, in the temperate zone of Europe, large-scale forests supplied ample wood for palisades to enclose the villages. The talayots evolved, and the excavations of Professor G. Lilliu, for example, show the successive stages in the development of talayotic villages, where new towers were progressively added.

Not far from the settlements, the funerary monuments of these populations include, first and foremost, the curious navetas, sepulchres on a grand scale which look like the hull

131 Naveta, Es Tudons (Minorca)

of a capsized ship with the keel in the air; hence their name. The one at Es Tudons in Minorca is one of the most famous and best preserved. It boasts a trapezoidal façade and a rounded apse. These navetas were entered through a low rectangular opening in front of the majestic burial chamber, which was sometimes supported on pillars. The naveta is the best known of the funerary structures and many variants are in existence: micro-navetas, circular or rectangular tombs like the ones at Sant Margarita, recently excavated in Majorca by the Bryant Foundation. But the most classic navetas, which may be as long as 30m, seem to be located in Minorca. Here, too, the radio-carbon criterion has been most useful. G. Rosselo-Bordoy obtained a date of 1350 BC for the naveta at Pula and 1250 for the one at Son Marge.

It is in Minorca, too, that one of the most curious and distinctive monuments of the Mediterranean is found, the taula. It is an enormous rectangular pillar, which may be as much as 4m high and 2.7m wide, as at Trepuço. A rectangular table rests horizontally on the pillar in a feat of equilibrium which is approaching a miracle, so much so that at times it has been necessary to support the whole structure with a small secondary pillar placed obliquely. Sometimes this taula, sitting in the centre of the village, is surrounded by a rectangular or circular structure, often in a poor state of preservation.

What was it for? Here, too, imagination has run wild. In the days of 'Celtic' interpretations, it could only be a magnificent sacrificial table, thrusting heavenwards, intended for human sacrifice, of course. Unless it was a place where the dead were exposed until the flesh had gone, before their bones were buried in hypogea or navetas. But the

132 and 133 Lloseta treasure talayot period (Majorca)

134 Votive dove, bronze, late talayot period

rationalists were on the watch and Emile Cartailhac, not wholly convinced, put forward the idea that it was simply a central pillar supporting beams which radiated out to carry the roof of a house; a big pillar, indeed, but one that was functional and not ritualistic. The imposing size of the taulas, however, is difficult to understand if they only played a supporting role, and the complementary structures are often too poorly preserved to settle the question. So we come back after all to the idea of a religious function, linked, perhaps, with a cult of the sun: a bit of Stonehenge, in fact . . . so long as we are not seeing, as Mascaro did, a symbol of the cult of the bull: the great lintel representing the horns, with a lot of imagination, it is true. Professor Pericot Garcia leans towards the theory of a cult monument, too, but, wisely, he does not try to be too precise as to the details of the ritual.

The culture of the talayots belongs to the Bronze Age in its early phases; classic triangular daggers and arrowheads made of copper are found. But very soon some local creations were to characterise the Balearics; bronze-hilted swords for example, a distant echo of the central European *Vollgriffschwerter*: the grip is distinctive, narrow at the centre and widening out at the level of the pommel. The blade is leaf-shaped. G. Rosselo Bordoy dates them to between 1200 and 800 BC. They are accompanied by a few tools, flat axes, which had a very long life in the Iberian world, chisels and curious instruments shaped like gigantic arrowheads, which no doubt had a ceremonial purpose. Examples of Balearic swords occur in the famous hoard of Ria de Huelva, in the south-west of the Iberian peninsula, showing how these types lasted right to the end of the late Bronze Age. A few socketed axes, inspired by western models, appear sporadically, as well as a few small jewels. In the later talayots, dating to the Iron Age, iron daggers have been found with handles topped with antenna-like appendices, recalling Pyrenean styles; some bronze collars were found too, together with a whole range of animal art celebrating birds and bulls. Magnificent bulls' heads in an original, local style, testify to the persistence and vigour of that Mediterranean cult. The talayot culture seems not to have had much contact with the Iberian peninsula apart from a few episodic trading exchanges. It is linked much more closely with the great insular architectural centres of Corsica and Sardinia.

Still in the Balearic Islands, the islets of Formentera and Ibiza are famous mainly for their occupation by the Carthaginians, but the Bronze Age is represented there, too. It takes the form of isolated objects ranging from the little tanged daggers of the Chalcolithic to the flat and socketed axes of the latest Bronze Age. A few dealers in bronze weapons and tools must have stopped off there very occasionally.

Corsica: torre and Shardana

In 1840 the writer Prosper Mérimée was carving out a fine literary success for himself by publishing that masterpiece of the short story, 'Colomba', in the *Revue des Deux-Mondes*. It was the outcome of an official mission to Corsica in 1839; for Mérimée was then Inspector General of the Historic Monuments of France and in that capacity he undertook various regional journeys, bringing back precious 'Travel Notes' in which he recorded the precise location of the monuments he had been able to visit. He revealed the ancient and pre-Roman works of Corsica. We are indebted to him for the first description of the Corsican dolmens and menhirs; in those days the dolmens were called 'Stazzone', 'devil's forges', and the menhirs 'Stantare'. Mérimée even records that when a child was amusing itself by

135 Alignments of stantari (Corsica)

spinning round like a top, it would be told' 'Don't act like a Stantare.' He described the monuments at Tavaro, Cauria and the district round Sartène and drew parallels with the Breton megaliths.

But one of the stones that pre-date the Romans intrigued him more than the others. He had stopped near the ruins of the church at Sagone to look for 'a statue of a knight with a helmet on his head', which had been mentioned to him, but he could not find it. Then a friendly old Corsican, with a white beard, offered to show him an 'idolo dei Mori' in the neighbourhood. It was at Apricciani in some burnt 'maquis' or scrub: a block of granite 2.12m high and carved at the top.

136 Statue-menhir at Scalsa-Murta (Corsica)

But let Mérimée describe it: 'The face is hewn from the naked stone and is a little worn now. And yet the rather well drawn eyes, the nose, the mouth expressed by a single straight line, the pointed beard can all be distinguished. The hair is parted in the middle and forms two projecting tufts, level with the eyes. That is where the stone is widest, about 40cm. Breasts and pectoral muscles are indicated but the rest of the slab is completely smooth. Behind, the hair is cut short and does not cover the nape of the neck. The shoulder blades are indicated as crudely as the chest. In a word, it is a flat bust on a stand.' Mérimée adds an important detail: 'Perhaps someone might see horns in those two lumps which I took to be tufts of hair.' We shall return to those horns. At first sight, Mérimée, who was used to Roman antiquities, thought of an ancient Terminus, a Priapus perhaps. 'But the essential attribute is missing,' he observed maliciously. So it could only be an earlier work representing some Ligurian or Iberian hero. And he concluded wisely that he could not go further until other, more characteristic, finds had been made. The future was to acknowledge that Mérimée was absolutely right and we can justly consider him as one of the pioneers of Corsican prehistory. But for that almost a century was needed and the

137 Statue-menhirs at Cauria (Sartène, Corsica)

heroic work of the late lamented Roger Grosjean, who died on the job while he was preparing one of the excavation sites from which he conjured up Corsica's magnificent past. It is to him that we are indebted for the extraordinary series of statue-menhirs and torre, the answer to the nuraghi of Sardinia, which had remained buried until then. And his memory will always be linked with the amazing site at Filitosa, guarded for eternity by its cohort of stone warriors carrying their swords crossed and their daggers at their side.

For Grosjean the first menhirs appeared in Corsica associated with the coffers of the megalithic period. Small at first, and often buried, they became progressively more imposing. A major step forward came with the release of the head from the shoulders giving the stone a decidedly more anthropomorphic shape. At a later stage the face became clearer with the appearance of a nose and chin and the depiction of eyes and a mouth. The final stage has representations of weapons and details of warriors' clothing. The big sword,

138 Statue at Filitosa (Corsica)

in the Aegeo-Mycenaean style, is worn at the side or perhaps vertically hanging from a scapular cross-belt. The dagger remains at the side, often on the right, which is a little surprising, but no doubt it was a complementary weapon to the sword which was worn on the left.

The defensive armoury included a helmet, indicated on the stone by a strongly marked occipital pad. Often two holes at the top show where horns, either real or artificial, could be inserted. The horned helmet was very popular throughout the Bronze Age, from the Mediterranean to northern Europe. On the back, ridges fanning out from the central axis of the menhir represent leather corselets which protected the warrior. In front some pectoral padding can sometimes be seen too. Last, some statues like the ones at Cauria have a kind of escutcheon in relief at the bottom of the swords; perhaps it is a buckler, although Grosjean saw it rather as an apron, a sort of leather loincloth which, again, was intended to ward off blows.

Interpreting these statues raises a great many problems. First of all there are the abundant depictions of weapons which, by their crescent-shaped pommels seem likely to belong to the Aegeo-Mycenaean type in use from 1400–1200 BC. It is true that some observers thought they recognised antennae in the shape, which would bring us up to the

Iron Age, but this remains doubtful. These abundant depictions of weapons are recorded in a country where finds of that type in excavations are exceedingly rare. Only a few isolated finds of daggers are known, some triangular from the Chalcolithic and early Bronze Age periods, others, with antennae, from the beginning of the Iron Age. R. Grosjean interpreted the position as follows: the statues were put up by the peaceable megalithic populations of Corsica, whose weaponry was still Neolithic, based on arrow tips of flint or obsidian, and who had had to repulse invaders armed with bronze weapons, and he evokes a text of Aristotle to the effect that the Iberians surrounded their tombs with obelisks as numerous as the enemies they had killed. R. Grosjean recalls the well known fact that the British General, Montgomery, hung a picture of Rommel, his valorous adversary in the African campaigns, in his HQ. He also quotes the custom of painting crosses on tanks and aircraft to mark victories over the enemy, another undying tradition in warfare.

But then we must identify these warlike intruders in Corsica. With this in view, R. Grosjean introduces the famous Egyptian relief from Medinet Habu as the prize witness. Indeed amongst the adversaries of Pharoh's soldiers we can recognise some horned warriors, equipped with corselets and neck pads, who look like the warriors of the Corsican statues. These were the invasions of the 'Peoples of the Sea', as they are called in the archives of the Pharaohs of the nineteenth dynasty, which list the peoples in coalition

139 Statue-menhir, Genna Arrele (Sardinia)

140 Warrior with a horned helmet, bas relief
from the temple of Rameses III at Medinet-Habu

against Egypt. Among them are the Shardana with horned helmets – a name which it is tempting to identify as that of the Sardinians. These Shardana, then, would have been occupying both Sardinia and Corsica. This hypothesis, which is certainly a little romantic, was very attractive, especially as the Egyptian relief could be dated to 1190, thus giving an unexpected synchronism for Corsica. But it is very difficult to subscribe wholeheartedly to this thesis and a lot more work and excavation will be needed to verify it. That in no way detracts, however, from the merit of R. Grosjean in making the marvellous prehistory of the 'Beauteous Isle' known far beyond Corsican shores.

The statue-menhirs accompanied megalithic monuments which were often grouped in real alignments on a small scale. But a great proportion of them have been broken at different periods, either from sheer vandalism, or at the injunction of the clergy, anxious to destroy traces of a pagan cult; a few more were Christianised by the addition of a cross. But the greatest destruction was the work of prehistoric populations, the builders of the torre.

The torre are the Corsican variation of the watch-towers protecting villages in the Mediterranean world. Again it is to R. Grosjean that we are indebted for their discovery and publication from 1955 on. Mérimée would have been delighted, for he had heard of the 'Nur Hags' in Sardinia and was a little disappointed not to find anything similar in Corsica. The torre are often sited on easily defendable heights, mountain peaks or spurs. Frequently they are situated on rocky escarpments which are extended by walls made of big blocks and stones, amongst which were found from time to time fragments of statue-menhirs. How surprising! Here is proof that the latter were no longer in use and that they had no doubt been destroyed by the torre-builders, who were probably invaders and had dealt harshly with the previous megalithic cultures.

The torre is complicated in detail. It is organised around a central or lateral tower from which the wall enclosing the whole unit starts. Sometimes it covers a small area, sometimes it protects a little village with dry-stone huts. Occasionally the village lies alongside the

141 A Corsican torre

main structure of the torre and has its own fortified wall, as at Cucuruzzu. The torre have false corbelled roofs like the tholoi of the Mediterranean Chalcolithic. They are entered along a passage which may be open to the sky or covered with large stone slabs. Often the structure is complicated by the addition of benches, either inside or outside, side chambers, niches and irregular diverticula.

What were these torre for? To defend the villages, no doubt, but they were also places of worship, as is shown by the many hearths and remains of animal sacrifice. They are forerunners of the fortified churches which were to be both places of worship and defences in just the same way in historic times. The torre do not share the extraordinary size of the great nuraghi of Sardinia. In fact some are tiny, like the one at Cecia, which is 10m wide with a cella of only 2m, and Grosjean uses this to support his argument against their role as a refuge. It seems that the earliest circular monuments of the 'torre' type were not fortified and that it was only later that they played a part in defence.

Radio-carbon datings together with various correlations have led R. Grosjean to date the blossoming of the torre culture to about 1400–1000 BC. Thus pieces of carbonised wood from the cella at the monument at Pagliaiu yielded dates ranging from 1200 to 1000. The furnishings of the torre, although generally poor and atypical, have yielded a few metal objects which would seem to date it to the late Bronze Age. Thus in the Castello de Cucuruzzu, fibulae, axes and pieces of sheet bronze with small bosses were recovered, fragments of body armour perhaps. Pottery has a distinctive local style with flat cups and basins, some of which have Italianate or Sardinian affinities, which is hardly surprising.

About a hundred of these monuments are known now. R. Grosjean believed that this civilisation had vanished at the end of the Bronze Age when the only objects known in Corsica are imported winged or socketed axes of Italian make, fibulae and little bronze daggers with antennae, harbingers of the Iron Age. So the culture of the torre would not have flourished as brilliantly as that of its Sardinian neighbour, with the nuraghi which have amazed the world ever since the days of antiquity. However, some researchers like F. de Lanfranchi think the torre were still being used, belatedly, in the Iron Age, stressing at the same time the uncertain element in the dating of many of the fortified sites.

With its megalithic culture, the astonishing phenomenon of the statue-menhirs and the religious elements of the torre, Corsica is an example of a distinctive island civilisation, which still holds many mysteries for R. Grosjean's successors to unmask.

Sicily and the Aeolian Islands

The plan of this book inevitably implies a choice. But it would be impossible to pass over in total silence the early days of Sicily and her northern neighbours, the Lipari or Aeolian Islands. At first sight, for the layman at least, their prehistory is less spectacular than that of the other great western Mediterranean islands, Sardinia and Corsica, renowned for their Cyclopean monuments and their statue-menhirs. And yet a whole series of distinctive cultures succeeded each other in Sicily, from remote Palaeolithic times onward, known through rock carvings like those of the curious dancers in the Grotto at Levanzo.

In the fifth millennium Neolithic cultures prospered in these islands. One of the sources of this wealth, in the Aeolian Isles mainly, was trade in obsidian, the black, vitreous volcanic rock which could as readily be made into sharp knives as into murderous arrowheads. Through the pottery styles we can follow the development of several human groups, linked at times with eastern civilisations from which they adopted little statuettes of Mother Goddesses, testifying to a fertility cult.

In the Chalcolithic these local pottery styles were in competition with Bell Beaker wares, possibly imported. Metal made a timid appearance. Funeral customs evolved and the burials in trenches of the early period gave way to rock-cut tombs which were common at that time in many Mediterranean sites. In the Bay of Palermo the tombs at Conca d'Oro show a vertical access shaft leading to little circular grottoes cut into the sub-soil. In the Bronze Age, at Castellucio in south-east Sicily, the tombs, which were still hypogea, were closed by stone slabs carved with fine spiral motifs. Bone plaques decorated with bosses recall the jewels of Lerna in the Peloponnese, or even Troy. Sicily was one of the forward trading posts of the merchants and navigators from the eastern Mediterranean. The earliest bronze weapons in Sicily were to be Aegean or Mycenaean swords: sites like the ones from the so-called Thapsos Cozzo period, in the time of the great Mycenaean expansion (around 1400–1200) seem, by the abundance of Mycenaean imports, to have been real Mycenaean 'shop windows' towards the west.

At the end of the Bronze Age a flourishing bronze industry developed in Sicily: local products included vertical shaft-hole axes, razors and fibulae, the bow of which suggested a violin bow. A few of these products were to be exported as far as the French Atlantic regions and even to the British Isles. Sicily had reduced her relations with the eastern Mediterranean and turned towards the western world.

The Aeolian Islands, too, show signs of very distinctive cultures. The villages occupy promontories protected by inaccessible cliffs. The huts had sub-foundations of dry-stone walling. At Portella great water vessels have been recovered and other pots, too, used for burying the dead, a tradition stemming from the Near East and found again in the early Bronze Age at El Argar. However, in the final phase of the Bronze Age, cremation was adopted in Sicily too; the fashion arrived from central Italy, starting with the proto-Villanovian cultures. But soon Sicily's destiny was to be closely linked once more with that of the Aegean world: it became a Greek colony, the 'Great Greece', evoked by a whole network of Greek legends as well as the wanderings of the Odyssey.

The nuraghi of Sardinia

How many volumes would be needed to describe in detail the six or seven thousand nuraghic monuments strung out along the mountains and plains of Sardinia? Their geographic distribution is eloquent, showing an almost total coverage of the island, with areas of heavy concentration in the north-west and the centre where at times some sixty monuments to the square kilometre are recorded.

The nuraghi have been discussed for a long time. As early as 1840 in Paris the learned Count Alberto Ferrero della Marmora, a friend of Mérimée, brought out his *Journey to Sardinia* which unveiled this astonishing civilisation. Since then there has been a succession of studies, down to the syntheses of Professor Giovanni Lilliu and Margaret Guido, not to mention countless artistic impressions, including the fine art album of Christian Zervos. Every encyclopedia of art feels obliged to have a photo of a nuraghe, sometimes accompanied by a small Sardinian bronze statuette, a 'bronzetto'. But there were other things besides nuraghi in the Sardinian past.

The prehistory of Sardinia is rich and fascinating. Like her neighbours, Sicily and the

142 Nuraghe 'Santu Antine' (Torralba, Sardinia)

Aeolian Islands, she experienced brilliant Neolithic and Chalcolithic cultures. It was to these islands, too, that the first Aegean and Anatolian navigators ventured forth, and contacts were maintained subsequently without a break, bringing cultural stimuli and novelties in the sphere of economics as well as metalwork.

The influence of Cycladean art is manifest in the little marble statuettes from Senorbi or Porto-Ferro. They show the same stylised faces and small conical breasts, but they are not imports for there are details of form which denote local manufacture and this has been confirmed by petrographic analysis: the marble used comes from the local deposit at Orani. About twenty statuettes of this kind are known, coming from rock-cut tombs or sanctuaries.

Alongside these eastern influences, the Chalcolithic in Sardinia is characterised by features which are distinctly western. The most typical are, once more, Bell Beaker wares, about thirty small vases with *pointillé* decoration, either classic beakers or large shallow basins or again bowls with small feet. As often in Bell Beaker hoards on the Continent, archers' wristguards, sometimes laid in a stone case, and 'buttons with V perforations' – bone buttons, so called because of the shape of their perforations – also accompany western-type Bell Beaker wares.

So Sardinia seems to be the crossroads of Atlantic and Mediterranean influences and this is illustrated notably by the burials and the architecture.

The Bell Beaker material that we have just mentioned, which is still Chalcolithic, is found in rock-cut tombs which are often remarkable. The most famous one, at Anghelu-Ruju, shows wall decoration which includes reliefs of cattle horns: here too the cult of the bull held sway. Burial under dolmens was practised, too, as it was throughout the western world at that time.

Following these early hypogea and dolmens, the curious Giants' Tombs were to show the mastery already acquired by the Sardinians in the matter of megalithic architecture. The chamber of the dolmen, which is longer now, is surrounded by a kind of peristyle, or enclosure of stones, preceded by a crescent-shaped courtyard. Here again we can recognise the emblem of the sacred horn in the shape of the monument. The entrance was often monumental: an enormous stone slab was raised, rounded at the top and slightly suggestive of a boat raised up with its prow in the air. At its base a narrow rectangular opening gave access to the tomb. The sacred stone in front of the kingdom of the dead was visible from afar and reminded the living, at work in the nearby fields, of the frailty of human life.

But Sardinian prehistory is chiefly famous for its nuraghi. These are the supreme achievement, the consummation of the Cyclopean architectural art which took shape in the western Mediterranean in the Bronze Age.

The period of the nuraghi lasted on into the Iron Age until the island was conquered by the Carthaginians and this brilliant regional development came to an end.

The basic element of the nuraghe is a tower in the form of a truncated cone, built with big, carefully dressed stones with a platform on top and step-like tiers all round. Openings are few and narrow and an exiguous corridor leads to the chamber. The simple types of nuraghi were to appear around 1300, probably at the same time as the talayots in the Balearics or the torre in Corsica. But soon the nuraghic unit was to diversify. Chambers with corbelled roofs were to be introduced in the towers and several storeys were inserted with access by an 'inside staircase'. Secondary towers were arranged around what amounted to a central 'keep'. The whole structure took on the appearance of a small medieval castle, but we must not forget that these imposing structures were built entirely of big blocks with no mortar. The function of the nuraghi is far from being completely clear, but, like other Mediterranean monuments of that type, they were undoubtedly both sanctuaries and defensive towers.

143 Nuraghic village of Barumini (Sardinia)

'Nuraghic villages' grew up in the shadow of these monuments. The huts, with low, circular dry-stone walls, were probably covered with branches and thatch. Near the village dry-stone enclosures served as cattle pens; the dead rested in hypogea or 'Giants' Tombs'; places of worship were provided and sacred springs were protected by structures consisting of an encircling wall approached by a flight of steps and sometimes roofed with a cupola or with large stone slabs.

The Sardinians exploited the local ore, but only belatedly. At first they imported Cypriot copper. In the earliest nuraghi, copper ingots in the shape of oxhides have been found, typical of the Aegean world. The first copper and bronze tools were also imported from the east: axe-adzes or double-ended axes. Around 800 BC Sardinia was trading with the western world, and finds at, for example, Monte Sa Idda, include swords with narrow points, the famous 'carp's-tongue' swords, which were the fortune of the Atlantic zone from Brittany to Spain. Similarly finds of palstaves and two rings of Iberian make testify to lively trade with the west. In that period of great prosperity the finest nuraghi were constructed and the remarkable bronze statuettes, or bronzetti, which were housed in the sanctuaries, were beginning to be produced in abundance. These bronzes, which are the

144 The 'tribal chief' (*left*) and an archer (*right*)   nuraghic bronzetti (eighth century BC)

glory of the museum in Cagliari, are datable to somewhere between 700 and 500 BC and are surprising for their expressiveness, shape, and their modernism. Archers stretch their bows or carry them casually on their shoulders. The faithful greet the deity by raising the right arm as though to take an oath. Others argue, fight or carry vases of offerings. There are touching scenes involving both masculine and feminine figures, a mother and child or a weeping woman holding on her lap a son who had been killed or wounded in battle, a true Pietà. Animal art is no less vivid. Bulls and stags claim a large part for themselves, as they

145 Aegean ship, fresco at Thera, Minoan period

do in the rock carvings of the late Bronze Age in Italy. The Sardinians were artists in bronze as well as wonderful architects.

So the barbarians had raised remarkable architectural creations in the western Mediterranean. The 'civilised' peoples, Greeks, Latins, Etruscans and Carthaginians were about to consume each other in the attempt to win control of the seas. In their thirst for conquest they brought the distinctive cultures of the large islands to a brutal end. In the sixth century Barumini was destroyed and Sardinia conquered by the Carthaginians. Corsica was the subject of bitter fighting between the Phoenicians – who founded Alalia in 564 BC – the Etruscans and the Carthaginians. In the Balearics, Greeks and Carthaginians were in conflict: but except in Ibiza and Formentera, which were occupied by the latter, the conquest seems to have penetrated less deeply into the life of the Talayot culture which continued for some while, well into historic times.

Chapter 9

Carved Stones, Stelae and Statue-Menhirs

Some peoples then were past masters in the art of architecture and had built castles and grandiose tombs. Others had achieved complete mastery of metals and were unrivalled as creators of works of art in gold and bronze. Still others had learned to form clay into splendid pots or were master-craftsmen in wood and cane. But barbarian art took many forms and a whole art of rock carving flourished both on the glacial rocks of Scandinavia and in the high peaks of the Alps: the themes occur again frequently on stelae and rock or cave walls here and there in Europe.

Curiously, it is a sprightly concrete art which was to bring all these Bronze Age men, in their joys and sorrows, to life, with countless scenes of everyday existence, very patriarchal and agricultural in the Alps, hingeing on boats and travel in the north. Warfare is brilliantly depicted, too, by very many representations of weapons or by showing actual battle scenes. Hunting, too, has a place of honour as the indispensable complement to agricultural resources. This figurative art presents a strange contrast with the abstract or symbolic style which decorated not only humble everyday pottery but also the weapons of war through the greater part of the Bronze Age. Cave art, on the other hand, was far removed from the 'old European geometrical style', indulging in exuberance – nowadays we might even say lack of inhibition – but in those happy days there was no need for psychiatrists and sociologists.

For a long while all this art was unknown, or appeared to be unknown, first because it would have meant going to places that were inaccessible, at least at certain times of the year, to find the carvings; and then, too, because for a long while they were seen as examples of witchcraft, the fruits of witches' sabbaths. Indeed the uninhibited quality of some scenes may well have shocked puritan souls. Merry little Bronze Age men were hardly ashamed of their virility and sometimes they even added on a bit. . . . And there was a tendency to see in them simply the products of mountain shepherds amusing themselves.

Dating was difficult, moreover. Certain groups of carvings consisting of thousands of figures were certainly not made at one sitting. The same places were frequented over thousands of years and bits were remodelled, different periods were juxtaposed right down to the Middle Ages. Nothing could be decided until progress in prehistory and typology of bronze weapons made it possible to identify the carvings. Very soon, in the Alps, halberds and swords were recognised dating the greater part of those carvings to the Bronze Age. In Scandinavia the great S-shaped trumpets proved beyond all doubt to be representations of the famous lurs, so dear to Bronze Age musicians. The study of these rock carvings is making great strides at the present time both in northern and southern Europe. One of the surprising things is to discover, from examination of these 'petroglyphs', that beyond the schools and regional variations there is a homogeneity which reveals a common attitude of mind in the European world of the Bronze Age.

Scandinavian rock carvings: boats

From the end of the last century a relationship has been recognised between the bronze weapons found in excavations and those carved on rocks in Scandinavia. Not only can the drawings and the objects be compared, but in some Bronze Age tombs like the one at Kivik, the funeral slabs themselves are adorned with carvings of a type similar to those on rocks scattered about the Scandinavian landscape. H. Nilsson drew the parallels as early as 1862. Identification of weapons rapidly became a means of dating, inaugurated in 1869 by B. E. Hilbrand, who recognised the typological characteristics of the Bronze Age swords. Since then, numerous representations of razors or horns, like the ones at Wismar, have led to more accurate dating of this art, which flourished principally from the middle Bronze Age on into the Iron Age. Detailed discussion between the specialists is still very academic, as witness publications which followed the appearance of Sverre Marstrander's work on the carvings in the Oestfold district, south of Stockholm. A complete catalogue of the different districts, which would allow comparisons to be made, is still a long way off.

The main groups of carvings appear in southern Scandinavia. In present-day Sweden there are large numbers in the Malmö district, around Lake Vanern, on the coasts of Bohüslan and in some of the islands, like Götland in the Baltic. They continue along the frontier with Norway in the Oestfold district, but also further west, on the coast in Rogaland or further north in Trondeland where the main concentrations are found. Denmark also has numerous rock carvings, often isolated, but with some groups as well, like the one on the island of Bornholm.

146 (*left*) Scandinavian rock carving with boat, Bohüslan (Sweden)
147 (*right*) Scandinavian rock carving with boat, Ostergötland (Sweden)

Frequently the carvings appear in open country, in the middle of woods and fields, on large smooth surfaces, polished by glaciers long ago. The carvings often depict complex scenes with lines of people amongst boats, peasants ploughing, symbols (both solar and other) and weapons including the inevitable halberd – and boats.

The boat frequently figures in them, confirming the importance of the theme of navigation, whether temporal or spiritual. For the scenes could equally well represent daily activities or impressions of the afterlife. We will leave aside the question of interpretation for the moment – it is always subjective anyway – and apply ourselves to discovering how the ships were constructed, since they obviously represent contemporary models.

The oldest representations simply show a line turning upwards at both ends, to give a schematic impression of the poop and the prow, with short vertical lines running off from them. These are raised oars or even the sailors themselves, very stylised. These carvings are early, some, no doubt, even dating back to the Neolithic. They are identical with the ones found, for example, in the passage grave at Mané-Lud in Brittany. But soon the ship became more complicated: a second line represented the keel fitted with a spur. The prow and poop became higher still and twisted, ending in stern posts in the form of monsters – dragons, serpents, themes which were to be taken up again by the Viking lords, which shows the tenacity of regional maritime traditions. The rowers became more and more numerous, with up to twenty pairs of oars, and in certain carvings there seem to have been two banks of oarsmen. Sails continue to be an exception and representations of them are hotly discussed. One of the carvings at Ekjeberg seems to show two steering oars. Certainly a whole fleet of swift ships propelled by oars must have forged their way gaily over the Baltic, the North Sea and the Atlantic. No wrecks of Bronze Age boats are known in Scandinavia, but a more recent craft, with its keel extended to form spurs and dating from the Iron Age, was discovered in the peat-bog at Hjortspring. This boat measured 18m and contained iron javelins; it was astonishingly like the boats in the rock carvings. Pollen analysis confirmed its date to around 400 BC.

In the boats carved on the rocks little men are often moving about, wielding halberds or playing lurs. Some of them even have an acrobatic quality or seem to be being thrown overboard. Are they divers or is it a picture of a naval battle? Often there are pictures dealing with everyday life, but not always, and it is probable that these carvings had a religious significance as well. It is impossible otherwise to explain solar discs, frequently associated with boats, which are then transformed into the vessels of the Sun God. They have a role too in funeral ritual and boats transporting the souls of the dead over the oceans beyond the grave have turned the head of many an archaeologist.

Other, more finely executed, boats decorate the razors of the Nordic Bronze Age. Sometimes we find further details in them: the probable existence of a great fan-shaped sail and, on one of them, a row of little circles along the gunwales which could be interpreted as a row of bucklers, without in any way trying to see in them forerunners of the Viking craft.

Fertility cults

In the repertoire of rock carvings, agricultural scenes, particularly scenes of ploughing, play a major part. Generally a ploughman is driving a team consisting of a pair of oxen. They pull a big ard made of a piece of forked wood. The draught animal was the ox, only exceptionally the horse, which was reserved for a role in religion or warfare: for war chariots in the Mediterranean world or for cult chariots in temperate Europe like the famous Trundholm sun chariot. The plough was wooden. A forked branch was cut and the longest part was attached to the team while the other, shortened and stronger, was shaped into a ploughshare. A second piece of wood which was slotted through a hole level with the ploughshare was used to guide the team. Other ards have been found in Nordic peat-bogs. The one from Hvoslev in Jutland was recovered from a small bog which yielded a sub-boreal date by pollen analysis; that is, at the end of the Nordic Bronze Age. It was made of ash. Subsequently many other ards were found of slightly later date, ranging from the middle of the first millennium to the beginning of the Christian era. Oak and birch were used too. Another more recent model was made of several pieces, the main one for the shaft or the beam, a second for the share which would be shod with iron later, and a third for the stilt.

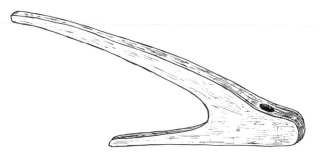

148 Type of wooden ard, Nordic Bronze Age

149 Ard with team of bullocks, rock carving, Bohüslan (Sweden)

It was thought that these ards must have been thrown into peat-bogs during some kind of sacred ceremony. Professor P. V. Glob laboured this point, referring to a great many spring ploughing rites described by ethnographers. Certain ards made of soft wood could only have been used for a first ploughing, probably symbolic. Moreover the presence of some ithyphallic figures in the carvings has been linked with this probable fertility cult. Ploughing was also one of the rituals in certain funeral ceremonies; that is how the presence of furrows under some tumuli in areas unsuitable for agriculture and apparently uncultivated outside the bounds of the tumulus have been interpreted. So gradually the religious customs of the barbarian world are taking shape. It is known how persistent these farming rites were, those associated with ploughing and harvest, and only the mechanisation of agriculture has finally destroyed them in our own countryside – and not so very long ago. It is possible that the ploughing scenes carved on rocks were also linked with periodic ceremonies celebrating nature and the return of the sowing season. We are a long way from the trivial pastimes of shepherds!

Val Camonica

Hidden in the Italian Alps, Val Camonica in northern Brescia shelters the most extraordinary series of rock carvings of the proto-historic world. After being hidden for a very long while under moss and earth piled up through the centuries, they only came to light again quite recently. However, tradition had preserved the memory of strange or wonderful sites, which it was perhaps not always wise to frequent, as placenames in the area remind us: 'Witches' Peak', or the 'Fairy Horn'. But occasionally shepherds made bold and in about 1914 they went so far as to talk to a professor in Brescia, G. Laend, who was the first to inform the learned world of the existence of these petroglyphs. Gradually further discoveries were made but it was chiefly the work of Emmanuel Anati, from 1956 on, that revealed the splendours of Val Camonica.

Anati's first expedition was carried out with the help of painters from Montparnasse, with just whatever means came to hand. But the harvest from this initial campaign was so eloquent that soon official encouragement and material assistance, both French and Italian, proliferated. A series of publications catalogued this amazing find and made it known to a wide public. Studies and conferences have been continuously analysing this world of carvings revealing the social, domestic and religious life of the Bronze Age. There can be no question of giving more than the broad outlines here.

One of the main interests of Val Camonica comes from the amazing duration of this art which stretches from the end of the Neolithic down to historic Etruscan and Latin civilisations. So we can watch here the gradual evolution of proto-historic tools, weapons and social customs.

In this way progress in weaponry can be followed because the likenesses are faithful and easily identifiable with bronze models used at the same time in Europe. Only in Period I, the earliest, are weapons less numerous and their identification more doubtful. By contrast, from the beginning of Period II there is an abundance of small ribbed daggers, reminiscent of the Chalcolithic culture of Remedello. They are accompanied by halberds, the actual 'type fossils' of the early Bronze Age. The earliest have long handles and rather rigid blades like the Italian ones or the daggers from the Iberian culture of El Argar. At the beginning of Period III of the Camonican art, daggers are evolving, the handles are ending in fine crescent-shaped pommels, which occur again in the Aegean world, at Mycenae itself. Halberds, with handles that are shorter now, and sturdier blades, indicate some central European influence from Únětice. At the end of Period III, swords or daggers with leaf-shaped blades are datable to the late Bronze Age, that is to the period of the Urnfield culture. Finally Period IV sees the unfolding of a whole new defensive weaponry: crested helmets, sometimes fitted with little tubes at the sides, which make the warriors look oddly like modern motorcyclists, or even, in the eyes of the more imaginative, like Martians or extra-terrestrial beings. In reality they are simply the helmets with crests or tubes which are classically identified with Italianate or Etruscan Iron Age cultures.

Carts; the ard

Carts and vehicles show a different type of evolution. A representation of a two-wheeled chariot can be compared with war chariots on Mycenaean stelae. Pictures of four-wheeled carts are more frequent. Carts pulled by oxen are often associated with wooden ards, also pulled by cattle. They are the same as we have already seen in the Scandinavian rock carvings. Moreover wooden ards have been found in peat-bogs in Italy and even, from the late Bronze Age, at Lake Ledro.

Later carts were pulled by mules or horses. They date from the Iron Age and certain details of the body are reminiscent of traces found in funeral carts of the early Iron Age.

Ards had evolved, too, and in the most recent scenes became a composite whole with a more sophisticated share and one or sometimes two stilts. The evolution in technique was the same as in Northern Europe.

Primitive ards certainly cut furrows, but because they lacked a coulter or blade they

150 Houses on piles, rock carving, Val Camonica

left great clods which had to be broken up with hoes. This is the explanation of the little figures in the Val Camonica carvings, following an ox-drawn ard carrying adzes to finish the job: an interesting example of the way agricultural work was organised.

Many other aspects of rural life are depicted: geese or ducks for example were plentiful in that marshy land; there were horses, cattle, goats, sheep, pigs, not to mention dogs which must have been domesticated. In this district of lakes fishing supplied an important element in the diet and there are carvings of fish being caught in nets or wicker pots. But hunting has the place of honour in the carving of Val Camonica with a host of scenes which celebrate the stag, either singly or in herds. Stags are caught in nets, trapped or driven into enclosures; they are attacked with lances or even pursued with packs of trained hounds. We have here an indication of the noble rite of hunting and also of the sacred nature of the stag, a horned, male symbol essential in the religion of the age. This is confirmed by the imposing size of some of these pictures of stags and by the occurrence of pictures of stag-men, no longer the quarry but the Stag God.

The Stag God

The religious role of the carvings is beyond dispute. Many of the figures are at prayer in attitudes of adoration with both arms raised. Others plainly have the accoutrements of sorcerers and in some scenes they seem to be conducting ceremonious rituals or funerals. The corpse lies on the ground, surrounded by his mourning family, his precious weapons laid around him. This tradition is illustrated, for instance, on late Bronze Age stelae in the Iberian peninsula or the South of France. Lastly there is the supreme deity, represented symbolically in many of the scenes, the Sun. Sometimes it is a disc emitting rays, but it can be changed into a circle, a dotted circle or a wheel. Often it is associated with man, but female representations are rare. There is even one instance of a wheel directly associated with the phallus of a male figure. Sun-Male-Stag or Ox: these are the key symbols in Bronze Age ritual.

But it is not all ritual and religion: many of the scenes tell anecdotes from everyday life. There is the smithy with its anvils and hammers and perhaps even some rudimentary bellows; weavers with their great wooden looms fitted with weights are often honoured as well. Last, woodwork and house-building provide us with valuable documentation too. The houses were made of wood and built on a platform: access was by an outside ladder. The roofs were ridged and the timbers large. But as Emmanuel Anati observed, there is great variety in the 600 illustrations of dwellings. They range from a simple hut to little wooden chalets executed with great care, indicating a society which, despite its patriarchal aspects, experienced profound social distinctions marking the economic standing of the individual. At the end of Period IV, there even seem to have been a few more imposing houses for chieftains, real little castles intended to keep watch over the lord's territory.

161

The society of Val Camonica, as we have tried to interpret it, seems to have led an enclosed existence, accepting technical innovations from outside, it is true, but forming a closed world, wisely keeping aloof from the great upheavals that were shaking Europe. This society of artisans and tillers of the soil, which was also a people of hunters and fishers, has left the modern world the most vivid testimony possible of the manners and customs of the Bronze Age.

The whole sequence of Val Camonica carving is not an isolated phenomenon. Towards the west, both in the South of France and in the north of the Iberian peninsula a whole proto-historic cave art developed and is at present being studied extensively.

Mont Bego and the Val des Merveilles

The centre of the earliest known Alpine cave art is on the Franco-Italian frontier and follows its vagaries through the course of contemporary history. In the neighbourhood of Tende, in a glaciated hollow dominated by the 2873m of Mont Bego, a wild region lies hidden away, snow-covered and inaccessible for a great part of the year. Precipitous rocks with evocative names like Pic du Diable or Testa dell'Inferno dominate the string of Lacs d'Enfer, and it is there, on grey or red schist polished by the glaciers, that an extraordinary series of some 50,000 carvings were made; there may be even more, according to the latest census. They flourish at an altitude of between 2000 and 2750m. Maurice Louis has already drawn attention, in his guide to Mont Bego, to the fact that they were mentioned as early as 1650 by Gioffredo, the historian of the Alpes Maritimes but that, there again, they were seen at the time as no more than 'lively jokes' attributable at the most to a few rough shepherds. In 1877, Emile Rivière was sent there by the French government and brought back some sketches and descriptions which he presented to the learned assembly of the French Association for the Advancement of Science. But the 'discoverer of Alpine cave art', to repeat an expression of J. Combier, was an Englishman, Clarence Bicknell, who devoted the greater part of his life to it, as the result of a combination of circumstances. The young Clarence was delicate, and after studying brilliantly at Cambridge, he left the mists of Britain and sailed towards the Mediterranean, eventually settling at Bordighera in 1878. As a botanist he used to go collecting plants in the mountains until the day when he stood thunderstruck, looking at the first carvings of the Val des Merveilles. The naturalist became an archaeologist and that seems to have been beneficial to his health, since he reached the respectable age of 76. At that time, in 1918, he left records of more than 12,000 carvings, preserved in the museums at Bordighera and Genoa: this documentation is the more precious in that since then erosion has blurred if not destroyed some of the carvings which were the earliest to be described, not to mention the depredations of war.

Many Italian scholars have carried on Bicknell's work, in particular Carlo Conti who started a systematic catalogue and published a first series of records. The last war brought

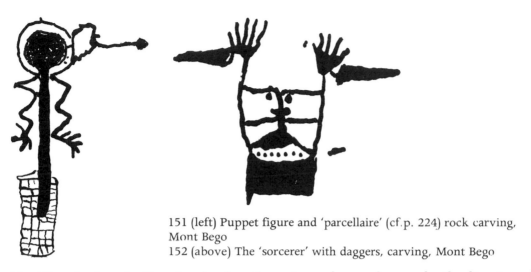

151 (left) Puppet figure and 'parcellaire' (cf.p. 224) rock carving, Mont Bego
152 (above) The 'sorcerer' with daggers, carving, Mont Bego

Mont Bego back under French rule. Since then a team of researchers under the direction of Professor H. de Lumley has been engaged in extending the written accounts and ensuring photographic records of the carvings.

Around Mont Bego the pictures are distributed in great sectors; Carlo Conti distinguished twenty, based on the nature of the objects represented or the sites, but also on reasons of convenience in publishing. They can in fact be grouped in three main centres: the first stretches from the region of the Lakes to the Vallée des Merveilles; the second is centred on the area around Fontanalba, where Clarence Bicknell had a little chalet built so that he could pursue his work there; the third is more remote, in the neighbourhood of the Sabbione Pass. There do not seem to have been any notable chronological differences between the groups.

The carvings were executed by pecking, using an instrument that was harder than the schist, made of quartz or flint and, no doubt, of metal, bronze and, later, iron. Sometimes the whole carving is pecked, but often the artist seems to have wearied of his work and left it unfinished. In other pictures, only the outlines are dotted. Life-sized daggers were engraved, no doubt, by drawing carefully round the contours of the object which was placed against the rock.

153 Carvings from Mont Bego

163

The first studies carried out at the Val des Merveilles simply aimed at dividing the objects into categories: horns or horned animals, weapons, human figures, enigmatic or geometric shapes. Progress in the study of rock carvings has made it possible now to identify chronological sequences, although research of that nature requires a good deal of caution.

In 1960, on the strength of his experience in Val Camonica, Emmanuel Anati attempted a classification of the Mont Bego carvings. He distinguishes a first phase, characterised by pictures of horns, enclosures and mazes. It could go back to a very early, Neolithic period. It is always difficult to make a direct link between carvings and material from excavations, but we must stress that one stratum at Val des Merveilles yielded some very early Neolithic pottery of the Cardial or impressed shell type, datable to before the third millennium. Phase II of the valley belongs beyond any doubt to the earliest Metal Ages, with daggers and the inevitable halberds. Horned objects are more varied, and some twisted horns could represent ibex. Phase III is more classic and includes teams of oxen pulling the Bronze Age ard, triangular-bladed daggers, swords, axes and, in the most recent period, more complex scenes of a religious or mythological nature. The latest weapons herald the Iron Age.

The catalogue of objects in the Mont Bego carvings is less wide-ranging than in Val Camonica. The carvings are stiffer and there are no large compositions. We should stress, however, that this set is not yet known in its entirety, but in many respects, what we know already is distinctive and attractive.

Symbols and interpretations

Teams of oxen, often stylised with a rectangular, pecked head, equipped with two large horns, are among the most distinctive figures, as are small men waving halberds with enormous handles, four to five times as tall as themselves. Sorcerers draw amazing compositions. The 'tribal chief' in a praying posture decked out with a horn on his chest wears a kind of chasuble over an animal skin. The 'evil genius', the 'dancing girl' and the 'Christ' are so many curious human figures. Some geometrical drawings are interpreted as houses or stockyards. But others, more mysterious, seem to be symbolic signs and have been thought at times to be hieroglyphs or even a primitive script, but the hypothesis

154 Stags engraved on a rock, Peyra Escrita (Pyrénées Orientales)

remains unverified and unverifiable. The great mass of the Mont Bego carvings, however, returns to the classic themes of proto-historic cave art mentioned above: horns, the ard, weapons and male figures. Serpents seem to join these traditional subjects, which is hardly surprising in an area where even today there are places where vipers are said to abound.

The centres at Mont Bego and Val Camonica were two exceptional poles in proto-historic cave art. In Val Camonica a society with a talent for graphic art continued the tradition for millennia. At Mont Bego, which is more inaccessible, it seems likely that the phases of occupation were only temporary, associated with the movements of shepherds who were already practising transhumance. Another theory sees them as religious centres where at certain times of year, such as springtime, people came to carve ploughing scenes in order to make sure of a good harvest. The long walk to reach these remote places was a kind of ordeal which was endured to propitiate the gods, a tradition which continues in our own day with the rite of pilgrimage. The carving could represent the same act of faith as the modern ex-voto which people deposit at Lourdes after a long pilgrimage. But of course these are only theories and highly debatable.

155 Ard and team of bullocks, Mont Bego

Languedoc, Iberia and the British Isles

Outside these great centres of cave art, there is a scattering of carvings, often more difficult to interpret, along the southern edge of the Massif Central from the Alpes Maritimes to the Pyrenees. At an early stage they attracted the attention of that great specialist in Palaeolithic carvings, the Abbé Breuil, the 'pope of prehistory'. Indeed his knowledge of cave art was universal; he showed himself at times to be an excellent proto-historian and did not fight shy of a study of the Metal Ages. He pointed out the interest of these southern carvings and since then recent investigations and discoveries have brought the question to the fore again: it has been studied for Languedoc and the Pyrenees in very many publications by Abbé Glory and by J. Guilaine and J. Abelanet, while J. Combier has published an exhaustive catalogue of the carvings on grottoes and sites in Ardèche. Dating and interpretation of these small pictorial groups are a delicate matter. A very early section may draw its sources from the Iberian peninsula. An ancient storehouse of pictures may go right back to the Mesolithic and come on down through the Neolithic, but a large part of the carvings containing human figures are attributed to the Metal Ages – mainly Chalcolithic and Bronze Age.

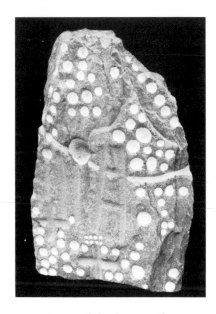

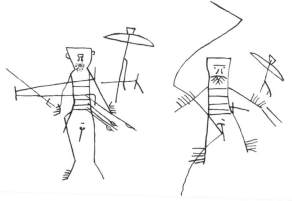

156 (*left*) Rock with cup-mark engravings (Denmark)
157 (*above*) Human figures, crossbow shapes, engravings from Peyra Escrita (Pyrénées Orientales)

Some of the human figures are reminiscent of the ones in Mont Bego or Val Camonica with characters in a praying posture. The wheel and the circle appear again and a few wagons – but these are more distorted and hypothetical. However a tendency to schematic treatment led to curious matchstick figures of which the modern painter, Bernard Buffet, would not be ashamed. Man became a kind of disjointed puppet, waving stick-fingers at the end of arms represented by a single line. Other signs became crossbow-shaped, roof-shaped or just shapeless. Alongside the human figures groups of dots are recorded like the purplish-red ones round the man in the Gilles grotto in Ardèche. Other signs are cruciform, 'cup-marks' or the curious horseshoes which have sometimes been seen as the final derivation from the face of the Neolithic Mother Goddess. Signs painted in the form of stars or dotted circles have recently been discovered in Savoy, in the Trou de la Féclaz, showing this art extending northwards.

In other regions of France sites with carvings or paintings, often forming large groups, have been attributed to the Metal Ages. A few petroglyphs in Loire-Inférieure, with cruciform and cup shapes have been compared with signs in Galicia and Ireland and taken to be the marks of Bronze Age prospectors. Unfortunately it is often impossible to distinguish them from Christian symbols which flourished subsequently in historic times. It seems, likewise, that the strange sculpted rocks at Saint Aubin de Baubigné in Deux-Sèvres which bring together both signs and human figures also belong, in the main, to historic times.

Iberia is rich in post-Palaeolithic cave art which continued into the Metal Ages as Professor E. Ripoll Perello has shown. A distinctive centre developed in Galicia and Portugal and Emmanuel Anati has recently been engaged in tracing its evolution. Realistic figures appear from the Neolithic onwards. In the Chalcolithic, idols reminiscent of the Mother-Goddess statues are accompanied by weapons: daggers, but also long, tanged swords analogous with the copper weapons recovered in Spain. In the Bronze Age the daggers diversify, solar images appear as do figures which often have the appearance of 'sorcerers'. Abstract art seems to predominate in the Iron Age: wheels, palettes and mazes proliferate, accompanied by new shapes like the swastikas.

Another mysterious sign is the cup-mark found in many European Bronze Age groups, particularly in the British Isles, where the work of R. Morris has made them better known. In Scotland, E. W. Mackensie has recorded numerous series. They are common in the county of Argyll, among others. They adorn natural rock-faces, as at Kilmichael, where cup-marks of different sizes, sometimes associated or linked together, form a language which has remained indecipherable. But they may also adorn standing stones. At Temple Wood the central stone of a stone circle is adorned with cup-marks in this way. Bronze Age burial chambers are themselves covered with cup-marks and with pictures of weapons – an interesting detail which enables us to date some of the cup-marks. In the tumulus at Ri Cruin, again in Argyll, there are flat axes and a halberd associated with cup-shaped marks.

Stelac and statue-menhirs: the last Mother Goddesses

Wall art cannot be treated separately from the stelae and statue-menhirs which combine statuary and graphic art. The same themes recur. We have seen that some of the horseshoe signs on the grottoes and rocks of the South of France could be considered as the very last derivatives of the representations of Mother Goddesses which were common in the Chalcolithic of Provence and Languedoc.

Pictures of weapons are common both to the statues and to the rocks. We may recall briefly the weapons of the statue-menhirs of Corsica, but still nearer to Val Camonica, the amazing group of stelae which was discovered in the region of Lunigiana in Italy and constitutes the main curiosity of the Museum in Spezia. There is a recurrence of the tradition of the Neolithic idol with schematic nose, the same position of the arms which end in clumsy fingers, pairs of breasts and sometimes the 'object', in the shape of a crook, which the gods of the South of France seemed to appreciate. Often in the Lunigiana statues it tends

167

158 (*above left*) Late Neolithic Stela of Sant'Anna d'Alfaedo (Verona, Italy)
159 and 160 (*above centre and right*) Stelae from the Lunigiana area (La Spezia, Italy)

to become a handled axe. But there are many differences between them and the statues of the South of France. First of all some of the heads are carved in a crescent and call to mind the two-cornered hat of the *carabinier*; then there is the presence – and this is the most important thing – of daggers with cruciform pommels which are somewhat analogous with the pictures in Val Camonica and which date the statues at La Spezia to the Chalcolithic and the Bronze Age.

The statue of Filetto II undeniably shows on its sides a dagger with antennae pommel which brings us on into the Iron Age. So it seems that this astonishing series of stelae had a long life, a phenomenon we have already observed in Val Camonica.

Still in Val Camonica, one of the carvings depicts a dead warrior, surrounded by his family and his weapons: some of the carved Iberian and southern French stelae of the end of the Bronze Age are in the same vein. The most famous is the one at Solana de Cabanas, Caceres; the warrior is depicted on the right, lying on his back; near his shoulder a mirrror and a razor testify to his personal vanity. At the top of the slab are grouped his array of offensive weapons: a spearhead and a great leaf-shaped sword. The centre of the composition is occupied by a large shield, crescent-shaped at the sides and adorned with small bosses. In the lower part a four-wheeled, horse-drawn wagon is depicted. So all the classic themes of Bronze Age cave art right across Europe are there.

In the South of France another carved stela, which is to be found at present in the museum at Montpellier, comes from Substantion (or Sextantio) in Hérault. The drawing is more difficult to recognise but the great late Bronze Age shield decorated with concentric circles and cut away to a crescent shape at the side, a spearhead and at least three wheels

161 (*far left*) Stela from Sextantio (Hérault)
162 (*left*) Statue-menhir from Saint Bénézet (Gard)

can be clearly distinguished. The sides of the limestone block are decorated with more abstract geometric signs.

The typical symbolism of the Bronze Age recurs in these stelae: evocations of travel and the sun, by means of chariots and wheels, and the glorification of the masculine hero surrounded by his weapons. Moreover, at Substantion, two small motifs represent flight: those sacred ducks, first known in the Dupljaja chariot and which will proliferate in the Hallstatt period.

163 Rock engraving: daggers, 'parcellaire' (cf. p. 224), dignitary with pectoral, Mont Bego

164 Bronze mask, Kleinklein (Styria, Austria), Hallstatt period

The precursors of the Celts

The end of the second and the beginning of the first millennium BC saw an acceleration in progress towards history. Soon we shall meet the names of our nearest forebears – such as the Gauls. Great human and cultural upheavals were to affect Europe, with the appearance of people of the Urnfield culture, then of the Hallstatt horsemen. They are often described as the harbingers of the 'Celtic invasions', but many of these groups, or those deriving from them, were to beget ethnic units other than the Celts: for if we find proto-Celts in western or central Europe, we shall also see, further north, proto-Germans or proto-Slavs appearing, and further south, proto-Illyrians or proto-Thracians.

Now is a period of great changes, the true proto-historic period.

Chapter 10

Lake-Dwellings and Urnfields

The winter of 1853–4 is a landmark in the annals of European prehistory. It was one of the driest and coldest of the century and, in Switzerland, this led to an unusual lowering in the level of the lakes, since water remained locked in the glaciers. Here was an unexpected opportunity for the dwellers along the shores of Lake Zürich, to enlarge their small vineyard plots. Everyone hastened to build walls as near as possible to the low water level and the areas thus marked out by dykes were filled with silt and loam from the lakes. But that proved not at all easy: whole strange networks of wooden stakes made the task extremely tricky. Moreover strange objects were picked up: bits of pot, bone and antler, not to mention metal objects, particularly bronze.

The villages on piles in the Swiss lakes

All this was not surprising since fishermen in the Swiss lakes had often cursed these submerged posts on which their nets regularly got caught. But little attention was paid to them; generally the objects themselves were thrown back into the water without more ado, and it was only exceptionally that a few antlers or potsherds were taken to the local museum. Some districts yielded quantities of pottery and the story is told of small vases, more or less intact at the time, being used as targets for shooting practice! Venerable proto-historic pottery was a good substitute for the earthenware pipes of shooting ranges.

But at Zürich the veritable forest of stakes that was uncovered, the abundance of bronze objects, including some very fine axes of unusual shape, eventually intrigued people. It was decided to bring them to the notice of the learned authorities. The people at Ober-Meilen broached the matter to their schoolmaster, Johannes Aeppli, who, in turn advised the distinguished Dr Ferdinand Keller, who already enjoyed a reputation as an archaeologist, founder of the Züricher Antiquarische Gesellschaft, excavator of tumuli and a well read and much travelled man of culture. The ideas of Thomsen, the Dane, were already known in archaeological circles all over Europe, and Keller had come to support them. He undertook the first systematic investigations. His conclusion was quite clear:

these were traces of prehistoric villages. The stakes had been used to support platforms on which houses had been built and later burned down. These *Pfahlbauten* or structures on piles were the subject of a report by Keller as early as 1854.

This small work had a great success all over Europe, and in the lake districts of Switzerland, Italy and eastern France, people began looking for and finding these *palafittes*, a term (from the Italian *palo*, a stake, and *fitto*, pushed into the ground) proposed by E. Desor following his discoveries in the Lake at Neuchâtel. A few more dry years like 1858 and 1859 brought about some magnificent harvests. In addition to collecting objects, E. Desor was trying to reconstruct the early chronological sequences. Despite the undeniably serious qualities of his research, the methods he used, in common with many other investigators of the day, raise a smile nowadays. Outside the dried areas 'fishing for objects' went on amidst the submerged pickets. A drawing by E. Desor even shows his 'fisherman', B. Kopp, at work in his punt. He is using two main implements – a 'hand-hoe', a spade with a long handle for dragging axes up from the bottom as if they were oysters or clams, and a pair of 'tweezers with handles' on the end of a piece of string, by means of which small objects like pins and knives could be gathered in. Primitive tools of these heroic periods of archaeology!

Nevertheless many of E. Desor's observations are still valuable. He observed that the stakes were sometimes driven into the silt, sometimes held in place by heaps of stone blocks, brought from the bank to support them in rocky places. These heaps formed small submerged hillocks which the lakeside people called *ténevières*, and could measure more than 80m in length, as at Auvernier. There was even a dug-out canoe full of these big

165 Tools from Swiss lake settlements: winged axes, sickle, socketed axe (Morges) and horse bit (Corcelettes)

172

blocks that was recovered. This craft, which was too light, had sunk while being used in a transport operation and could not be refloated. Desor observed, too, the distribution of the sites and introduced the now famous names of Cortaillod, Auvernier and Corcelettes. F. Keller, for his part, continued to gather together all the information on the lake-dwellings, which he was the first to 'invent'.

In France other pioneers like L. Rabut started investigations on the shores of the Lac du Bourget in Savoy in about 1860. Gradually a whole vast literature was devoted to the lake-dwellings which had their moment of glory at the beginning of this century. Even school textbooks popularised the romantic image of these wooden huts, built on piles emerging from the midst of the waters. At the same time there was a keen trade in finds from excavations and from barefaced looting. In the showcases or storerooms of more than one museum in Europe can be found pottery or metal remains, christened 'lake-dwelling' pots and bronzes, often with no more accurate provenance.

166 Reconstruction of a lake settlement, as envisaged at the beginning of this century

Besides the pins, axes and potsherds, carbonised organic material was often found, particularly remains of food. This too was a revelation. Plant debris, burned or not, had been marvellously preserved throughout millennia of uninterrupted submersion in the depths of the water and provided remarkable evidence: basketry, woven matting, wicker baskets, bowls and wooden vessels. In 1865, E. Desor was able to draw up a whole list of the food of these prehistoric groups: apples, cherries, beechnuts, strawberries, raspberries and even water chestnuts, nowadays almost vanished from Switzerland. Since then a few grape pips have been discovered which lead us to suspect that grapes were grown from the beginning of the Bronze Age.

The 'myth of the lake cities'

Studies have obviously proliferated since that time. Not much credence is given now to the idea of the great lake cities, erected in the middle of the lakes. In 1958, O. Paret denounced the 'myth of the lake cities' which had enchanted generations of young prehistorians. There was lively controversy between the protagonists of genuine 'lake' settlements and those who thought that these houses on piles were simply raised up on the edges of the lakes, in muddy or marshy areas which in themselves offered some kind of natural protection.

For Paret, the dimensions of the stakes are often too slight to support houses, admittedly wooden, whose walls, in the interests of privacy and also of protection against fire, would have had to be liberally coated with a considerable weight of puddled clay. As for the 'breakwaters' which were described as consisting of rows of stakes, O. Paret reckoned that they were very flimsy for lakes where the storms are still powerful enough to smash modern stone-built jetties. The palisades could only have surrounded stockyards, built on dry land. If the lake-dwellings were drowned, it was as a result of climatic deterioration which is vouched for by pollen analysis. They were built and used on dry land and abandoned as soon as they were surrounded by water.

Built near the lakes and occasionally the victims of severe flooding, such then were the 'lake cities'. Moreover the general style of construction in the Bronze Age seems often to have been of the same type: the rock drawings at Val Camonica have shown us single-storey houses entered by means of a ladder. The basement could have been fitted out as an accessory barn or cowshed. Sometimes the houses had stone foundations, particularly in the high mountain areas. E. Vogt and R. Wyss have made remarkable reconstructions of Swiss houses in the Sissach region.

Much modern work, often on the occasion of excavations made necessary by major roadway or urban construction schemes, has enabled us to reconsider the problem of the lake-dwellings, using means very different from those available formerly. Programmes of aerial surveying carried out over the waters in calm weather, have given photographic coverage of the sites and made it possible to reconstruct overall plans on the basis of large numbers of photographs. More recently, a series of remarkable studies by M. Egloff has made it possible to give a general plan of the lake-dwellings at Auvernier, both of the villages and of associated enclosures. This is not always an easy matter. Indeed, in many of the lakes violent currents have often disturbed the structures, leaving a haphazard muddle of broken stakes and giving the archaeologist nothing but a puzzle which is difficult to piece together. Even when they have remained in place, it is difficult to distinguish the series of stakes. More recent stakes have often been driven in beside earlier series. Frequent subsidence of the land may have played a part, too. C. Strahm's excavations at the lake settlement of Yverdon show clearly the complexity of the problem. On that site, with numerous layers going from the Neolithic to the Corded Ware period, careful examination of the stones in the *ténevière*, for example, has been very instructive: there were flat round stones, which were often broken and had obviously been fired. These were not wedging stones, dating from the first period of construction, but a gradual collection of 'heating stones' underneath or near to the dwellings. Pebbles or flat stones were heated, rather as a modern cast-iron griddle might be, in order to cook flat loaves and pieces of meat. This operation, repeated over and over again, caused the stones to break and they were then thrown away. After several decades these composed part of the *ténevière*.

On the ground, or rather under water, the wish to excavate *in situ* has led to the development of a new branch of archaeology: underwater excavation. Archaeologists have become divers and, thanks to modern techniques of pumping, of location by means of balloons or metal staging, of suction cleaning, they can release objects or structures on the spot, identify archaeological layers, register the objects as they leave the water and, in addition, treat the remains of wood and organic matter, using complicated techniques. Many lake sites are being actively excavated in France, by P. Laurent and later A. Bocquet at the Lac du Bourget in Savoy for example, or by M. Petrequin at Clairvaux in the Jura.

167 Kidney-shaped bronze bracelet, lake settlement at Morges (Switzerland)

The lake-dwellings, in or beside the lakes, lasted a long time. They started, in fact, in the Neolithic and continued down to the Iron Age. But the majority date from the Bronze Age and, at the end of that period, they yielded abundant and magnificent metal material, evidence of a booming industry. This production has often been linked with the series of late Bronze Age cultures, known as the Urnfield cultures. We must now turn to their development, which is often obscure and complicated, but without going too far into controversial details about their structure and chronological phases.

The 'second end of the world' in the Aegean

Between 1200 and 1000 BC great changes were taking place throughout Europe, though the causes are far from clear. Again it is the Mediterranean world that first came to the boil. Destruction and catastrophes, both human and natural, followed each other at such a pace that H. van Effenterre did not hesitate to see it as that 'second end of the world' which put an end to the splendours of the Aegean Bronze Age with the final destruction of Mycenae.

Of course destructive invasions have been evoked: bands of blond looters from the north, carrying iron weapons – a very great novelty in metallurgy – are supposed to have sacked and burnt the Achaean citadels. These were the 'Dorians' of Greek legend. Their existence and the part they played are being called into question more and more. No doubt they were merely the occupants of smoking ruins which were the work of others. On the

175

sea, elements of the famous Peoples of the Sea, routed several times by the ships and armies of the Pharaohs, were still prowling around. Falling back towards the Aegean, they might this time have achieved their object, the conquest of a great empire through the total destruction of its cities.

But Greece was not the only land to be completely destroyed in this way: the Anatolian and Syrian coasts were affected too. To explain a phenomenon on that scale repeated seismic upheavals have been suggested – with some appearance of probability: earthquakes may be associated with a devastating volcanic explosion of which there are real signs. The epicentre was in the south of the Cyclades, in the island of Santorini. Small neighbouring islets like Thera are simply the remains of an immense volcanic cone, which still at times emits rumblings and flames. The effects of the 'tsunami' – the tidal wave – of Santorino have been found in the ruins of ancient cities and also in traces of ash beds and burned houses. Radio-carbon dates, however, would tend to place it somewhere around 1500 BC, three centuries before the most important upheavals in the Aegean world. But was there only one eruption? The memory of these cataclysms, perhaps, was at the root of the myth of Atlantis. Oddly, the people of Atlantis are supposed to have been swamped in a Mediterranean tempest.

'Lusatian' and 'Celto-Illyrian' migrations

The causes of these vast destructions remain shrouded in mystery, but a few undeniable facts remain. Around 1200–1000 BC a great change took place in customs, material equipment – with the notable arrival of iron in the Mediterranean countries near the Aegean – and in religious and funerary rites – in particular, cremation became widespread from the Aegean to central Europe. Hounded by the gods, or by men, did whole tribes jostle each other in a gigantic movement of populations? It is difficult to envisage the reality of such a romantic vision; and we come back constantly to the same question: are the appearance of new weapons, new types of pottery, a change in funeral rites, as striking as the replacement of inhumation by cremation on a large scale, always due to a new influx of people?

For a long time people thought so. Long migrations would have started, it was thought, in the distant steppes of eastern Europe. For example, at a time when styles in ceramics were less well known, the illusory notion arose of a 'Lusatian migration' which was thought to have overrun the whole of Europe. Based on a few tubby biconical vases decorated with raised bumps – which are common in Poland and north Germany – this theory was built up, abandoned at one stage, but seems nevertheless to have supporters once more. The 'Lausitz culture' existed, but within its well defined Nordic European confines; it is generally difficult to reconcile it with what was going on further south and west.

Another theory also sees migrations, originating this time in the plains of present-day Hungary, where the rite of cremation in funeral pots spread very early. And indeed a great phenomenon occurred: central Europe was gradually covered with cemeteries in which the ashes of the dead were placed in or beside an urn, often accompanied by broken urns and secondary offertory vases.

Was this widespread phenomenon a sign of a great, uniform culture resulting from the successive arrivals of waves of conquerors of the same origin who subjugated the previous populations? In other words, invasions? The Urnfields have in fact been attributed at times to a preliminary 'Celtic' wave.

This was believed, in the past – and is still believed by some. People have also spoken emphatically of 'Celto-Illyrian migrations', harbingers of the great Celtic expansion that was to take place some centuries later. The nearness in time of the two phenomena and the parallel nature of their movement may encourage belief, but the question still remains highly controversial. For detailed study of the groups, and particularly of those of the so-called preliminary phase, show that there were not always obvious signs of brutal destruction or a clear break with the previous Tumulus culture. The same vision of these preliminary waves of Celts had also, by extension, attached the label 'Proto-Celtic' to the middle Bronze Age Tumulus culture: so the Urnfield peoples would simply have been descendants of the Tumulus people, suffering, at the most, a religious crisis which overthrew their funeral styles, and a series of technical innovations which refashioned their furnishings – both pottery and bronze.

But the complex skein of cross-fertilisation, of local peculiarities which have come to light in the wake of the most recent excavations and studies increasingly pushes this epic theory back into the ranks of romantic daydreams.

And yet. . . . How can we fail to admit certain facts indicating a real diffusion? For we should not go to the other extreme and reach the point, as some would like, of suppressing even the name of Urnfield culture.

Methodical study of the bronzes and pots reveal some undeniable characteristics of regional diffusion and even the appearance of undoubted novelties over wider areas; in short a few general features justifying the title 'Urnfield cultures'.

It is true that the original beginnings and the mechanism of these diffusion phenomena remain unclear. Nevertheless we are aware that 'classic' groups in south Germany, for example, really spread in successive 'waves' southwards. These 'waves' reached France from the east and were followed by diffusion north-westwards and southwards. What exactly are these 'waves' covering? Brutal invasions with the sacking of the villages and settlements of the middle Bronze Age Tumulus culture? This romantic picture, too, becomes blurred in recent studies: we are witnessing a slow impregnation rather than massive migrations. In any case the existence of fortified high places shows that insecurity was indeed the rule. The Urnfield penetration was peaceful at times and at times gave rise to local clashes.

The end of the tumuli: the Fremdkulturen

During the centuries of the middle Bronze Age, the great Tumulus culture had spread over the greater part of Europe. Now the Tumulus peoples would have to come to terms with foreign elements: either new arrivals, bringing with them new funeral rites, originating probably in central Europe – cremation, and soon urnfields – or at least with the rites themselves penetrating westwards by the simple diffusion of new beliefs. Let us repeat: change is rarely brutal; it is only slowly, even insidiously, that something strange and intrusive is taking place in the Tumulus culture. This justifies the German name *Fremdkulturen*, 'foreign cultures', that F. Holste gave to several small groups of people, said to be 'transitional' between the Tumulus and the real Urnfield peoples. They can be placed to about 1200 BC.

168 Rixheim-type sword

169 Lausitz urn, Schlieben (East Germany)

One of the most typical is the Riegsee group, so called after a lake in upper Bavaria. It is known by its tumuli, an ancient tradition, but it cremated its dead, a new 'foreign' tradition. Weaponry changed too. The last *Vollgriffschwerter*, swords with spindle-shaped handles, often decorated with spirals and with bronze hilts, also belong to the Tumulus tradition: but they are gradually replaced by narrow rapiers, with a handle consisting of a simple tang, the Rixheim swords. This was an innovation: the founders were becoming mean with their metal, so the hilt is formed from a simple tang on which supplementary plaques of bone or wood were fastened and held in place by rivets. Small knives with blades curved like a donkey's back accompanied the swords, and this is another novelty in the range of tools. Adornment still consisted of the eternal wheel shapes and a few pendants in the form of bronze spirals. But bracelets testify to the birth of new ornaments: the panels with incised geometric motifs are replaced by hollow cast bracelets with ribbed decoration. Pottery was changing too and we find a decoration of rilling or wide grooves on vases which grow more and more globular or biconical. Finally, the pins, those good indicator fossils of the Bronze Age, diversify. Their heads are adorned with miniature vases, for example, and these vase-headed pins were to last a long time.

The necropolis of La Colombine

In France, several cemeteries in the basin of the lower Seine and its tributaries show notable changes reaching as far as the departments of Yonne, Seine-et-Marne and Aube in particular. One of the most revealing of these necropolises is undoubtedly that of La Colombine at Champlay in Yonne.

Near a ford on the Yonne and a crossing of communication routes, the place was ripe for a settlement. On a slight eminence, it could be easily defended and moreover the area provided good agricultural land, a not unimportant factor. It was known for a long time that a settlement existed at that spot and in particular that there were burials which for more than a century had been shamelessly and randomly pillaged by ruffians. It was a veterinary surgeon, Georges Bolnat, who undertook a methodical excavation of the burials some time before 1938. He kept precious notes of his digging, made plans of the tombs, drew and photographed the skeletons and objects *in situ*, all for the purpose of producing a great monograph which he was never able to complete. The war prevented him, and then after that his own premature death. It was Abbé Bernard Lacroix who finally published this exceptional report based on the documents painstakingly accumulated by G. Bolnat. Abbé Lacroix's remarkable memorandum, published in 1958, made it possible to analyse in detail one of these 'transition groups' in eastern France.

Despite the repeated depredations of earlier years, the necropolis still sheltered some handsome remains. The tombs were flat with no mound covering them, aligned east–west in accordance with the ancient rite. Inhumation was the rule. In the finest tomb at La Colombine lay the skeleton of a woman, on her back, her arms slightly away from her body. Although, to judge from details of her skull and her teeth, she had seen some fifty springtimes, it was impossible not to respond to her charm, heightened as it was by magnificent bronze jewellery. But we shall see how she appeared to the diggers at La Colombine.

They had approached the skeleton from the feet, of which only a few scattered fragments of bone remained. Then they unearthed two well preserved tibias encircled by those magnificent leg spirals that were the glory of the Haguenau tumuli. They had been worn by women, then, and unless we concede that we are dealing with women-soldiers, we may assume that these heavy spirals, which were not easy to wear, were simply for adornment and not 'cnemids' or shin protectors for use in battle.

After the tibias they moved up towards the pelvic girdle where G. Bolnat found about fifty small spiral tubes of bronze intermingled with blue glass beads. Fifty-five bronze buttons were lying near the knees in two or three long rows. This Bronze Age lady wore a skirt of linen or wool which was adorned with this stock of bronze. She must have jingled delightfully as she moved. Incidentally, this fashion had been very popular in the Tumulus cultures, especially in north Germany.

But the finest object at La Colombine was a huge boar's tusk which had been encased in a mounting of bronze leaf bearing repoussé decoration of geometrical motifs and surmounted with little bronze spirals. It is a masterpiece of Bronze Age jewellery and one of the glories, now, of the Musée des Antiquités Nationales at Saint-Germain-en-Laye. Abbé Lacroix describes it as a 'diadem'. It is possible but unlikely, for it would be worn very low down. This doubt was voiced by Professor R. Joffroy who discovered a similar 'diadem' in one of the tombs at Barbuise-Courtavant in Aube: it could simply be an object worn on a belt, something like the bronze discs with which elegant Danish ladies decked themselves at the same period.

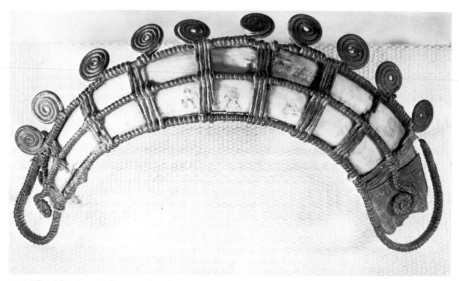

170 The 'diadem' of La Colombine (Yonne)

The lady at La Colombine had other jewels, too: bracelets, a necklace, earrings, rings, all in bronze, not to mention a little bracelet of amber beads. She was a wealthy and noble princess. For the great journey she was supplied with food: two ribs of wild boar and a little beaker that had contained some beverage or other, we do not know of what type.

This female burial is exceptional in its wealth. It shows the climax of the bronze art of the Tumulus people in the famous 'diadem'. But other tombs are more revealing of the changes and human upheavals that were going on at the time. Pottery ornamented with wide channels, unpublished till then, which could only come from regions further east, was deposited in the tombs. The kinship of these pots with the 'transition groups' of the Riegsee type is undeniable. Those 'men from the east' had passed through La Colombine too.

Other burials in Yonne show the same characteristics: at Vinets, for example, where some fine leg spirals were found, but in association with enormous channelled pins (there were also some at La Colombine) – another 'foreign' type of adornment. In Aube the burials at Barbuise-Courtavant betray the same phenomenon of cultural 'accommodation' between the 'Tumulus' people and the 'Foreigners'.

Beside these 'transition groups', with mixed influences, we find 'preliminary groups', to use the archaeological jargon. They are not yet true, classic Urnfield people, but irregular troops. They existed about 1200–1100 BC. The rite of cremation in pots was becoming more frequent, particularly for women, at least at first. Such a one is the Rixheim group, named after a tomb in Alsace and characterised by male burials with knives and the typical swords already mentioned, and female cremation burials, where poppy-headed or pyramid pins of a baroque style were deposited. The 'poppy heads' are huge balls with alternate horizontal and vertical grooves. Often in these burials in the east the corpse was to be burned with its equipment, and sometimes the sword was even broken in two: nothing that had contributed to the glory of the dead warrior must remain with the living, and eternal fire must consume or purify men, adornments and weapons alike.

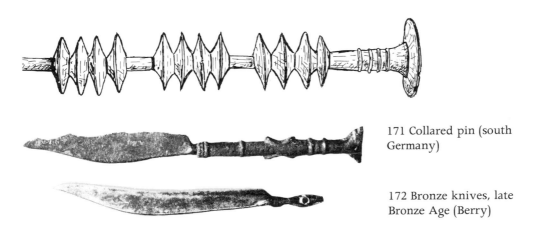

171 Collared pin (south Germany)

172 Bronze knives, late Bronze Age (Berry)

A second 'preliminary group', well known through the work of Professors W. Kimmig and J. P. Millotte, is marked by another type of pin, no less curious than the preceding one – the collared pins. They could be as long as 90cm and their wearers were in no danger of passing unnoticed. On the bronze stem, which ended in a disc, small bronze rings, discs and biconical collars were strung or cast. Pins like that could fasten a large piece of cloth – the peplum of the living or, more probably, the winding sheet of the dead,

181

unless they were simply status symbols. The distribution of this very characteristic type shows the spread of new industries towards western and south-eastern France. Soon the true Urnfields were to follow.

The classic urnfields

A typical urnfield – *Urnenfeld* in German – is a necropolis in which funerary urns are buried very close to each other and are often accompanied by accessory vases and other goods, weapons or jewels. The principal urn is often globular or biconal, covered with a plate or a vase in the 'Chinese hat' style. But there are many variations on this basic theme. The urns may be placed in natural caves as in the west central or southern France. Moreover urnfields are not always found in isolated necropolises that are characteristic and belong to a well defined period: often the urns appear in cemeteries that were used over a long period, and are interspersed with inhumations of the middle Bronze Age Tumulus culture and Iron Age burials. So the situation is often very complex and has a host of regional variations.

The influence of the urnfield phenomenon radiated far and wide. It spread from the Danube region to Normandy and from north Germany to Catalonia and Italy. In France the first urnfields appeared in the east, Alsace, then Burgundy, and spread rapidly north-westwards to Aube, Yonne and Seine-et-Marne; they reached the centre and south-west by the Loire route, the south, Languedoc and the Pyrenees by the age-old Rhône axis. The urnfields were misunderstood for a long time and then, by reaction were over-estimated and there was a tendency to bestow the epithet urnfield on almost anything, and certainly

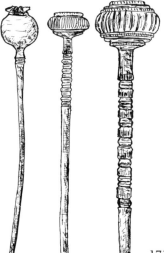

173 Poppy-headed pins (Switzerland)

on everything which might be remotely linked with the cremation rite. But this funeral rite was in use at several different periods and appeared with renewed vigour in the Iron Age. It seems reasonable to restrict the term to the 'classic urnfields' as defined by Professor W. Kimmig.

From a study of the material, especially the pottery, he distinguished four basic phases. The first phase, UF I, takes in the 'preliminary groups' with the poppy-headed and collared pins already mentioned. UF II and III include the two great late Bronze Age sequences datable broadly from 1150 to 750 BC. Finally UF IV consists of the ones that lingered on into the early Iron Age, co-existing with the first typical Hallstatt cultures.

Detailed analysis of the pottery shows groups clearly identifiable by their material possessions, who later spread outwards leading to the development of other urnfield groups. In southern Germany and northern Switzerland one of these early centres can be recognised by large urns with necks shaped like truncated concs and cover plates attractively decorated on the inside with festoons, swags or dog-tooth designs and highlighted with white encrustations or red paint. This group, known as the Rhine-Swiss, was to exercise a strong influence on the earliest French urnfield centres.

The Main-Swabian group is distinguished by grooved decoration, sometimes with raised protuberances, which would have been called 'Lusatian' at one time, and by curious beakers, very narrow at the base. It, too, was to play its part in the westward spread of the urnfields. Further north, groups were identified very early on in the lower Rhine basin and in Belgium, but this type is relatively poorly supplied, in the beginning at least, with accessory vases and bronzes. Similar cultures were flourishing towards south-east Europe, from Austria to Yugoslavia and Hungary. In northern Europe, Lausitz too adopted biconical urns and cremation of the dead. So we have a whole mosaic of centres more or less related.

Westward spread of the urnfields

As far as France is concerned, the great Joseph Déchelette had noted in his *Manual* the importance of the pottery that was then called 'Lusatian' and had placed these pots with their channelled decoration at the end of the Bronze Age. There was still no talk of urnfields in France. The phenomenon would have to be thoroughly studied in south Germany and Switzerland; the main sources of its influence, before its repercussions were discovered on French soil. The early work of A. Brisson and Professor J. J. Hatt in the Marne department helped to disclose the new funeral rites. Professor J. P. Millotte's synthesis on the Jura and the plains of the Saône, and the excellent detailed studies of Professor W. Kimmig, confirmed the expansion of the phenomenon and soon Miss Nancy K. Sandars was able to present her study of the urnfields in the framework of the French Bronze Age. Since then countless regional studies have proliferated on all sides, more particularly as the development of large-scale earth-moving operations in urban sites and road construction schemes made rescue digs essential, so that often archaeologists had to go and hunt under the wheels of the bulldozers to find their precious potsherds.

Age-old land over which invasions from the east passed or stopped, Champagne enjoyed the urnfield phenomenon on a rather grand scale. A. Brisson and J. J. Hatt had studied the many ritual and funeral enclosures in the cemetery at Aulnay-aux-Planches. More recently, B. Chertier devoted himself to a patient, detailed reconstruction of the funeral customs, approaching the study of the ritual graves with exemplary method. Great variety reigned in the structures: the simplest is a hole the size of the urn dug in the chalky soil for it to be buried in: this is the classic urnfield, which is found at Bannes and Broussy-le-Grand, for example. But often these venerable remains were better housed; a great trench was prepared, two or more metres long and 1m wide in which the urn was carefully deposited and protected by a stone surround.

Even more substantial protection was a tumulus surrounded by a ditch. B. Chertier has described these 'flat tumuli' which might seem a heresy or a flight of fancy if we did not know that the mounds were later rased as is proved by the filling of the external ditches. Indeed, in section, these show a deep chalky area resulting from the collapse of the sides of the holes shortly after the tumulus was built. Then there is a filling of black earth, stuffed with bits of bone and pot: this indicates that, at a later date, when the dead were no longer feared, the funeral mounds which could have been 8 to 20m in diameter, were simply levelled. The ditch was annular, about 1m deep, reviving the ritual circle, adopted by the Chalcolithic and early Bronze Age people long before. But there is one difference: the enclosure is broken, often on the south side (the direction of the sun again) to allow a small access to the centre of the monument. Perhaps a few beasts were sacrificed to the glory of the dead a certain time after the ceremony, or at regular intervals. We might well think so from an analysis of the soil in the ditch where animal remains are frequently found: sheep, ox, pig and even dogs, probably domestic ones. But we cannot be sure, for another possible explanation of these animal remains has been given: often soil was raked up from round the settlement to build the funeral mound, and this soil also contained refuse from meals, channelled or finger-impressed pottery and sometimes humble bronze buttons lost by one of the inhabitants. One was found in the ditch at Aulnay-sur-Marne.

The enclosures were not all funerary. The urn may be missing from the centre and its place taken by a simple cremation directly on the ground. It seems that there were enclosures of religious significance, too, little open-air chapels or temples amidst the settlements or necropolises.

These enclosures long remained popular in north-west Europe. Usually they were circular but a few are known of rectangular shape, especially religious enclosures. Sometimes they have a more distinctive shape. So in the Netherlands, the necropolis at Wessinghuizen sheltered urns amongst enclosures curiously shaped like some gigantic key-hole, whose significance still eludes us. The first bronze keys did indeed appear at about this time, but key-holes no doubt were circular then, not trapezoido-circular as they are today.

184

174 Funeral urns (late Urnfield period), (*left*) from Millas (Pyrénées Orientales), *right* north Germany

We cannot describe in detail the numerous necropolises of the period. Amongst the latest to be recorded, one of the most interesting at Marolles-sur-Seine in Seine-et-Marne, excavated by the brothers C. and D. Mordant, proves that inhumation was very long-lived in places: here it continued with channelled pottery but soon the bronze razors characteristic of the urnfields and typical pottery reminiscent of the classic groups would be adopted. Cremations under a simple lid of pot and numerous accessory vases either in or beside the urn show quite definitely that current fashion had won the day. At that period too the circular ditch reappears, protecting the slumbers of the dead.

Classic types of pottery are strung out towards the Alps and the South of France, but there are regional forms, too, like the little beakers of the lake villages of Le Bourget. Is this, too, a hint of the arrival of new ethnic groups? A long series of bone samples would be needed in order to detect the physical characteristics of the newcomers. Unfortunately by adopting the rite of cremation for their dead, the urnfield people played a really mean trick on the poor anthropologists.

The great age of bronze: tools and weapons

In the area encompassed by the spread of the urnfields, and particularly in the Swiss and Alpine regions, strong schools of metallurgy proliferated, producing an enormous volume of metal. It is the climax of the art of the founder and much has been said about the 'fine Bronze Age of the lake-dwellers'. The bronze objects come from tombs – a few; from settlements – a few; from lake-dwellings – a great many; and also from 'hoards' buried in the ground, one of the curiosities of the Bronze Age. A 'hoard' or 'cache' consists of either a stock of new wares intended for sale or broken objects collected for re-casting. It fulfils some of the functions of monetary treasure: in those days the smallest piece of copper or bronze had a certain value, just as our coins have. We must not include here certain votive collections, offerings to the gods, like the golden objects tossed into lakes, rivers or bogs. The tiniest chips of metal in the 'hoards' are interesting to the archaeologist. Gone are the days when a certain cache in the Alps is said to have met a strange fate: the finest bronzes were kept and the rest were melted down to make a handsome plaque commemorating the discovery. Whether this is fact of fiction we cannot say, but it is a fact that in the past the 'waste' simply went to the foundry.

Founders' hoards consist above all of fragments of swords and massive winged or socketed axes in which an elbowed handle could be inserted. But the novelty is the invention of very many gadgets of everyday life which were to remain in use down to our own day. This is the time when the socketed or tanged gouge was created, when numerous variations of chisels, paring knives, spokeshaves, chasing tools, gravers, etc. appeared. Hammers continued to be socketed, and anvils made it possible to make sheet metal and sharpen razors or swords. The razors, which were numerous, must have been tricky to use but the men of the Bronze Age did not hesitate to scrape their faces in order to please the ladies. Another speciality of the Swiss and Alpine workshops was the knife – already! Times have not changed much, but forms have changed a little more. Knives developed from the early blades with curved backs and wooden handles down to the fine specimens with flanged hilts, lap-jointed, and later fitted with thin sheets of horn until finally they were made entirely of bronze with baroque shapes and a ring to hang them by. A recent study of all these tools by G. Gaucher and J. P. Nicolardet has shown the variety of instruments offered to the craftsman, who from then on almost totally abandoned his traditional tools of bone, flint or horn.

175 Late Bronze Age razor (Bavaria)
176 'Lost wax' casting: the nails are made in clay in a central column (*right*). After removing the clay the raw casting is obtained

The workshops were producing for agriculture too. Small sickles were made in series, with small tangs fastened by rivets or studs to very elaborate wooden handles. At Briod in the Jura, one hoard contained 300 sickles, many of which were lost at the beginning of this century. This abundance of sickles gave rise to the notion that the peoples of the east and south-east, who were somewhat hastily identified as Ligurians by J. Déchelette and others, were agriculturalists who supplied wheat to almost all the rest of Europe. More simply a new phenomenon appeared in that area, as in the Atlantic zone – the manufacture of series of objects, a step towards industrial production. The foundries at Briod, Larnaud, etc. were an early version of Creusot's workshops or the factories at St-Etienne.

So bronze was making its way then into everyday life. It was no longer a luxury article for use by the powerful, the priests and the soldiers. Everyone took advantage of it and loved to be adorned with countless trinkets: pendants, and, above all, pins – myriads of pins, vase-headed, collared, ring-shaped, disc-shaped, shepherd's-crook, bubble-shaped, conical, biconical; with necks that were straight, curved, ringed, twisted, swollen, grooved, decorated with incisions, with hollow heads filled with some precious substance – amber or cornelian – finished with a ring to hang by, double-headed, etc. *Rhythme et composition du décor des epingles* (*Rhythm and Composition of Pin Decoration*) is the title chosen by the distinguished specialist F. Audouze, who uses the most modern mathematical techniques to find his way out of this forest of pins, enlisting the aid of V. Elisséef's scalogram.

177 Sword with antennae, late Bronze Age, Corcelettes (Switzerland)

The choice pieces of this sophisticated metallurgy are the bronze weapons: we are back to the swords with massive handles – Liptov, Auvernier and Mörigen swords, each with a distinguishing mark by which we can identify the various workshops. Then there are the swords with antennae pommels where the handle is surmounted by two elegant bronze spirals. The great novelty is the defensive weaponry. Like those described in the *Iliad*, the warriors girded themselves with bronze. On their heads a helmet, at first a simple riveted metal chape, then an elegant headdress with crests or cabochons and small cones or tubes at the sides. They get dredged up from rivers such as the Moselle or the Seine, when they are not found in caches like the famous crested helmets from Bernières d'Ailly in Calvados. The first cuirasses, in sheet metal adorned with bosses, appear at the end of this period, too. Their kinship with the accoutrements of war from the Aegean has been emphasised by Professor H. Müller-Karpe, and bronze leg-pieces were being worn now, analogous with the cnemids which protected Greek calves. Lastly the shield completed the urnfield warriors' panoply of war. Another discovery is the presence of horses for riding, and chariots. Bits of assembly pieces for harness such as buckles, etc. proliferate, as do objects of military decoration: tintinnabula, charms, phalerae, to adorn the head or breast of the noble chargers. Bronze wheels testify to developments in casting. We are far removed from the flimsy wheels of the Trundholm chariot. The massive wheels have great bronze hubs cast by the lost-wax method: such are the wheels found at Fa, a commune of Rennes-les-Bains in Aude, described by J. Guilaine – masterpieces of casting at the end of the Bronze Age.

The founder's workshop: mine workings

The equipment of the founders included the hammers and anvils already mentioned and also a host of complex moulds made of the most varied materials such as earth and clay sometimes reinforced with wood, but few of these have been preserved other than in a state of advanced decay. On the other hand, moulds made of stone, Alpine clay and bronze abound in finds, in a good state of preservation. Big pieces were cast in moulds consisting of two valves, small ones in multiple moulds which enabled a whole run to be cast at once. In founders' hoards the tiniest bits of waste were collected. They lie alongside large plano-convex ingots and 'saumon' ingots with a central perforation. These copper ingots probably originated in the Alps.

Finally the mine, the real centre of metal extraction, which at that time almost always produced finished articles on the spot, was beginning to be a feature of the industrial landscape. From the end of the Bronze Age on, important copper workings are known to have existed in the Salzburg area and in the Austrian Tyrol. On the Saalach, the mines at Viehofen show an early stage in copper workings, when circular cavities were dug in the ground with, here and there, shallow vertical shafts. But it is at Mitterberg that really serious workings are found: entrances to mining galleries were spread out along a front of some 1600m and at times penetrated for up to 100m. The standard extraction procedure was by fire-setting. The rock was subjected to intense heat and then water was thrown

178 Stone hammers (Vaucluse and Pyrenees)

over to make it split. This implies a network of wooden channels with Archimedean screws to bring the water up slopes; in addition there would be ladders or stairways, wooden sledges for bringing the ore out, not to mention the indispensable woodwork supporting the galleries. Vestiges of this equipment have been found in great numbers, and so have the great stone pounders and bronze socketed picks which were used in the final stages of extraction.

Outside the mine, the ore had to be finely crushed and concentrated, often under water, and hence the construction of more reservoirs and complex systems of conduits. Finally the hearth represented the last operation and by no means the least delicate. Smelting hearths loaded with ore and charcoal produced plano-convex ingots of metal. Spectrographic analysis and electrolysis carried out on these ingots caused some surprise: the metal was of a very high quality – almost pure copper. Using their cunning and some 'tricks of the trade' our metallurgists had succeeded in refining the metal to perfection.

179 Bronze armour: helmets (Paris and Auxonne) and cuirasse (Fillinges, Savoy), late Bronze Age

They had discovered the procedures empirically and had seasoned them with a little magic. For all primitive people, the smith has always been something of a sorcerer. This assumption does not rest only on ethnographic comparisons: in Val Camonica one of the carvings shows us a smith at work and he is wearing a strange feathered headdress, which, in the series as a whole seems to be the prerogative of sorcerers or priests.

Social life and religious beliefs

This prolific production of bronzes cannot have taken place in a period of disturbances, rather it suggests a time of prosperous trading. It implies a sophisticated organisation of trade routes, in the first place, to bring the raw metal, in the form of ingots, to the manufacturing sites, which were often a long way from the mines. Then there was the casting of large quantities of objects in series. The Barbarians had to be transformed into skilful organisers, champion planners of distribution networks, shrewd creators of a highly organised work force.

Religious life was still characterised by this dual nature, pastoral and industrial. Animal cults were still vigorous, as is shown, for example, by votive clay horns in many settlements in Alsace and elsewhere. In addition, at La Colombine and at Courtavant, there were the famous boar's tusks mounted in bronze which must have distinguished people of high rank. Perhaps it was more than mere adornment: the deification of an animal which was dear to the tribe. In Val Camonica, with its pictures that are so precious to us in our attempts to understand something of the mind of Bronze Age man, the stag was clearly the sacred animal. In the regions of Aube or Yonne, it may have been the boar.

The other time-honoured standby of religious beliefs was the fire–horse, sun–wheel association – fire, most of all, since it is the main funeral rite. The theme of the sun appears again in the abundance of small bronze wheels or gold discs with simulated rays. The horse is known by harness mountings found in hoards and also, at the very end of the late Bronze Age, by the appearance on pottery of small stylised horses, especially in the South of France. Last there are the wheels. The ones found at Fa, from the late Bronze Age, have been interpreted by J. Guilaine as belonging to cult wagons. He draws a parallel between them and the famous group from La Côte-Saint-André in Isère, though this was later, early Iron Age work – G. Chapotat has analysed it minutely and interpreted it as a processional wagon. It is an early discovery; the deposit was found in 1888 between the Rhône and the Alps and consisted of four fine bronze wheels together with a bucket and a pan of the same metal. The whole group was sold to the Musée de Lyon. The wheels, more than 50cm in diameter and weighing more than 10kg, have six spokes. The hub is massive and made of bronze. The metal rims overlay an oaken frame. This wagon bore the weight (4kg) of the great bronze bucket 645mm tall, which could hold 80 litres. The small bronze pan was with

180 Tintinnabulum, Urnfield culture, Hoechst (Germany)

it. There is no doubt that this was a wagon associated with religious practices. The arrangement of the wheels is difficult to reconstruct. The standard arrangement divided the wheels, two to each side, but the initial distribution at the time of discovery, which may have been fortuitous, showed one wheel in front and three behind.

The wagon of Côte-Saint-André brings us close to the Iron Age cultures which were to introduce a profusion of bronze buckets or situlae. But wheels appeared earlier, in the late Bronze Age: besides the ones at Fa, they have been found in the lake dwelling at Cortaillod in Switzerland, at Langres in Haute Marne, at Hassloch in the Palatinate and as far away as Staden near Hamburg. Rites involving wagons, as we well know nowadays, plunge their roots into the very middle of the Bronze Age. It is probable that the Côte-Saint-André wagon was uniting an ancient tradition with a technical innovation, that of the bronze situla. It shows the power of survival of these wagons, often linked with the sun cult. Hallstatt cultures in the Iron Age were simply adopting a tradition that was already almost a thousand years old.

Chapter 11

The Cassiterite Islands

The Mediterranean world used up large quantities of bronze in the classical period and was constantly looking for new workable deposits. Tin was becoming rare and had to be fetched from remote barbarian territories either by land or by sea. It would be interesting to have accurate information about the deposits of the time, for it is reasonable to suppose that the sources were more or less the same then as in the Bronze Age: but ancient texts tend only to make the question more confused.

They locate the western deposits of tin in three regions – Iberia, the Cassiterite Islands and the British Isles. But they are sparing with further details and the reason for this is very simple: the tin trade brought vast profits and it is obvious that the holders of the monopoly had no wish to divulge the sea routes that led to prosperity.

There can be no doubt that the first well organised traders were Phoenician businessmen, but they have allowed very little information to filter through. Strabo, in his *Geography* written at the beginning of the Christian era, tells of a Phoenician captain, pursued by Roman ships, who deliberately altered course to run his ship on to treacherous shoals, thereby causing his adversaries to be lost as well. The Phoenician, who escaped, was generously rewarded for this act by the aediles of his city, who reimbursed him for the price of his cargo. This anecdote was probably not had at first hand but it confirms the ruthlessness with which the secrets of these sea routes were defended.

The tin routes and the Phoenicians

Strabo situates the famous Cassiterite Islands off Artabria, in other words beyond the north-west tip of the Iberian peninsula. Other authors have suggested the British Isles. But I humbly admit that I do not understand Greek and leave scholarly exigesis of Greek texts to my historian colleagues. Countless modern writers have tackled the problems of the Cassiterite Islands and the 'tin routes' of antiquity. The celebrated islands have been moved from the coasts of Spain to Ireland, though with a preference for either Armorica or south Cornwall, in which connection the Scilly Isles have frequently been mentioned.

181 Bronze warrior, Roca Rotja
(Majorca), late talayot period

J. Ramin, who worked out a new theory of the *Problem of the Cassiterite Islands*, inclined towards the southern coasts of Armorica and his arguments seem very convincing.

But might it not be of interest to examine the deposits known in our own days? Some veins were worked very early in Saxony and Bohemia and their presence undoubtedly contributed to the development of the Únětice culture in the early Bronze Age. But ease of working certainly played a part as J. Ramin points out, and the most sought-after deposits were the alluvial ones along the coasts which produced natural concentrations. In Spain and north Portugal rich deposits are known nowadays in Galicia, in the provinces of Orense, Zamora, Minho and Tras-os-Montes. But we should also note with interest the presence of small tin-bearing deposits in the south-east, in the hinterland of Almeria, which may have contributed to the birth of the El Argar culture in the Iberian early Bronze Age.

In the British Isles tin has been recorded in Ireland, sometimes in association with gold, but it is chiefly in the southern part of Great Britain that tin can be found, with important deposits in Devon and Cornwall. As is often the case, the mineral is formed round small granite masses where they meet beds of schist. The alluvial deposits were worked in preference to the veins and in the last century a few traces still remained near St Just and St Austell, but two or three thousand years' working had almost exhausted them. Another point of interest in the south British deposits is their association with seams of copper. This cannot have failed to favour the birth of the Bronze Age cultures in the British Isles, particularly in Wessex.

In central France a great many sites are known, like the one at Montebras in Haute-Vienne. Several deposits of tin lie within the confines of Brittany, as recent investigations by the Bureau de Recherches Géologiques et Minières (the BRGM) have confirmed. But ancient authors gave some practical hints as well. Sometimes the ore was at ground level, which suggests alluvial workings; at others it had to be extracted from the rock by means of galleries. This was a difficult undertaking, for techniques of crushing rocks *in situ* were only perfected in the Roman period. Traces of ancient workings in Armorica show this clearly.

In Loire-Atlantique the open-cast mine at Abbaretz-Nozay were still being worked between 1952 and 1957, until fluctuations in the market brought about their closure. Some 4000 tons of cassiterite were extracted in six years, which gives some idea of the magnitude of the deposit. Modern exploitation uncovered an ancient working and, thanks to the goodwill of the mining engineers, a distinguished lawyer turned archaeologist, C. Champaud, was able to study it. He showed that the ancient traces went back to the beginning of our era. Wooden spades and hoes, remains of channels and lumps of iron had been abandoned by the Gallo-Roman miners. But some bronze axes and even a small torc of twisted gold from the middle Bronze Age were evidence that the site had been used from those times. No doubt the neighbouring streams had been searched for cassiterite and the small gold jewel could very well have been exchanged for tin ore.

Other ancient tin mines, at La Villeder in Morbihan, also date from the Roman period. There is no doubt that it was alluvial tin that was mostly highly prized by proto-historic populations. It abounds at the mouth of the Vilaine where the site of Pénestin, the 'Cap d'Etain' (the 'Cape of Tin') with its beach called 'La Mine d'Or' ('The Gold Mine'), reflects a dual wealth which still brought fortunes to a few people in the last century. The Comte de Limur reported in 1878 that three workmen from the tin mine at Piriac, a little to the south of Pénestin, collected 600 to 700kg of cassiterite from the beach in a matter of a few weeks by panning. We can only guess how rich such a deposit was at a time when it was still untapped.

The last deposit still being worked in Brittany is at Saint-Renan in the north of Finistère. It is a huge flat, a shallow alluvial basin near the sea where the cassiterite has already broken away and is found mingled with sand and silt. All that needs to be done is to screen and dress the sand. It is understandable that this method of extraction suited ancient peoples ill-equipped with tools. A few fibulae and some slag have been found at Saint-Renan, testifying to workings dating from the Iron Age. As regards earlier times, we can only be struck by the large numbers of Bronze Age tombs in the district followed at the end of the Bronze Age by numerous founders' hoards. Moreover the huge menhirs at Plouarzel and Saint-Renan could have been markers for the famous deposits.

Armorica took full advantage of its coastal and fluvial tin resources: many small streams in the interior also proved to contain tin. This allowed the development of distinctive Bronze Age cultures and the maintenance of strong trading relations all along the Atlantic face and even towards the Mediterranean through the Narbonne gap, as A. Soutou and G. Gaudron have suggested.

British tin had to cross north-west France too. The source of the wealth of the Burgundian tumuli of the Hallstatt period, and in particular of the famous Vix burial, so dear to R. Joffroy, has often been sought in a prolongation of this trade towards the Mediterranean via the Rhône. We should note the importance of tin in some preliminary urnfield groups as early as the bronze period. At La Grève de Frécul and Barbuise-Courtavant in Aube, R. Joffroy has collected little white ingots of a bronze that is very rich in tin. Others had been reported previously in the same district.

Ingots: gold and lead

It has been thought that, in the early days, tin was not cast in ingots but added directly to copper in the form of cassiterite. This might account for these early ingots of white bronze: it was one of the forms in which this trade normally took place. The case is not isolated and the hoards at St Denis-de-Piles in the Gironde also contained little bars of tin bronze in the shape of the moulds in which they had been cast. It was only later that large ingots of tin were cast. One of them was picked up off the British coast at Falmouth. But we must bear in mind a purely chemical phenomenon, which is the very poor preservation of tin in the soil; this might explain why so few ingots of pure tin have been found.

Gold, for its part, was extracted from numerous European rivers. France has a few gold-bearing deposits which may still be of interest to prospectors with plenty of time. But not much is left after the activities of tens of generations of gold-panners.

Lead acquired economic importance at the end of the Bronze Age when it appeared almost routinely in alloys. Indeed it is one of the criteria used by British writers to distinguish middle bronze which had a low lead content, from late bronze, which often used, and at times, even abused it. The lead came from Spain, as did silver; mines there were being actively worked from the earliest times. In Brittany there is an abundance of lead and this natural wealth made its contribution to the economic prosperity of the late Bronze Age in the Atlantic zone. But we must see what was happening in the Cassiterite Islands at the time when the Urnfield culture was flourishing in the east.

The great Atlantic hoards of the late Bronze Age

Fortuné Parenteau was the first Conservator of the archaeological collections in Nantes, which were then housed in the little Musée de l'Oratoire. He described himself as 'not wrapped in but scarcely covered by his ragged cloak' (an allusion to the poor means at his disposal), 'a pioneer of the future, with a mattock in one hand and a lantern in the other', who was trying to uncover traces of the men of the past by interrogating the tiniest remains of ancient times. In December 1867 a new discovery came to nourish his consuming passion for archaeology – but let him tell us about it himself.

'Louis Ménard, a clog-maker by trade, who preferred to earn a few halfpence a day by toiling on the land in those days of unemployment and deserted workshops, discovered a coarse clay pot from which amidst some greenish dust one hundred and fifty fragments of bronze covered with a fine green patina spilled out on the ground. "Gold!" cried the first witness of the find. "Copper," said the second, sadly. "Rubbish. Let's sell the lot to a dealer in old copper and go and have a noggin." ' But Louis Ménard intervened and told them about the Musée de l'Oratoire; and so the find was saved, thanks to the goodwill of Dr Ecorchard, director of the Jardin des Plantes at Nantes, where this scene took place. And the lyrical Fortuné concluded: 'And so, thanks to the intervention of two men at opposite ends of the social scale, a remarkable find was preserved in its entirety without anything going astray or finding its way into the hands of the second-hand dealers – the plague of archaeology. All praise to Dr Ecorchard and to Louis Ménard.'

The publication of the hoard – which consisted chiefly of remains of axes, swords and bracelets – appeared under the name of Parenteau in 1868 in the brand new *Bulletin de la Société Archéologique de Nantes*. The description as a whole was very good for the period and the hoard was attributed very pertinently to the 'secondary Bronze Age', which was soon to be named Larnaudian by de Mortillet, from the site at Larnaud, a vast hoard of some 1800 bronzes discovered as early as 1865 in the Jura.

The 'Jardin des Plantes' is not the most important of these late Bronze Age hoards in Armorica but it was the first to be recognised and published in the modern manner with sound comparisons. In passing, the account shows us the fate of bronze remains, which at that time were frequently taken to a scrap metal dealer and melted down. Unfortunately this tradition was of very long standing. A letter from a Monsieur de la Roque, dated March 1713, is an important piece of documentary evidence and quoted in *Le Chef d'Oeuvre d'un Inconnu* by Dr Chrisostomus Mathiasus (undoubtedly the pen-name of some noble man of letters, perhaps Albert-Henri de Dallengre, author of a certain *Eloge de l'ivresse (in Praise of Drunkenness)*). M. de la Roque relates that, in the year 1707 at Mesnil-Hue in the Manche department, peasants discovered a large quantity of copper axes when they were planting apple trees. There were enough to make up a load for a horse and they sent the lot to 'the township of Villedieu', a command post of the order of the Knights of Malta, all of whose inhabitants were founders or coppersmiths. The town was, of course, Villedieu-les-Poêles whose glowing copper ware still tries to lure well-heeled tourists.

182 Hoard of small socketed axes (7 to 8cm long), perhaps currency axes, Moidrey (Manche)

'Hollow bits' by which we understand socketed axes, were found in profusion in the Cotentin. For a long time the interpretations of these tools were very varied and amusing: at first they were seen as Roman weapons, the heads of catapult missiles, or grapnels for scaling walls used by Caesar's legionaries, or, again, as reinforcing pieces for the poles of standards. We will pass over the prosaic or romantic descriptions, such as 'feet of cauldrons' or 'lachrymatory vases'. However, there were precursors in this field, like Christopher-Paul de Robien, Speaker of the Breton Parlement. In 1756 he wrote a *Description historique et topographique de l'ancienne Armorique*, which was published in 1974 by J. Y. Veillard – one should never despair of seeing one's works in print! Speaker Robien described bronze axes as Gaulish, which was a very honourable attribution at the time, and gave the first coherent classification, foreshadowing modern work. But with what result? It remained unpublished.

From the end of the last century a host of hoards were recorded along the Channel and Atlantic seaboards. They testify to the lively activity of the foundries in the western zone at that period of the late Bronze Age. Indeed the development of bronze industries in the Atlantic zone was merely the outcome of a movement which started in the middle Bronze Age. Many types from that period, such as palstaves, were to remain in use for a very long time, concurrently with the winged axes, originating in the east. The same economic community included the French Atlantic zone, the Netherlands and the British Isles. Regional differences there certainly were, but a common basis was maintained throughout,

183 Late Bronze Age axe, 'Portuguese' type (Spain)
184 Axe of the late Bronze Age from Iberia (Spain)

thanks to repeated exchanges all along the shores of that 'inland sea' which the Channel remains to this day. The new element in the late Bronze Age is undoubtedly the expansion of trade relations southwards: after its great megalithic and Argaric period in the Chalcolithic and early Bronze Ages, the Iberian peninsula had only produced undistinguished cultures in the middle Bronze Age. Now, in the late Bronze Age, she roused herself and experienced a renewal of the bronze industry all along her Atlantic face, especially in the north-west.

Contacts with continental peoples increased even if a certain reluctance to adopt new cultural or economic ideas can be detected at times. Normandy and the west central areas were subjected to a more profound influence from the Urnfield culture than was the Armorican peninsula, whereas the British Isles remained loyal to their own tradition of funerary urns which sprang from the local middle Bronze Age period. Weapons from the east, for example rapiers of the Rixheim type, were exported as far as northern France and Brittany (some have been dredged up from the Vilaine at Rennes) but often the people preferred to transform the technical innovations from the east in their own foundries and workshops.

Thus, from the beginning of this late Bronze Age period, they were making rapiers at Rosnoën with notches or rivet holes like those from eastern Europe. The tang of the dagger was rectangular, one small detail amongst others which distinguish it from its Rixheim cousin with a triangular tang. Copying took place, but with a distinctive style. The rapiers were joined by spearheads with long sockets, razors, socketed hammers and some winged axes. Palstaves had become more massive and were regularly fitted with a ring on the side. Rosnoën is a hoard in Finistère which has parallels in Normandy and as far off as northern France. Neighbouring groups arose in the British Isles, with small-tanged swords, and swords which were sometimes leaf-shaped – that is the blade was widened two-thirds of the way down, and could slash like a sabre. These British groups have been studied extensively by Colin Burgess, who stressed their continental affinities. Thus from their earliest phase, the influence of the urnfields was felt in the west, giving rise to a renewal of material equipment.

Leaf-shaped swords

This Urnfield influence was to increase subsequently throughout the late Bronze Age period. In weaponry, in particular in swords, the development is clear. The narrow rapiers of Rosnoën were rapidly abandoned in favour of the manufacture in series of a whole range of leaf-shaped swords. The small tang became 'tri-partite', to take up the technical term proposed by G. Gaucher and J. P. Mohen who specialised in this proto-historic weaponry. That is to say that it is clearly divided so as to give a V-shaped guard, a central part which was widened at the base, and a splayed pommel in the shape of a fish tail. Rivet holes or else a long slit for riveting made it possible to fix the bone or wooden plaques which completed the handle, using small pins. The small size of the sword hilts always surprises the uninitiated. They could almost be taken for children's playthings, forgetting that they may have caused a man's death. It is simply that the way of holding them differed from that of today. The thumb and forefinger pressed on the blade, but without injury, whence the device known as the ricasso. At first it was quite unobtrusive: the blade was either hammered lightly or left as it came from the foundry, unsharpened. Then a milled effect was made by tapping with a burin. Finally in the latest swords of the Atlantic Bronze Age, small rests were provided for the fingers, sometimes outlined with some moulding or other decoration.

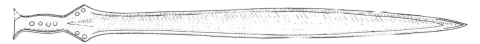

185 Leaf-shaped sword, Monts d'Arrée (Brittany)

Many of the finest swords have been dredged up from rivers where they are often found in surprising concentrations. Why are there so many swords intact in the water? This phenomenon is not peculiar to the Atlantic area and J. P. Millotte, for example, has stressed the importance of such discoveries in the Saône. He notes their associations with fords and places where important roads cross the river: places where commercial activity sometimes clashed with warlike ventures, trading posts or factors' premises having provided interesting objectives for plunderers and raiders down the ages. But other theories may be put forward: for instance the votive gesture, a perfectly plausible explanation when we know that both Gauls and Romans readily endowed springs and rivers with divine powers. The tradition must have been very ancient. Or did the warriors sacrifice some of their finest weapons to the river god in order to make sure of victory?

199

Traditional or ritual combat at fords, where tribal territories met, has been suggested too; the study of medieval Irish texts, which show a long tradition of heroes fighting near rivers, lends support to this theory.

The estuary of the Loire yielded a series of leaf-shaped swords at the beginning of this century both at Nantes and at St Nazaire, while the Bassin de Penhoët was being constructed, and this deserves an anecdote. The engineer, René Kerviler, tried to construct a 'prehistoric chronometer' on this basis. He observed the layers of silt, which had been deposited regularly, and tried to date them. A coin of Tetricus, an ephemeral emperor of the Gauls in the third century AD, was found one and a half metres below the present low-water mark. Since the bronze swords were discovered 2.5m lower still, he deduced that the Bronze Age dated from the fifth century BC and this brought the wrath of G. de Mortillet down on his head, accusing him of confusing the 'Bronze Age' of the Homeric tradition with the real Bronze Age which is a fine modern discovery. It is true that though Kerviler's aims were very laudable, the speed of silting and the exact recording of objects found in the bustle of the huge Penhoët construction scheme were highly debatable.

The Nantes swords are leaf-shaped, of the so-called 'Loire type' with a ricasso that was becoming more and more elaborate. Detailed analysis suggests that they are imitations of prototypes from south Germany: once again local series of weapons were being manufactured on the basis of models from the Urnfield culture. They were very popular and, long before the Atlantic shipyards, the Nantes region was a centre of considerable economic activity. It is represented by objects dredged from the river but also by three large late Bronze Age hoards in Nantes itself: the Jardin des Plantes, the Prairie de Mauves and the Ecobuts.

Atlantic bronze

The prosperity of the Nantes region may be explained in part by the development of forges, but is also due to its role as a commercial crossroads for the region. Nantes was ideally placed, at the mouth of the great Loire waterway which brought in the imports from the Continent, and in exchange it could offer products of the Atlantic region, including tin. Its prosperity was long-lived and it is thought that it may have been the site of the famous Corbilo of the ancient texts, which was said to have even aroused the envy of Marseilles, the ancient Massilia, in its transactions between the Greek world and that of the barbarians. Nantes was only some ten leagues from the tin mines at Abbaretz, which were being worked in the Gallo-Roman period, as we have seen, and possibly well before.

The earliest large hoards of leaf-shaped swords contained many innovations as well. In Brittany, the hoard at Saint-Brieuc-des-Iffs in Ille-et-Vilaine, included winged axes and spearheads but also a whole spectrum of new bronze tools: gouges, chisels, hammers, burins, narrow-bladed chisels, scrapers, etc. In the west as in the east bronze had become commonplace, a part of everyday life. Among the characteristic pieces of this fully

186 English socketed axes: *left* Givendale (Yorks), *right* Lakenheath (Suffolk)

developed late Bronze Age period, we should note the bronze chapes. To protect the blade of the sword the leather or canvas scabbard was reinforced with long, bronze, lozenge-shaped terminals, measuring as much as 60cm – another technical achievement, produced by casting as opposed to simple hammering.

Throughout the Atlantic zone these swords and their chapes are found: in Normandy, in northern France and even across the Channel in the Wilburton group whose affinities with the Bronze Age of north-western France have been stressed by our English colleagues, Professors C. F. C. Hawkes, J. Coles and Colin Burgess. Even so, some very British objects are found with them: indented socketed axes, or spearheads with perforated blades. Every workshop – particularly the British ones – felt bound to proclaim its individuality. In Spain the same development is in evidence and analogous sword types demonstrate that trade relations were very active and exchanges frequent between Ireland and the Iberian peninsula, by way of the British Isles and Armorica. Hoards like St-Denis-de-Piles at the mouth of the Gironde belong to the same late Bronze Age community.

The climax of the Atlantic Bronze Age was to be the group of carp's-tongue swords, a strange name, but one which, curiously, was honoured by international agreement. The carp's tongue, *Karpfenzungenschwerter, tipo de carpa*, etc., flourished everywhere. The term was chosen to designate a sword which narrows sharply towards the point, like a carp's tongue, it seems. This homogeneity of nomenclature is particularly felicitous when we remember that these swords often had pommels in the shape of fish tails. They are sometimes very big, as long as 80cm. The parallel-sided blade is strengthened by a marked central rib, and two large ricassos under the guard accommodate the fingers. If we include the fragments found in hoards in Europe we can reckon that thousands of them were made. The leaf-shaped swords had been very varied in form: by contrast, the carp's-tongue swords had few variants. In the hoards they are found with a few novelties: hog's-back knives and particularly socketed axes with very varied decoration, simple vertical lines, globules or wings simulated in relief, reminding us of the winged axes in earlier use. Objects of adornment abound and include bracelets, either solid or hollow and decorated

187 'Carp's-tongue' type sword, Nantes

with geometric motifs. There are all kinds of beads: discs, round balls, bronze spirals, etc. On the other hand pins become rare – very different from eastern France.

Pieces of harness, buckles and bit mountings for horses are fairly frequent; in addition a few large rings with pendants, known as rattle pendants, hung and jingled from the chargers' breast straps. Bronze-wheeled carts are known, either from small votive wheels (as at Longueville, Calvados) or from the remains of wheel-hubs. Quantities of unidentifiable bronze fragments may be connected with decoration on cart frames. Other fragments of metal sheet may come from helmets, cuirasses or cnemids. All this confirms that bronze was in common use.

The founders' equipment included anvils, hammers and numerous bronze moulds. Specialists think that by using a good lining, the layer inserted between the mould and the object, it was possible to cast objects directly in these moulds. It has been suggested that they may sometimes have been used simply to make wax models. The smallest bits of waste metal were carefully collected after casting, hence all the casting jets, and miscellaneous debris. Pure copper – very pure, in fact, since analysis shows a degree of refinement of 98–99 per cent – was stocked in the form of plano-convex ingots. They took on the shape of the crucible in which they were cast, even including, sometimes, the pouring lip. These plates were used as required, either whole or, more often, in pieces. Analysis of bronze objects shows the increasing proportion of lead in the alloys and a certain discrimination in the alloys. Thus, swords still had a reasonable lead content, from 4–5 per cent, but axes could reach a proportion of 15 per cent. The lead made casting easier, but another phenomenon may have played a part: the tin deposits were becoming exhausted after more than a millennium and so another component had to be used to remedy this deficiency, to some extent at least.

The 'Atlantic community' from Ireland to Iberia

Commercial copper came from Iberia, Cornwall and from the Alps by way of the basins of the Loire and Seine, providing the trading posts on those great rivers with the source of their prosperity.

Carp's-tongue swords have a huge distribution, geographically. They are found from northern Germany to the south-east of the Iberian peninsula. They were even exported to the Mediterranean and variations of these swords have been recorded among the bronzes of the Nuraghic culture in Sardinia and in continental Italy. This testifies to widespread and lively trade relations in this late Bronze Age period, around 800–700 BC. The most important centres are scattered from south-eastern England to the Iberian peninsula with major groups along the French Atlantic seaboard. The connection with other British industries and with those of Ireland was a close one. We cannot enter into a detailed description of all these styles, but we must at least draw attention to a distinctive Iberian trade (that of palstaves) and, later, socketed axes fitted with two loops, which were

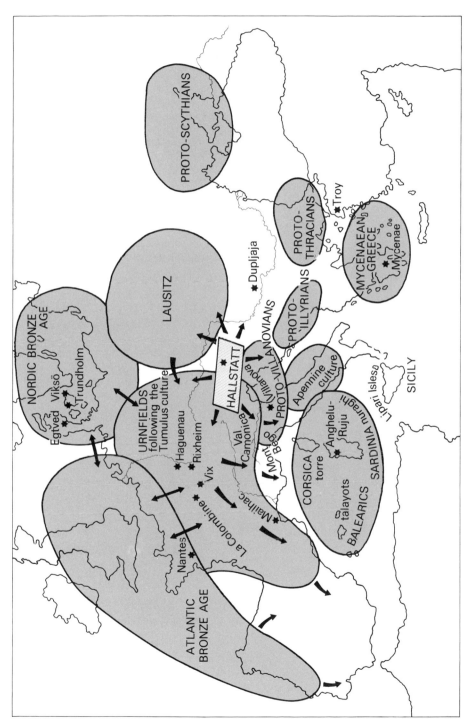

3 Europe in the Urnfield period

188 'Atlantic'-type leaf-shaped sword, Bellevue, near Nantes

189 Spanish Atlantic sword, late Bronze Age, Rio Esla (Leon)

exported as far afield as England. Hybridisations with cultures attributed to the urnfields appeared in the Paris basin and west central France, with large hoards like the one at Vénat. Alpine or eastern Swiss types mingled with western types at this period when economic exchanges were still commoner than warlike confrontations. The first concern of the Urnfield peoples was to cast their important production of bronzes and perhaps, too, to assure their supplies of tin from the countries in the west.

The uniformity of style of the carp's-tongue swords shows a definite 'Atlantic community' at this time: its existence has often not been recognised, eclipsed as it was by the great 'protoceltic' phenomena on the Continent at that time, the Tumulus and Urnfield cultures. But it was a period of great economic prosperity based on western supplies of tin and also on the complex organisation of trade to routes linking the British and Atlantic worlds with ethnic groups on the Continent. But if the trade in metal objects carried on in the Atlantic regions is easy to demonstrate, other aspects of these cultures are often difficult to detect: the lack of burials, monuments and settlements in certain Atlantic regions often deprives us of any accurate information about their social life and religious beliefs and of points of comparison with that of the Urnfield peoples.

Cremation burials

In this late Bronze Age period, groups of Urnfield peoples settled in Belgium, deriving classic characteristics from southern Germany. In the British Isles, too, the dead were being cremated, but the latest urns, known as Deverel–Rimbury (which were massive and barrel-shaped with fingerprint decoration) are derived from an ancient local tradition. Cremation had begun very early in the Bronze Age in Britain. The clumsy pots had no connection, moreover, with the often very fine ceramics of the continental Urnfield areas. Normandy and west central France were also subject to the influence of the new fashion in funerals which had come from the east. By contrast the Armorican peninsula was more conservative and both cremations and inhumations there are found only in tombs without any

204

characteristic grave goods. Spain, too, practised cremation, but with some distinctive cultural features: cave drawings and funerary stelae like the famous stone with the dead warrior of Solana which was mentioned earlier.

The decorative style of this period supplies little information about beliefs except for a few of the everlasting sun or wheel symbols, etc. Geometric art still held sway but was soon to give way to the livelier Hallstatt style of the early Iron Age. A few harbingers were already appearing like the little stylised stag's head, found in the hoard of carp's-tongue swords at Challans in the Vendée. Nor must we forget the use of carts and chariots, whose part in worship has been alluded to many times in these pages.

The economy: the salt trade

Very little more is known about domestic life in the late Bronze Age period of the Atlantic. The British Isles provide a little information on settlements: small circular huts with thatched roofs have been reconstructed; they had stone footings, sometimes protected by a bank of earth. Traces of cultivated fields have been found in the neighbourhood of the settlements. Querns and bronze sickles indicate the importance of agriculture. There are even distinctive British types of sickle which were sometimes exported to the Continent. They were socketed, a fortunate characteristic by which they can be distinguished from the tanged or knobbed sickles of the Alps.

It has been possible to study diet as a result of pollen analysis, which has shown the presence of graminaceous plants. Rubaceae, plants from clearings and forest margins, testify to the clearing of land for pasture. Remains of cereals have sometimes enabled us to identify the plants grown. At La Roussellerie in Loire-Atlantique Dr Tessier pointed out the presence of wheat and seeds of vetch, a kind of wild pea, which radio-carbon methods were able to date to 770 b.c. At Questembert in Morbihan there were charred acorns associated with the remains of wattle from huts. At Cherbourg there were hazelnuts: gathering clearly supplemented agricultural production.

Animal husbandry, from the evidence of bones collected from settlements and bogs, extended to the large ox, the sheep of the lake dwellings, and pig. At St Pabu in Finistère, two little horses of the steppes – the species known as Przewalski horses – were lying besides some bronze axes. Hunters stalked deer and wild boar. In fact the technical innovations had hardly affected hunting and pastoral activities which are the normal complement of these types of society.

However, one new feature appeared: it was at this period that the first traces of the salt trade were to be found. Salt had long been collected periodically, probably from dried-up pools beside the ocean. This must go back to the beginning of the Neolithic, for as soon as wheat or barley were being used, seasoning became a necessity. A loaf or porridge without salt is not very appetising, as unfortunate people who are ordered a salt-free diet will agree. The quality of the salt raked up from the sands or rocks must have been mediocre, not to speak of the purgative effects produced by the impurities. In order to refine it, a saline solution had to be obtained and set in settling tanks to eliminate the impurities before transforming the salt into small marketable blocks. The technique involved heating the brine in receptacles placed on hot charcoal. A few traces of such installations seem to go back to the late Bronze Age. The hearths, like the ones at Préfailles in Loire-Atlantique, were rudimentary: trumpet-shaped clay pillars supported flat stones on which the salt containers or troughs were arranged to heat the brine. Later, in Gaulish and Gallo-Roman times, the process was improved. The work of Y. Coppens and, later, P. L. Gouletquer has thrown much light on the techniques used in Brittany. The exploitation of sea salt was to develop in south-eastern England and the Basque country.

The sea played an important part in other aspects of life. Often settlements were sited on promontories or small coastal islands which were alternately linked with the mainland, or not, according to the tides. This type of settlement was still being used by Gaulish peoples like the Veneti in Morbihan and had the distinction of annoying Caesar: the coastal tribes were able to change positions rapidly by sea, and well organised sieges with towers and ballistae were of no effect against such mobile tactics.

The sea, which helped communications, also supplied raw materials: flint, which continued to be used for a long time, stones for querns and polishers, and occasionally whalebone, etc. Last, it was an inexhaustible source of food. The piles of shells mixed with sherds of Bronze Age pottery are legion. As always oysters, clams, periwinkles and other local seafood were eaten. The dish of 'fruits de mer' has changed very little since then.

Currency axes

Around 700 BC, after the carp's-tongue swords, tens of thousands of rectangular socketed axes with a high lead content were manufactured in Armorica. These are the 'Breton-type' axes of early authors, but the large numbers of them in eastern Normandy, particularly the Cotentin peninsula, would make the term 'Armorican' more suitable. They have been found in extraordinary quantities on some sites, 4000 axes at Maure-de-Bretagne in Ille-et-Vilaine, for example. They are rarely associated with other tools: a few fragments of waste from casting or broken remains of tools, one or two bits of copper slag and some sporadic bracelets which are shown by their bosses or more compact decoration to belong to the early Iron Age. Models differ in size: there are small axes, from 5 to 8cm, medium sizes of about 10 to 13cm and occasional large luxurious variations, often attractively decorated. Early authors saw them as genuine currency, with multiples and sub-multiples. Unfortunately the distribution maps show distinct areas, so the small axes are more numerous in the Cotentin and Ille-et-Vilaine than in western Armorica. Peculiarities more subtle than mere dimensions make it possible to identify the locality of factories in Côtes-du-Nord. So within this Armorican phenomenon we can recognise the production of local factories.

190 Arrangement in layers of the hoard of socketed axes at Cléguérec (Brittany)

These axes are found in jars or in hoards buried in the ground. They are arranged in circles in cylindrical cavities, sometimes lined with clay. Their wedge shape made it possible to arrange them with the cutting edge towards the centre, in several layers. In the last few years hoards of some 800 axes have been found at Loundéac in Côtes-du-Nord and Le Trehou in Finistère. At Moidrey in the southern part of the Manche department, G. Verron excavated a hoard in which the axes were attached to each other by a band of linen or hemp passed through the loops on the side.

Why have they been referred to as 'currency axes'? In the first place the storage of a large quantity of the same type of object is reminiscent of monetary treasure houses. Second, because the axes are often very badly made, badly cast, not trimmed, with a cutting edge that is not fit for use of any kind, or even with no cutting edge. Furthermore the socket, which is very deep, reaches the cutting edge, making them impossible to sharpen. Last, their composition is very rich in lead, from 30–60 per cent, and it seems likely that if the axe had been used as such, it would have bent or broken. There are even some genuine lead axes with no internal socket: these are undoubtedly ingots and so, most probably, are the others. Ingot or currency – the idea of exchange is the same. But it is rare to melt down currency in order to make something else. The socketed axes may have sometimes been ingots and sometimes currency.

They gave rise to an important trade, the details of which remain unclear. Indeed, thousands changed hands in the last century, too, and were exported as far afield as the Peabody Museum in Cambridge, USA. If their presence in America causes no confusion, axes of doubtful origin in Russian or Polish museums do seem rather a long way from our shores. The only reasonable certainty is that the trade reached at least as far as the British Isles, the Netherlands and north Germany. It reached the Alpine regions, Switzerland, the Rhône valley and the South of France. A few isolated axes reached the south-east. It is odd that none seem to have penetrated into Iberia, although socketed axes without loops are known there; but they would more likely be Mediterranean in origin – Launatian perhaps, produced in the neighbourhood of Montpellier, which we shall discuss later.

Finally, ancient texts report that some Iberian peoples paid for their transactions with pieces of metal, portions of silver bars, for example. The Armoricans must have offered their socketed axes. Did they grow rich or remain poor? Both possibilities seem plausible: rich, perhaps, because the hoards represent a vast production which overflowed into northern Europe; or poor because we can recognise that many of the axes, which were often of very bad quality, were not valued in the market and remained unsold, stored in the ground for the greater delight of future archaeologists. It is true, too, that at that period, when iron was arriving and replacing bronze, the Bretons were wrong to continue stubbornly making their traditional products. The frequency of the hoards possibly reflects a sudden problem of over-production, caused by the general upheaval in the European economy. This would also explain the general poverty of the early Iron Age in Armorica.

Chapter 12

Hallstatt and the Early Iron Age

Iron is plentiful in the earth's surface and is often found in shallow easily workable deposits. But it is not easy to handle. To separate it from its ore it requires higher temperatures than copper and therefore more sophisticated furnaces with very highly developed tuyères. It must be purified and refined in successive operations. The first attempts to smelt iron ore no doubt produced nothing more than a disheartening, slaggy mess, shapeless and of no use at all. And yet one day iron, too, arrived on the scene, and the people who were the first to possess it became formidable conquerors, for the iron sword was more manageable and tougher than the bronze blade which was fragile and quickly damaged by blows. It gave indisputable superiority to the warriors equipped with such modern weapons.

Even before the beginning of the second millennium, several barbarian peoples in Armenia or Asia Minor discovered the secret of iron-working. The first organised kingdom to guess at its importance was that of the Hittites. They probably bought the secret and guarded it jealously for several centuries. This explains their successes in war. But, they, too, fell victim to the wave of catastrophes and destruction that struck the Near East around 1200 BC. The secret escaped without more ado from the smoking ruins of the Hittite empire and led successively to the prosperity of neighbouring peoples until it gradually reached Europe. In Greece iron seems to have been in current use from the tenth century. It took longer to reach barbarian Europe, where for a long time it was simply an object of curiosity, occasionally of adornment. We may quote, for example, a certain late Bronze Age sword from the Alpine regions, the hilt of which was adorned with iron, then a precious metal. Soon the roles were to be reversed and it was bronze that was to decorate iron implements from time to time. The final introduction of iron into central and western Europe depended on the vagaries of the migrations of the cultures known as Hallstatt.

Hallstatt and the rock salt mines

Hallstatt lies in upper Austria in the heart of the Salzkammergut, the land of rock salt.

Today the wooden chalets of the picturesque little town are strung out along a blue-green lake with typical parti-coloured gondolas sailing on it. After an amused and slightly fearful glance at the skulls bedecked with painted gothic characters which are preserved in the old church, the tourists take the cable cars which carry them painlessly up several hundred metres to the salt mine. Then cheery groups sit astride the sledges that take them deep down to the galleries. A little further on, others stride more solemnly over the wooded slopes. These are the lovers of the past, making their pilgrimage to the most famous of Iron Age cemeteries, in which the tombs, which are now empty, can still be distinguished in the form of small circular excavations. A large commemorative plaque celebrates the discovery of the Hallstatt necropolis which contained more than 2000 individuals.

In November 1846 Burgermeister Johann Georg Ramsauer, Supervisor of the Imperial Forests and Waterways, was digging out gravel when he unearthed a skull with a bronze buckle. He was very intrigued and set to work systematically in the days that followed. There was not just one skeleton but, as in Grimm's Fairy Tales, there were seven accompanied by pottery and bronze jewels. The Hallstatt saga was beginning. With moral and by no means negligible financial encouragement from Baron von Sacken, the curator of the Vienna museum, Ramsauer methodically explored the cemetery with the help of an enthusiastic team of workmen and from 1846 to 1863 almost 1000 tombs were opened, yielding more than 6000 objects. The publication, embellished with watercolours in pretty pastel tints, makes a change from austere modern plans, but it was very advanced for the period. It shows the skeletons aligned east–west, surrounded by a circle of stones and sometimes covered by a makeshift mound. Cremations, of which there were about the same number as inhumations, showed that both funeral rites were practised concurrently.

Excavations became less frequent subsequently but we should note an important campaign by the curator of the Museum, Dr Friedich Norton, between 1937 and 1939. He studied some sixty burials. The total grave goods from the cemetery comprised almost 10,000 objects which are at present distributed mainly between the museums in Hallstatt, Vienna and Linz. The luxury goods, weapons or jewels, are bronze and then iron. The cemetery was in use over a long period stretching well into the second Iron Age. Besides the tombs, a few houses or small forts made of wooden logs are known: these date back to the proto-historic period.

One of the reasons for the prosperity of Hallstatt, of course, was the working of the salt mines. Modern mine workings have often re-opened or disclosed traces of Iron Age excavations and discovered interesting tools. Wicker baskets, spades, wooden tubs and sledges, torches of resinous wood were all used. The salt was cut out with antler picks but bronze ones with wings were used too. Even the miners' clothing, made of coarse cloth or leather, is known. Some workmen had been buried by the sudden collapse of a gallery; their heads were protected by leather hats and on their feet they wore sandals which were also of leather. The most fascinating of these remains is a cunning rucksack with a wooden frame. The leather pocket could be emptied at one go by means of an ingenious device like a trap door which was operated by a wooden lever.

191 Hallstatt dagger
(Austria)

The appearance of iron

Salt from Hallstatt was certainly exported far and wide, especially as the mine was situated near one of the traditional routes linking south Germany and western Europe with the Mediterranean world, by way of modern Yugoslavia and Greece. In return Hallstatt was the recipient of new influences and probably of an influx of foreign peoples. The style of the bronze weapons, ornaments and vessels is in sharp contrast with traditional Bronze Age goods. Of course we find the eternal bronze wheels or spirals but alongside these there is a sudden unfolding of a whole new figurative and animal art. A bronze cauldron has a long-horned cow followed by her latest-born clambering round its rim; a votive axe is surmounted by an amusing little horseman, one of the favourite themes of Hallstatt art. Fibulae are transformed, now baroque and enormous with dozens of pendants, now formed in the shape of animals. Bronze vessels diversify: there are cauldrons, already known in the Bronze Age, but great bucket-shaped situlae as well, an invention of the early Iron Age. Soon a whole range of receptacles, decorated with gryphons or motifs which testify to Greek or Etruscan influence were to be found mingled with native products of the Hallstatt cultures. All this hollow ware is linked in part with the trade in wine which the barbarians were so fond of. It is pointless to launch into a diatribe against the 'Celtic thirst' mentioned in many ancient texts.

Last, an innovation in cutting instruments: the introduction of iron which brought a change in weapons. The long iron swords of the horsemen were adorned with heavy pommels encrusted with bone or ivory plaques which were sometimes blended with amber. The chapes at the end of the scabbards were fitted with wide appendages at the sides, made of bronze, a metal that was now used only for the decoration of weapons. To supplement the sword there was the strong Hallstatt iron dagger, often fitted with a handle topped by antennae. At Hallstatt one of the daggers had a blade encrusted with gold and the scabbard was also overlaid with leaf of the noble metal. These warriors had expensive tastes!

The 'migrations' of the Hallstatt horsemen

Thrilled by the discovery of the wonders in the Salzkammergut tombs, Europe quite naturally christened the early Iron Age 'Hallstatt'. But there is a certain ambiguity in this. French writers, following the example of J. Déchelette, made a distinction between the

Bronze Age, which included the late Bronze Age Urnfield cultures, and the Hallstatt period. The German Paul Reinecke used a different system of chronology: he included the Urnfield cultures in the Hallstatt period. He made a distinction between the Bronze Age, divided into four phases, A, B, C, D, the last of which corresponds to the beginning of the late Bronze Age, and the Hallstatt period, which was also split into four phases. Hallstatt A and B in P. Reinecke's system correspond to the classic Urnfield period (W. Kimmig's UF II and III) of the late Bronze Age. Hallstatt periods C and D, for Reinecke, correspond to the traditional early Iron Age. But that is not all; to make things more complicated the term 'Hallstatt period' is applied to cultures that have nothing to do with the true Hallstatt cultures, but happen to be contemporary: this is the case with many late Urnfield groups.

Hallstatt by their age or Hallstatt by their metallurgical techniques, in which iron gradually replaced bronze, the new industries are found in various sites and well scattered over central and western Europe: hence the notion of a race of nomadic warriors, following where the vagaries of their raids and grazing land led them across the continent. What is there in the story of these Hallstatt 'migrations'?

Their origin is certainly complex. As soon as populations of horsemen are seen to be on the move the inexhaustible 'reserves of the eastern steppes' are invoked. On the evidence of a few right-branching horse bits, found in the lake settlements, Thraco-Cimmerian invasions have been postulated, starting in the last Urnfield phase, but these have yet to be proved.

The only firm fact is that, very early in the Iron Age, new societies appeared in Austria and south Germany led by a war-like aristocracy. Thanks to their superior weaponry, they were able to dominate part of Europe in the seventh century. They reached Belgium, eastern France and Burgundy, where an important group settled, while other waves rolled down the Rhône valley, extending the Celtic influence as far as Spain.

For these Hallstatt peoples showed themselves by many of their characteristics to be direct forerunners of the Celts, and indeed of warrior Celts. All this is an admirable 'trial run' for the 'great barbarian invasions' which, a thousand years later, were to follow the same routes and sweep away the Roman empire.

These troubled times are reflected clearly in the development of fortified settlements and even of large earthworks. One of the most famous is at Heuneburg near Siegmaringen; it watched over the upper reaches of the Danube. In the neighbourhood of this site huge princely tumuli were constructed: the one at Hochmichele was no less than 80m in diameter and 13m high.

All these south German tombs are very rich. It is a curious feature that the pottery returns to a style of decoration that had been interrupted by the Urnfield episode. There is a renaissance of *Kerbschnitt*, the technique of excision, often emphasised by polychrome encrustations, which had already been used by the Tumulus cultures of the middle Bronze Age. Weapons still included the great iron sword and the small dagger with antennae. There is evidence in the vessels of contacts with the Mediterranean world from which glassware was imported, little beads and bracelets of blue or emerald glass and even the first glass cups – a Phoenician invention, it is said. Even more extraordinary products reached south Germany, like the fragments of silk, found in the tumulus at Hochmichele, which had come from China by heaven knows what strange routes. We might comment at length on these manifold exchanges.

Religion and society

In the Hallstatt period the rite of cremation practised by the Urnfield peoples lost ground. We see the gradual reappearance of the ancient rite of inhumation and of the tumulus, so dear to the middle Bronze Age Tumulus peoples. At first it was in competition with cremation, then gradually it prevailed. The new element in funeral rites, in its most sophisticated form, was the cart burial: the chief was interred in his chariot of war or of state. Sometimes the chariot was dismantled – the corpse lay in the body of the chariot and the wheels were arranged carefully along the walls of the grave. The tumuli of the chiefs were often imposing like the one already mentioned, at Hochmichele. But in some groups cemeteries with many small tumuli are known (in Languedoc or Jura, for example).

Religious life still borrowed a great deal from the Bronze Age, with the adoption of the votive chariot. The most distinctive is at Strettweg in Styria. In the centre a grand lady, her waist encased in a corset, was carrying a huge bronze bowl on her head, no doubt intended to receive offerings. Smaller figures bustled around, some looking forward, some back. They were brandishing axes and leading a stag. Two horsemen with bucklers were placed on either side of the goddess, the one on the right facing forward and the one on the left in the opposite direction. Thus the goddess was guarded on all sides. The meaning of the

192 Funerary votive axe, Hallstatt (Austria)

whole arrangement escapes us but is no doubt linked with the mythology of the period. The stag is there again, an animal beloved in Val Camonica, but there is the horseman too, a new and important theme in religious beliefs.

The Hallstatt world marks a break in the economic and cultural unity of the European Bronze Age. The march towards history, which is quite close now, takes place through a complex maze of changes and innovations. But firmly established cultural and economic traditions persist. Sometimes the new groups jostle the older ones and then mingle closely with them, sometimes, on the other hand, they exist side by side with no clashes and with a tacit agreement as to territories. At the present time it is still very difficult to sort out all these complexities. The historic civilisations, for their part, continue their advance westward. They reach northern Italy; contacts with the barbarian world become more frequent now and Greek or Italianate pottery, cauldrons from Aegean or Etruscan workshops, found more and more frequently in Hallstatt tombs, testify to closer and closer relations.

The Hallstatt cultures were not, of course, uniform. They evolved with time, and, moreover, were transformed as their wanderings took them ever further away from their original centres. The earliest are close to the Bronze Age in their way of life and their tools, the latest show by their equipment, their customs – as for example the use of cart burials – that they are the immediate forerunners of the men of the second Iron Age, including the Gauls of the La Tène period; those Gauls whose name we learn from ancient texts and whom, not so long ago, little schoolchildren in France and even in a now dead colonial empire stretching from Indo-China to Equatorial Africa, learned to recognise as 'their ancestors', those Gauls who were preceded by millennia of prehistoric or 'barbarian' cultures. But we will take a swift, bird's-eye look at the arrival of the Hallstatt peoples on French territory, or, rather, the territory of that nation in gestation, independent Gaul.

Hallstatt and late Urnfield peoples in France

The Hallstatt migrations arrived via eastern France and proceeded southwards by the Rhône valley, north westwards and into the centre by the Seine basin. The first Hallstatt swords, made of bronze, have a pommel ending in a trapezoidal tang. The blade widens near the guard and this distinguishes it from the parallel-sided blades of the carp's-tongue swords. These swords are found with crescent-shaped razors, often perforated, and excised pottery. Soon the great iron sword with winged chapes was to replace them.

But the details of the settlement pattern are complex and J. P. Millotte has emphasised its many forms. The finest examples are found in the Jura group with the Hallstatt tumuli at La Combe d'Ain and Barésia, which yielded iron swords and bracelets decorated with grooves and incisions. Lorraine shows various affinities, some with the Belgian group at Court-Saint-Etienne, some with Bavaria. In Alsace, in Haguenau Forest, where the middle Bronze Age tumuli had developed distinctively, the new fashion caught on too. Soon

193 Iron Age funerary urn, (north Germany)

194 Reconstruction of an early Iron Age burial, Dohren Grab (north Germany)

magnificent belt plaques of bronze sheet decorated with delicate geometric patterns were to be made there. In Champagne the Urnfield culture lingered on.

Burgundy appealed to the Hallstatt peoples: they built large funeral mounds there, like the one at Magny-Lambert, a great tumulus 40m in diameter and nearly 6m high. In the middle lay a warrior surrounded by his jewels and his razor, his weapons and a fine situla of corrugated bronze which could have been made in the Hallstatt forges. Trade coming up the Seine valley and passing through the gap at Langres into the Rhône highway could be surveyed from the oppidum at Mont Lassois in the fair land of Burgundy. Tin came down from the north while Massalian amphorae travelled up to Mont Lassois. The prosperity of the region was to become more marked. At the very end of the Hallstatt period, the famous princely tomb at Vix was to mark its zenith. Who has not heard of the princess with her gold diadem and huge bronze krater? Pictures of that burial are known world wide.

A scattering of bronze or iron swords marks the progress of the Hallstatt warriors southwards, from south Germany towards southern France. They dawdled a little through the garrigues of Languedoc or on the edge of the Massif Central. In the Ravin des Arcs at Notre-Dame-de-Londres in Hérault, a pretty excised vase was found with the traditional weapons. Alongside Hallstatt tumuli we frequently find dolmens being re-used. At Argelliers a Hallstatt blacksmith had been buried under a megalithic monument. Near him a clay tuyére had been deposited, indicating clearly the calling of the deceased.

The Launatian culture

Urnfield groups continued to live alongside the new arrivals in Languedoc. But the most amazing instance of survival is that of a metallurgical industry which continued making typical Bronze Age products well into the Iron Age. Cazalis de Fondouce called it Launatian, following the discovery of the Launac hoard near Fabrègues in 1897. This 'post late Bronze Age', as J. Guilaine called it more recently, included socketed axes, conical spear ferrules, triangular scrapers, incised bracelets, wheels and socketed hammers, continuing a long tradition. Affinities between these axes and those from the Atlantic workshops are seen in the quadrilateral shape and the decoration of lines ending in dots which are sometimes enclosed in a circle. They are cousins to the Armorican socketed axes which were also being made until a late phase of the Hallstatt period. The Launatian is known from a whole series of large hoards which came to light in the Aude and Hérault departments. But the most surprising discovery, still partly unpublished, is that of the cargo of a ship that sank in 8m of water in the area of Cap de Rochelongue near Agde. The same bronzes as in the Launatian were found there and also some plates of pure copper. A Launatian trader, or one of his customers, had come to grief within sight of harbour.

195 Launatian spear ferrule (Hérault)

The Launatian culture remains something of an enigma. Some people have seen it simply as a miscellaneous collection of objects, the treasures of second-hand dealers collecting useless old bronzes. And yet socketed axes and conical spear ferrules are new products of a distinctive school. The bronze workers of Launac, like their Armorican brothers, were fighting a rear-guard action. They persisted in making weapons and tools in the old style, not only in the Hallstatt period, but even a little later. Were Languedoc bronzes simply objects of barter? The variety of the tools and ornaments made seems to undermine that hypothesis: pre-monetary objects were generally produced in large series, starting from one basic model. In any case, trade in Launatian products was held in esteem all over southern France and some belated derivatives of the industry are found in the Massif Central.

The oppidum of Cayla

Languedoc was very densely occupied in the proto-historic period. One of the most endearing of the Languedoc Urnfield centres is 30km north west of Narbonne: these, too, are belated Urnfield groups continuing a late Bronze Age tradition into the middle of the Hallstatt period. In the little village of Mailhac, hidden among the vines, Odette and Jean Taffanel have been conducting exemplary investigations over some forty years, often alone and – at least in the early days of their work – without official funds. Archaeology has become their everyday life and their big family house has quite naturally been transformed into a living museum where the treasures they have dug up are lovingly displayed.

The oppidum of Cayla, with its great limestone blocks, watches over the whole plain of Narbonne and commands the approach to the meagre pastures of the Causses. The dead were buried at the foot of the oppidum, in necropolises, where cremation was still the rule, and which the Taffanels named the Moulin and the Grand Bassin, names which are now classics in the annals of European proto-history.

The oppidum was occupied from the eighth century and the earliest Moulin necropolises date from that period. The new arrivals, probably coming from south Germany, practised cremation in urns. The pottery, with simple incised decoration, shows horses and men in a very schematic style. Cayla was a large village: the houses were wooden with stone footings. Hunting and animal husbandry were the main occupations of its inhabitants and often a quarter of meat was placed with the pots beside the dead in their tombs, as a reminder of that fact.

The second period of occupation at Mailhac, in the seventh century, witnessed the founding of the Grand Bassin cemetery, with the appearance of iron and of tombs with considerable grave goods. The most considerable are great pits dug in the ground with a narrow entrance covered by a stone slab and a small tumulus, which soon disappeared because the pits collapsed and the stones from the tumulus fell through to fill the underground cavity. In the simple circular trench, dug in the ground, a funeral urn was found containing the burned bones of a man of vigorous physique, leader of a band of horsemen, surrounded by no less than 57 items of pottery and the remains of his chariot, reinforced with bronze and iron and drawn by two richly caparisoned horses. The bits were of a Thraco-Cimmerian type, suggesting a remote origin whose nearest outpost was in the district of Baden.

In the sixth century the Cayla oppidum received some fortification: the pottery became more diverse in form: bowls with feet, amphorae with two handles, carenated or situla-shaped vases, etc. The metal objects were iron knives, daggers with hilts equipped with antennae, fibulae with their bows twisted like a serpent uncoiling. The horse bits confirm that these hunters are still horsemen. Soon they were to wear large bronze plaques with three hooks on their belts and curious fibulae, shaped like crossbows, that were to be found again in the Pyrenees and the north-eastern Iberian peninsula. But, on the shores of the Golfe du Lion, historic people had just arrived. Cayla's contacts with the classical Mediterranean world began in the sixth century and she imported Greek and Italian wine amphorae, fine 'bucchero negro' bowls, burnished black, which originated in Etruscan workshops, and Phocaean pottery. Mailhac provides an example of these Urnfield groups lingering on into the early Iron Age and contrasting with the traditional Hallstatt groups with their tumuli.

In the south-west, other groups with urns in their necropolises were to develop in the early Iron Age, some in the Pyrenees and some in the Arcachon area where an important group has recently been studied by J. P. Mohen.

196 Late Urnfield vessels:
left Agulanna (Gerona, Spain),
right Millas (Pyrénées orientales)

In the Pyrenees and Catalonia, Urnfield and Hallstatt influences became blended to give the so-called Celtiberian cultures at the dawn of history. But now the mutation is taking place everywhere in barbarian Europe: proto-history is passing into history.

Italianate cultures: the Villanovians

In northern Italy, one of the most important cultures of the Hallstatt period is that of Villanova, named after a suburb of Bologna. It is characterised by fortified settlements and necropolises with urns, continuing the Urnfield traditions. The Villanovians were contemporary with the first Celts in France. In the early or proto-Villanovian phase, the urns were biconical with incised geometric decoration: meanders, triangles and zigzags. The metal goods were still bronze: razors, simple fibulae, knives and daggers. In the Villanovian period proper, iron appeared both in weaponry, helmets and swords, and in tools. But bronze, now a noble metal, was used for making jewellery or fine cordoned situlae.

The funerary urns became highly original. In the Bologna area they remained classic, biconical, adorned on the carenation with Greek key motifs or triangles, as in the early phase. In Tuscany, the urn was covered with a clay helmet, sometimes accompanied by small iron plaques. They are exact replicas of bronze helmets with a strong sagittal crest in use from the late Bronze Age. The Latium group invented other shapes for cremation urns:

197 Villanovian fibula, Sassa di Furbara, near Rome

198 Villanovian funeral urn, topped with a helmet, Tarquinia (Latium)

they were clay replicas of small circular huts. The door, which was wide, was painted on and the roof embellished with motifs such as totems, ducks or persons. Sometimes the beams of the hut frame formed a succession of forks. It is odd to record that, some thousands of kilometres further north in Pomerania, this same rite of hut-shaped urns was to be used alongside others in which the human face can be recognised. This is more than a coincidence; it is a sure indication of links between the Nordic and Mediterranean worlds.

The Villanovians worked local mines and took part in the amber and possibly the glass trade. Agriculture and animal husbandry continued to supply their basic needs. They had horses and, if we are to judge by the furnishings of some female burials, the women were as adept as the men on horseback. Villages were well organised, so much so that some have tried to find the earliest signs of urban organisation in them. The Villanovians were to play an important part in the birth of the historic Etruscan civilisation which was to preserve some material features of the earlier equipment – helmets, sword types, etc.

Among the Villanovians' contemporaries, some groups developed a distinctive art in bronze, that of the situla. Classic Hallstatt situlae had a smooth surface which was then strengthened by horizontal cordons. The decoration, which was often Greek in inspiration

219

was restricted to the handle supports. In the Este region or in Carniole the surface of the situla came to life with the kind of processions known from earliest antiquity in the Aegean Bronze Age: now warriors march past with their weapons, helmets and bucklers; now women bear offerings to the gods on their heads; banqueting scenes show us footmen bringing in wild boar or mutton on spits with eager dogs running alongside. Sometimes musicians play the cithara, prizefighters clash using curious little dumb-bells, horsemen exercise their steeds. Animal friezes show stags, does, ducks and geese, but the bestiary is completed with fantastic beasts. On the famous situla of La Certosa at Bologna winged monsters go by, chimaeras spitting fire or devouring their prey.

Figurative and animal art was to surge forward further east or rather the 'royal hordes' of the Scythian civilisation were to adorn themselves with their jewels of gold or their felt hats decked with fantastic animals. But that is another story.

Epilogue

The Men of the Bronze Age

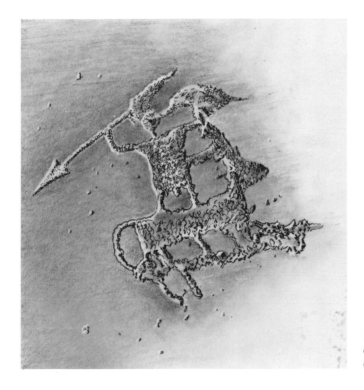

199 Horseman with shield, rock carving, Capo di Ponte (Val Camonica)

So the barbarians of the Bronze Age had had to give way to warriors armed with iron. Their territory had been reduced before the progressive westward advance of the Mediterranean peoples, some of whom claimed to hold a monopoly in civilisation. Soon the Gauls themselves would have to bow their heads before Roman imperialism. Either willingly or by force, they would all have to accept the civilising effects of progress. But did they need them so badly? What serious charges can be preferred against them? Perhaps that they preferred the easy-going indolence of a village life style to the feverish activity of the great cities? That they chose the delights of oral literature, which makes everything into a tale, rather than the stern training required by writing? That they defended fiercely the rights of the individual or small tribe in preference to the rigid structures of a great centralising power? Even wide-ranging phenomena which spread far and wide, like the middle Bronze Age tumuli or the late Bronze Age urnfields, displayed a host of local adaptations or regional peculiarities. Like many people in the past, if not the present, who have been considered 'barbarians', those of the Bronze Age were less barbarian than they were supposed to be. The technical and cultural contributions which Europe owes to them are eloquent proof of that fact.

Metallurgy and its techniques

The invention of, and progress in metallurgy must take pride of place amongst the contributions made by the Bronze Age peoples. The extraction of ores is a spectacular development, in the first place. The earliest skimmings of surface strata, sometimes supplemented by vertical shafts or small open-cast quarries, were enough for a long time. But demand increased in the course of the second millennium, leading to mining complexes like the one at Mitterberg with wood-lined galleries, ventilation systems, water channels and sledges, in other words to exploitation of copper on an almost industrial scale.

Prospecting for alluvial tin deposits, with a view to alloys, and techniques of treating ores were to evolve side by side. The range of ores being sought widened. Hotter furnaces allowed the reduction of more difficult ores like the sulphides. In addition lead was being sought and was to be in common use in the late Bronze Age. Sublety in varying the proportions of alloys led to the manufacture of compounds to order, more or less rich in tin or lead according to the purpose of the product; bronze rich in tin, which was very hard, was used for hammers while the pre-monetary axes required a high lead content. What progress, too, from the earliest moulds, crudely hewn from stone to bronze moulds with several parts, valves and matrices, or again clay moulds cunningly reinforced with wood!

As the cultures evolved so the tools of the artisan were renewed and their range increased. The countless forms of Bronze Age flanged axe, winged or socketed, were later abandoned and in more recent periods there was a return to the old model with a vertical shaft, invented by the Iranians or Sumerians and used in the Aegean. But, on the other hand, how many modern tools were conceived in a Bronze Age brain – socketed gouges, and chisels, knives, awls, goldsmith's graving and chasing tools, etc.

Metal weapons were already setting firmly in the forms that were to last down to modern times. The sword, developed gradually from the little Chalcolithic daggers, has hardly changed in general conception down to our own day. In defensive weaponry, bronze helmets and cuirasses, the only advances, down to the time of Napoleon III, were in the greater strength of the metals used.

Ornamental work benefited from the progress in tool-making: gravers and hammers produced bracelets with incised decoration or fine gold and bronze objects patiently adorned with repoussé work, like the Avanton cone or the Danish shields. The anvil was no longer simply a nondescript flat stone, but a complicated tool with stakes, horns, and a working surface that was often milled, allowing gold bars or rings to be made to order and more elaborate repoussé techniques to be evolved. The invention of the lost-wax process, still in use today, made possible the manifold and delicate decorations achieved by moulding.

200 'Flesh hook', late Bronze Age, Antrim (Ireland)

Means of locomotion made remarkable progress. The adze-blade certainly played a great part in the development of boat-building, as in the building of houses. Above all, the horse was domesticated for the first time.

The accoutrements of carts and horses, in particular, made great strides. The earliest wooden wheels of the Beaker peoples, both Corded Ware and Bell Beaker, were solid. The hollow wheel was probably invented somewhere in the Italian lake settlements and then later the spoked wheel. Finally in the Urnfield period bronze craftsmanship led to the casting of those magnificent bronze wheels which are undeniably technical masterpieces. The horse was arrayed in leather and bronze, from the bits and harness buckles to the countless trinkets that excited it in battle or in games.

Agrarian structures

The proliferation of bronze axes had a reason: woodland was being cleared more rapidly everywhere, because of the need for wood, of course, but also because of the development of animal husbandry and tillage. Wood was used to build dwellings, on piles or not, and for making palisades to form cattle pens or fortifications. Even roads were built of wood in marshy districts.

Plant selection made it possible to grow several varieties of wheat or barley. Millet was grown as well, and an improved type of wild pea: no doubt fruit trees, apple, pear and cherry, were also being bred selectively. But this was not peculiar to Europe.

The bronze sickle replaced wooden sickles reinforced with flint. As G. Gaucher observes, they were not always intended for cereals, as witness the famous gold bill-hook, beloved of the Druids for the cutting of sacred mistletoe.

223

The ard developed, and traces of wooden ones from Danish peat-bogs, as well as Scandinavian or Alpine drawings show how it evolved.

Animal husbandry increased dramatically, with pigs, cattle, etc., and, above all, in the later period, a newcomer of great standing, the horse. A few bits have been found, it seems, in late Neolithic lake dwellings but it is in the Bronze Age that horse raising developed on a large scale. This creature, which had been hunted since Palaeolithic times, was finally conquered by Bronze Age man – man's finest conquest, it is said – and has been a familiar part of our environment ever since. Cattle and diary produce, as we may deduce from the cheese drainers, played an important part in the diet. Danish costumes show, too, the economic importance of wool, an indispensable complement to garments of linen or hempen cloth. Trade in skins and leather must also have been considerable : we assume this from the fragments of leather shrouds or scabbards found during excavations, or from the attire of those unfortunate miners, trapped in the workings at Hallstatt, not forgetting, on a much more sumptuous scale, the furs of the kurgan princes of the steppes.

If agriculture had been known since Neolithic times, a new feature now saw the light : agrarian structures. The first true fields appeared at the dawn of the Iron Age in western Europe : banks or ditches now began to separate plots of cultivated land. These 'Celtic fields' have been thoroughly studied in the British Isles. The separation of cultivated areas is suggested, too, by the 'parcellaires' or networks of geometric shapes in cave drawings, but the interpretation of these is still a matter for debate.

Harnessing techniques were perfected : the simple ard was drawn at first by bullocks, then by mules or by horses in the late Bronze Age. Four-wheeled carts were used to transport produce from the fields to the villages and to exchange large quantities of goods. Not all the carts were used for burials or for warfare.

The artistic contribution

The barbarians of the Bronze Age were not all great builders. In western Europe the famous temple at Stonehenge or the last great menhirs in Brittany really belong to an earlier tradition. But in the great islands of the western Mediterranean, magnificent architects emerged : the builders of the Maltese temples were followed by those of the talayots, torre and nuraghi. Unfortunately we are not acquainted with architecture in wood, but the little temple at Bargoosterveld in the Netherlands leads us to suspect its existence, nevertheless.

Throughout the whole of this period, decorative motifs remain essentially geometric : incised motifs are arranged in panels on bracelets; wheels and spirals decorate the blades and pommels of swords; incised or excised motifs adorn the pottery. This art remains rather stiff and cold, in strong contrast with the liveliness of the extraordinary cave drawings of Scandinavia, the Alps and Iberia. Elsewhere simple cup-marks and solar symbols appear in wall paintings. Statuary art is exceptional and is restricted to the Mediterranean groups of statue-menhirs. However some very late groups like those from

201 Fibula, Hallstatt period (Italy)

the Nordic Bronze Age regions take up, in their normal decoration, subjects and an animal art which were often borrowed from the early Hallstatt cultures which were their contemporaries.

Small figurines are rare. At first they are found only in the Danube world, near to the Aegean sources, but skilfully transforming the initial models. We should remember the charming little goddesses – or gods – in multi-coloured skirts, from the Danube. Bronze statuettes remain rare and confined to a few exceptional pieces like the horse of the Trundholm chariot. Only later, in the Hallstatt period, did they become more frequent. The small votive bronzes of Scandinavia or the Sardinian nuraghi are outside the traditional chronological framework of the Bronze Age.

Finally, the most astonishing artistic contribution made by the Bronze Age was probably the creation of the first copper musical instruments, the trumpets of Ireland and the lurs of Denmark.

Societies and religions

The Neolithic world had glorified the cult of fertility and representations of Mother Goddesses proliferated. Society, which was essentially agricultural, continued to be patriarchal, without notable social distinctions. Burials were generally collective. Starting in the Chalcolithic period, mobile bands of Corded Ware peoples arrived to upset the traditional religious beliefs and laid the foundations for the development of individualism: now real social classes began to develop. It was a world of petty chiefs who were to rule the barbarian Bronze Age at first: princes of Wessex or Armorica, potentates of Únětice or Leubingen.

These warrior princes of the early Bronze Age had to give way to the rich traders who had exploited the markets. Subsequently, it seems, chiefs emerged because of their personal qualities, or of chance circumstances rather than for reasons associated with religion or social hierarchy. But it is very difficult to determine the internal structure of these societies. The tumuli of the middle Bronze Age and the urnfields of the late Bronze Age periods reveal that differences between social classes had declined. The 'warrior chief' would not appear again until the arrival of the Hallstatt horsemen. Probably great diversity reigned in the mosaic of the peoples of Europe. In that society women played a significant part at times. Burials in Denmark, as well as that of the lady at La Colombine reveal ladies of high rank who were probably honoured in their lifetime as they were in time of death.

Whatever his social position, the individual had acquired the right to consideration, as the study of the cemeteries has shown. The Bronze Age witnessed the assertion of personality, the recognition of the value of a spirit of enterprise. This was a consequence of the increase in travel and contacts, made necessary by this burgeoning industrial society. In short it was the start of a more elaborate organisation of labour, with the appearance of new professions and social classes: prospectors, miners, smiths, traders and commercial travellers, not to mention the scrap metal dealers, and the warriors stationed at the toll posts and strategic points on the trade routes.

202 Ship with ritual scene, cave drawing, Bohüslan (Sweden)

The old animal cults, linked with stock raising, undoubtedly continued to be honoured – worship of the bull, votive horns, etc. – but the pantheon grew larger and birds and horses gained entry. Gods, solar discs or cauldrons were driven about in carts.

Most of all, the magic of fire, linked with the birth of metallurgy, gave rise to new religious concepts. Fire had always fascinated men, but in the Bronze Age its mysterious power provided the means for new miracles. Thanks to fire, green stones were transformed in the heart of blazing furnaces into beautiful red metal. Again, thanks to fire, bronze gushed from the jaws of the crucibles as a burning liquid, to solidify mysteriously inside the moulds into formidable swords, sophisticated tools or ornaments the range of which continually widened. The master craftsman was the smith, a sorcerer or god-man: invocations to the sun, the fire star, can often be seen in his work. For thousands of years legend and myth were to preserve in the memory of man the story of the fabulous conquest of metal; the legend retold all through these pages by the cart, the male god, sun and fire in their countless symbolic forms.

Appendix

The Method of Dating by Radio-Carbon

The principle of the method is simple: living plants absorb atoms of carbon from the carbon dioxide in the atmosphere, in order to build their cells. Almost all these atoms are 'normal' ^{12}C but a very small proportion, which is thought to be constant, is composed of ^{14}C or 'radio-carbon'. When plants die they cease to absorb these atoms and those already absorbed which are radio-active, and therefore unstable, 'disintegrate' according to the usual laws of radio-activity; that is to say, each year a constant proportion of them become normal carbon, ^{12}C, again: half of them disintegrate in 5730 years (a period known as the half-life of carbon), half of the remainder in the next 5730 years and so on. All that is needed, then, is to measure the 'residual' radio-activity of a prehistoric sample containing organic material (wood, charcoal or even bone or shell) and compare it with that of a present-day organic substance, which is obviously higher, to deduce in theory the absolute date of its death.

In theory – for there are complications. The first is the choice of sample: the prehistoric user may have used wood which had been long dead (several centuries, at times) and ^{14}C gives the date of death and not that of the use of the plant matter. The carbonised wood chosen for analysis may have been affected by a variety of contaminations or mixtures of the soil in the dig (landslides, moles, etc.). In practice only concordant series of dates can be obtained – never a single date.

Moreover we are at present correcting all the dates obtained so far! Libby's original method is only possible, as we have emphasised, if we assume the proportion of ^{14}C in the carbon dioxide of the atmosphere to be constant. Unfortunately it has been shown that the proportion has varied through the ages: when an attempt was made to check the ^{14}C dates by an independent dating method, dendro-chronology (which measures absolute age quite simply by counting the growth rings in wood one by one, and has reached dates as far back as the seventh and eight millennia BC, thanks to some huge, well preserved trunks, and using correlations between the observed series), it was found that ^{14}C dates were consistently too 'young' in relation to 'real' dates. Looking at a given period in detail, it was seen that the theoretical ages obtained by ^{14}C showed some dispersal, due precisely to the variation in the atmospheric concentration of ^{14}C in the course of the ages. Dendro-

228

chronology, which is more reliable because it does not depend on any hypothetical principle, has led to the establishment of scales of correspondence. These are one of the major preoccupations of archaeology in recent times: various dendro-chronological research programmes, notably in California, Ulster and Bavaria, are being followed closely by the scientific world, for from them will emerge – laboriously but surely – a definitive chronology by which to read our past.

Lazily taking up the Anglo-Saxon terminology, which is very exact if hardly elegant, prehistorians from now on will talk about 'conventional' dates – those obtained by the crude ^{14}C method – and 'calibrated' dates when the conversion indicated by the dendro-chronological scale of correspondence has been applied. This calibration pushes back the date obtained by ^{14}C: thus a 'conventional' date of 2000 b.c. corresponds to a 'calibrated' or real date – in 'calendar' or solar years – of 2500 BC. So far no agreement has been reached on a universal 'calibration' curve, so prehistorians, cautiously, prefer to continue using dates expressed in 'conventional' ^{14}C years, dates which are certainly false in an absolute sense but are obtained under the same conditions and basic hypotheses everywhere, so that comparisons of relative ages can be made. This curious situation which is theoretically unsatisfactory is clearly only provisional.

Further Reading

General

Déchelette, J., *Manuel d'archéologie préhistorique, celtique et gallo-romaine II. Archéologie celtique ou protohistorique, première partie. Age du Bronze*, Paris, 1910–24.
De Laet, S., *La Préhistoire de l'Europe*, Brussels, 1967.
Millotte, J.-P., *Précis de protohistoire européene*, Collection U2, Armand Colin, Paris, n.d.
Renfrew, C., *Before Civilisation*, London, 1973.

Some regional and national accounts

Anati, E., *Camonica Valley*, London, 1964.
Briard, J., *Les Dépots bretons et l'Age du Bronze atlantique*, Rennes, 1965.
Broholm, H., *Danmarks Bronzealder*, 4 vols, Copenhagen, 1943–9.
Courtin, J., *Le Néolithique de la Provence*, Paris, 1974.
Effenterre, H. van, *La seconde fin du monde. Mycènes et la mort d'une civilisation*, Toulouse, 1974.
Gaucher, G. and Mohen, J.-P., *L'Age du Bronze dans le nord de la France*, Amiens, 1974.
Giot, P.-R., *Brittany*, London, 1960.
Grosjean, R., *La Corse avant l'histoire*, Paris, 1966.
Guilaine, J., *L'Age du Bronze en Languedoc occidental*, Paris 1972.
Herity, M. and Eogan, G., *Ireland in Prehistory*, London, 1977.
Holste, F., *Die Bronzezeit in Süd und West Deutschland*, Berlin, 1953.
Joffroy, R., *Les Sépultures à char du Premier Age du Fer en France*, Paris, 1958. *La France de la préhistoire*, Paris, 1972.
Millotte, J.-P., *Le Jura et les plaines de Saône aux âges des métaux*, Paris, 1972.
Paret, O., *Le Mythe des cités lacustres*, Paris, 1958.
Renfrew, C., *British Prehistory: a New Outline*, London, 1974.
Rondil, J.-L., *L'Age du Bronze en Languedoc oriental*, Paris, 1972.

Sandars, N. K., *Bronze Age Cultures in France: the Later Phases from the Thirteenth to the Seventh Century B.C.*, Cambridge, 1957.

Schaeffer, C.-F.-A., *Les Tertres funéraires de la forêt de Haguenau*, Haguenau, 1925.

Some reviews and collections

Many national or regional reviews are devoted to prehistory. Among the most important for France are: *L'Anthropologie; Bulletin de la Société Préhistorique Francaise; Gallia-Préhistoire.*

Inventaria Archaeologica, founded by M. A. Marien, publish the corpus of finds and the large hoards; La Sociéte Préhistorique Français edits volumes devoted to the typology of Bronze Age objects in France. *Prähistorische Bronzefunde* edited by H. Müller-Karpe deals with prehistoric bronze finds in Europe. For England the journal *Antiquity* and the *Proceedings of the Prehistoric Society* may be consulted, and for Ireland the *Proceedings of the Royal Irish Academy* and the *Journal of the Royal Society of Antiquaries of Ireland.*

Index

Numbers in **bold** type refer to illustrations and maps; the abbreviation BA is used for Bronze Age.